# PLAY
## ANTHROPOLOGICAL PERSPECTIVES

# PLAY

## ANTHROPOLOGICAL PERSPECTIVES

*edited by*
*Michael A. Salter*

1977 PROCEEDINGS
OF THE
ASSOCIATION FOR THE ANTHROPOLOGICAL STUDY OF PLAY

**Leisure Press**
**P.O. Box 3**
**West Point, N.Y. 10996**

## TAASP PUBLICATIONS

**The Anthropological Study of Play: Problems And Prospects,** David F. Lancy and B. Allan Tindall (eds.) available from Leisure Press, P.O. Box 3, West Point, N.Y. 10996.

**Studies In The Anthropology Of Play: Papers In Memory Of B. Allan Tindall,** Phillips Stevens, Jr. (ed.) available from Leisure Press, P.O. Box 3, West Point, N.Y. 10996.

**The Association For The Anthropological Study Of Play—Newsletter** (Quarterly), Brian Sutton-Smith (ed.) available from The Editor, Graduate School Of Education, University Of Pennsylvania, Philadelphia, PA. 19174.

## FRONT COVER

The drawing on the front cover is by David Frederick. We would like to thank Mr. Frederick and the Miami University Audio-Visual Department for granting us the privilege of reproducing it.

# PREFACE

The majority of the papers in this volume were originally prepared for the Third Annual Meeting of The Association for the Anthropological Study of Play, held in San Diego, California, during April, 1977. At this time TAASP met in conjunction with the American Ethnological Society, the Society for California Archaeology, the Society for Applied Anthropology, and the Southwestern Anthropological Association. The papers contained herein do not represent all those delivered by TAASP members at this gathering. Some were presented as part of the AES program while others were simply not available in time for publication. Abbreviated versions of the articles by Saegert and Hart, and by Riner, appeared in Volume 3 of the TAASP **Newsletter** and were solicited for this manuscript.

During the past decade or so, concern has been voiced over a number of factors associated with the study of play — to wit: the apparent inability to define such terms as "play", "games" and "sport" so that they can be operationally employed in a cross-cultural context; failure to clearly establish the parameters of the total field under investigation; and so forth and so on. While it is true that one needs the other — particularly if the criticisms are constructive in nature and the creators pay them heed. By-and-large the questions raised relative to the study of play have been legitimate and have served to provide direction to the field. It would be naive to suggest that this volume (or any other single volume for that matter) will serve to allay all the concerns expressed. To the contrary, its contents may, and hopefully will, lead to the formulation of further questions. On the other hand, individual contributions, such as Bateson's and group thrusts, such as the chapter on work and play, do provide fresh insights and partial answers to long-standing questions. We may never completely resolve some issues, but that, perhaps, is the nature of knowledge!

The strengths of this volume must be attributed to the individual authors, and to John W. Loy and Phillips Stevens, Jr. who spent countless hours reviewing manuscripts and to whom heartfelt thanks are extended. Weaknesses in the volume are mine.

Windsor, Ontario
December, 1977. M.A.S.

# ***Table of Contents***

## CHAPTER IV THE DICHOTOMY OF WORK AND PLAY

# CHAPTER I

# Theoretical Contributions to the Study of Play

## PLAY AND PARADIGM[1]

Gregory Bateson, University of California, Santa Cruz

I have had extraordinary luck at two moments in my life which are, in a sense, historic behind my finally arriving here at this podium. One was a longish time ago in New Guinea—about 1932 — when I saw a **Naven** ceremony for the first time. This is a transvestite ceremony in which a mother's brother celebrates an achievement of a sister's child and, so to speak, shames himself, though I didn't know this. All I knew was, he wore female costume, "drag," to do this; and I knew about the econo-mic exchanges that accompanied it. I had good native accounts of what happens, from 1929. But it wasn't until the Second Expedition, some time later, that I actually saw this thing happen, saw it done, and I discovered that it was **high comedy.** My notes had not recorded that simple fact. From the moment I knew it was high comedy, I began to be able to understand it, and this led into a very elaborate analysis which spread its roots through the whole culture. It was luck—and one of the things that was luck was the delay; that I was able to receive the fact, "It's funny," separately from the filling of my notebooks with the description of it, so that the fact of the funnyness stood out and became the thing to analyze —the new piece. That was the first piece of luck.

The next piece of luck, in a curious way, was rather similar. I was

7

working with Ruesch[2] in the Langley-Porter Clinic, and we began a conversation leading to the question of whether animals who exchange various sorts of signals (we'd all read Konrad Lorenz' **King Solomon's Ring** [1964] at that time) know that their signals **are** signals. For example, do the jackdaws, those "colonial crows" that lived in the top of Lorenz' house, do they **know** that the sounds which they exchange are in fact signals? A crow will go "kee-aw" (or something that sounds like "kee-aw"—ethologists, by the way, know absolutely no phonetics) and fly in the direction of home, and then other crows will say the same thing, and they too will fly in the direction of home, and evidently this utterance is somehow related to, "I'm going to fly home, you're going to fly home" (but who knows what the pronouns are). Do they know that this is a signal, or is it a sort of automatic thing, like blushing, for example? (Most of us do not recognize that we are signalling when we blush. We just wish we weren't blushing, if we know we are—and often we don't know we are.)

So, Weldon Keyes and I went down to the Fleishhacker Zoo[3] to look for the answer to this question, and we knew what we were looking for. You can't obviously, get inside an animal and know whether it "knows" something, but you **can** ask, "Has it the use of the information that its **signals are signals**?" If it has not the use of that information, for example, it could not deceive. Lying is a highly sophisticated operation, dependent on knowing that your signals are signals. It could not correct its messages, it could not utter a message which says, "I am going to utter a message." It might very easily not correct its signals for distance. A dog barks; does it bark louder to a dog that's far away? The answer is: on the whole, it doesn't; a dog barks louder to a dog that's close. Anyway, this was the question that we posed: can we find meta-communication among animals at the zoo, communication **about** communication, corrective messages, announcements of messages, and such things. You see, we **already** were asking about logical-type levels: "something" and "something and something **about** something."

When we got to the zoo we found something which everbody already knew—after all, we can't claim to have "discovered" it—namely, that animals play. The moment we saw **play** in the context we were in, in which we were asking ourselves about levels, about messages **about** messages (and I had, in the back of my mind, the Russellian[4] stuff on paradoxes and the trouble you get into with messages about messages and classes of classes, and such things), of course! Snap! Obviously, animals play — My God! — that means they can classify the components of their messages. It's not just us making classifications, it's **them** making classifications. We're in step with the native structure, not just imposing our nonsense upon it.

I then wrote to the Rockefeller Foundation and said, "Look, we are going to have a research project, and we want a lot of money." I knew at that stage that this was big, it was "hot," but I didn't know where we were going to go. Chester Barnard, who was then the head of the Rockefeller Foundation, said, "Come by when you're next in town." I was in town within three days. He said, "I don't understand, Mr. Bateson, what you're going to do, or what you're going to find. How much money do you want?" Incidentally, I knew, I had inside knowledge, that he had a copy of **Naven** (Bateson: 1958) at his bedside, so I though he would be a good person to go to. But, stupidly, I didn't ask for enough, I didn't ask for enough for long enough.

But we then did a study of otters playing. We did a piece of psychotherapy with them: we re-introduced play to otters in the zoo who had given up playing; we got them to playing again. We have the film[5]—we have actually the moment at which the psychotherapeutic change occurred. As far as I know it's the first piece of psychotherapy that was actually filmed at the moment when the "turnover" occurred. That was luck, and, you see, the nature of the luck is that the piece of insight comes at the moment when you happen to be loaded for that particular sort of bear.

Now let me jump straight forward; leave the history and jump into theory. The resilient point which, as I said, touched this off is, of course, the point that class is not a member of itself, and a class of classes is not one of the classes which are its members. And if you make a model out of this you won't get into the paradox of Epimenides,[6] the liar, the Cretan who said, "I always lie." Can the message, "I always lie," be a true one? If so, then it **isn't** true, because he made a true statement. If true, then untrue. If untrue, then true. The "then" connecting those, as we've now of course learned, first from Wiener[7] and now, repetitively, from George Spencer Brown,[8] has to be a **temporal** "then."

Now, what we began to discover is that the word "play" is a classifying term within the life of the creatures—or the natives, or whomever you're going to talk about; ourselves. If that is so, then of course it is quite different from the acts which constitute it; or if it is **not** different, if the message, "This is play," is itself a playful message, then the roof blows off and you don't know where you are, and somebody is either going to laugh, or be hurt.

You will create the Paradox of Epimenides when the message, "This is play," becomes itself playful.[9] This is the hazing common in initiations, when initiators may conceal the fact that the message, "This is play," is playful, and may make it into a pretense of discipline.

And now we have a disciplinary point, a point of **method**, not just for the study of play; but if you're going to study play, or any other meaningful behavior, you've got to carry in the forefront of your mind what sort of logical-type this class is. What is the level of classification, what does it enclose, what are the messages that label it, if any, and so on. I will try to make this clear by an example from another field.

You cannot, in general, teach a rat **not to explore** by giving him electric shocks when he puts his nose into boxes. The word "exploration" is not a word for any particular action; but people usually talk as though it were. But the class is not one of its members. So, if you put electric shocks in boxes, the rat will learn not to go into those particular boxes. He learns at that logical level, but he does not learn at the next logical level up, which would be "not to be an explorer." Obviously not, because he **is** an explorer, in order to find out which boxes are safe. And when he gets the shocks he has found which boxes are safe, and which are not safe. His exploration has been successful, so why should exploration be extinguished by a shock in a box? He will, if anything, be more careful to look in **every** box to see which has a shock.

Similarly, if you try to teach your dog who has once become a "thief" not to steal by smacking him down when he takes meat off the table, you'll get a dog who takes meat off the table more carefully. And for 2000 years or more, I don't know how long, we have assumed that "crime" is of the same logical-type as the criminal act, the act which we call "a crime." We feel surprised and hurt when we punish criminals, and they become more successful criminals; or change their field of activity. I mean, that those we punish for picking pockets may shift to putting their hands into other people's safes instead of pockets. They might learn, you see, not to pick pockets, which is an **action.** They will not learn not to be criminals by being punished for being pick-pockets. The problem of making criminals non-criminals is a much more complicated business, and I would refer you to the recent study, **Delancey Street,** by Charles Hampden-Turner (1976). The description of the brainwashing ex-convicts do to each other, to make each other not criminal, is pretty grim. It's not at all the same as slapping the wrist for the **action.**

In learning theory you must distinguish the **act** which is learned, the **learning** of that act, the **context** of that learning and the learning of that context. And, as for **play,** the whole notion of play and its complexities is one of the "hot spots" for looking into this set of problems. And I suggest to you that this set of problems is **absolutely central** for any scientific discussion of human behavior, or what they call "psychology." That much is established, I hope, after an awful lot of fooling around with this and that, and bits of New Guinea, and bits of animal behavior, and so on, which lies behind what I've just told you. The next thing is, since this is The Association for the Anthropological Study of Play, not to go roaming off sideways too quickly, but to take a good look look at this particular **levels** problem as it is associated with the word "play."

Let me set up a parallel. Let me tell you what scientists do. (Even in proper scientific labs they don't tell students what "science" is about, and of course still less do they tell anthropologists, and even less do they tell psychologists.) First they give a sort of general structural statement of some kind of something, be it play, be it gyroscopes, be it left-handedness, or what have you; and then they say, "Well, now, are there other sorts of phenomena in which similar sets of formal relations obtain?" We build what is called a "tautology" for the set, and we abstract that tautology and look for other phenomena to fit. That's called "abduction." It is abduction that give the whole of science its scope and body. It shifts science from being a series of mongoose-nosed insights and details, and creates a "scopish" picture, a broad scientific philosophy. The philosophy of science is that you **can** abduct, and the philosophy which is generated by science is a network of themes of wide scope.

In Iatmul, in New Guinea, there is a very sharp distinction between **wainga,** which is commercial buying, and **awa'ut** which is, literally tranlated, "in the direction of 'yes, yes'." That is true "giving," the sort of giving which is in the direction of reciprocity and not commercial relations. The term for reciprocity is **awa-awa,** "'yes, yes;" **awa'ut**, "in the direction of **awa,**" giving, as opposed to **wainga,** which is "trade." Here again, we've got a level, where the **content** of the action, from me to whomever, or from me, happening to be a mother's brother, to a sister's son, gets to **awa'ut**, because he will be compelled to give back valuables. The reciprocities of Iatmul are, in general, not symmetrical; they are, for example, valuables in one direction, food in another. That is, they **look** very much like trade, like **wainga,** in which valuables are given in exchange when buying sago in the market, or wherever. But the whole frame, as classified by the Iatmul, is totally different. And one of the things they will complain about is that a young man is behaving as though he **bought** his wife. Of course, he gave valuables for her, but these valuables were **awa, awa'ut**, in the direction of "yes, yes," and not in the direction of **wainga.**

Again, you see, we have the capacity, as human beings, to classify up into an abstract level. And this is what I'm talking about. That capacity gets to be more and more complex, and the analysis of it gets to be richer and richer, as you begin to think about it. When we were working with schizophrenics, what we found was that they were torn by what we call "double binds;" and a double bind is, in essence, a tangle of meta-labels. Suppose you think of the Iatmul **wainga** versus **awa'ut** discussion, and ask, what would happen to a man who had intended his act as reciprocity, when he finds that it is being classified by other people as a commercial trade act? This is where feelings get hurt, you see, because these levels of classification of behavior are where mammals really live. The fellow is put into a double bind by the deliberate or accidental criss-cross misunderstanding of the sort of behavior he's engaged in. Similarly, imagine that you intended your act to be play, but somebody took it seriously. Or, you intended it to be serious, and somebody took it for play. This can be painful. I am continually hurt because I make jokes when I talk, and people therefore think I don't mean what I said. **My** rule is, "never an untrue word spoken in jest." I don't know why people think that jokes really are not serious; or, indeed, why they would think that **play** is not serious. It's a funny sort of vulgarism we get into in this culture.

As you get into the more complex arrangements, where you can get cross-cuttings of these classes, **exploration** is taken to be **invasion,** and so on. Play is taken to be serious; the serious is taken to be play; the **wainga,** the commercial, is taken to be reciprocal; the reciprocal is taken to be the commercial, and so on. When you get up to those levels, you'll begin to discover that the way **out** of those tangles is largely dependent on a crow's-eye view. But it cannot be exactly an **intellectual** crow's-eye view. The intellect can talk about it, can dissect it, but you've got to get **up** there, not only with your intellect, but also with your diaphragm, or—perhaps it's your right hemisphere, or your heart—wherever you think, culturally, you carry your feelings. The analysis to deal with these hurts must itself be heartfelt.

Let's look, for a moment, at the sort of tangle I'm talking about, because "play" is a subset of this larger class of tangles. People will double-bind each other in "play." It's usually a rather cruel thing to do, I think; but you'll find it done by initiators to novices, in which the novice is essentially being "hazed," until he gets straight about the **logical-typing** of the hazing that he's suffering—until he can **transcend** his first view of that cruelty. When this happens the relationship between initiator and candidate undergoes a total change.

I'm trying to lead you to both feel and think about this matter of paradigms, so that when you go to places—as anthropologists should go to "places"—you may think and feel about such things **in the structure in which they occur in the places that you go to,** which will, no doubt, be different from ours. When you get to Bali, the contrast between **Yin** and

**Yang** won't be on quite the same diameter of the circle that it is among the Chinese. And when you get to the Chinese, **Yin** and **Yang** are not on quite the same diameter as they would be among Americans, or among the English.

Let me take the problem of addiction. The question is: you have an alcoholic or, indeed, a criminal, or, indeed, you and me; and you want him or her to make a deep change. You want that individual to make a deep change in the classification, the **paradigm,** of life. I use the word "paradigm" because I really am talking about the same thing that Kuhn is talking about in **The Structure of Scientific Revolutions** (1962); the "jump" from a learning of this order to a learning of that order; from a learning of content—not to put you nose into boxes—to a learning of how to be or not to be an explorer. And that is a very, **very** difficult jump to make, as looked at from before the jump. Looking back after the jump, you can't see what the difficulty was; but before it, you're stuck. A great part of every great religion is concerned with this particular business of being "stuck." And a great part of psychiatry is concerned with it too.

If you are going to understand what goes on on the Sepik River of New Guinea, or in Bali, or in San Diego, you have to be aware that these "stucknesses" are a part of the basic structure of the life of all people.

Take the simple case of a man who is stuck in alcoholism. The common-sense course from him is (let's leave out the ego problems and all that) to have another drink. He will feel uncomfortable if he doesn't; he's already beginning to feel uncomfortable and, if he does, he will, at least for a while, feel comfortable. He may become addicted not just to the comfort which **a** drink would give him, but addicted to **a progressive change in a given direction**; a next logical type of addiction. There are many alcoholics who are happy only when there is a positive gradient of alcohol in their bloodstreams. Such people become exceedingly skillful; they can keep that positive gradient going for a week, perhaps for ten days, slowly mounting. And that slow change is to them a stationariness, a static sort of bliss. But you cannot maintain that constancy, that constant positive first derivative, beyond a certain point, because at that certain point you land in the gutter.

How is the alcoholic going to get out of the logical-typing which says, "This is fine, the message is fine, and I am, **I am** the sort of person that enjoys that sort of message, and I'm going to have it. My personal culture involves that message." He can not get out, you see, by somebody saying "Don't," by somebody trying to cut him off from his alcohol, by somebody putting him in a tank of the local police station, or, indeed, by putting him in a local mental hospital, or by stuffing him full of various drugs, etc., etc. **He's got to get out by a change that will crack the whole paradigm.** And that which would crack the paradigm has got to be a **new** structure, a **totally** new structure.

Perhaps the first time he lands in the gutter at three o'clock in the morning will be a sufficient shock to be what Alcoholics Anonymous call "hitting bottom." That's a moment when it's worthwhile to try to help him. Between binges, you can't do much. But the **third** time he's woken up in the gutter at three o'clock in the morning, that won't work. You're going to have to wait until he takes the next step of bottom-hitting, because the bottom is changing. [10]

But in contrast to the alcoholic, there are people who deliberately put themselves into pain of this kind and "discipline themselves." They even "have fun." It is their "hobby," and the word "hobby" is somehow related to the word "play;" I don't quite know how. These people, for example, are people who climb mountains. Consider a man half-way up the mountain, his legs hurting, his breath coming short, his boots beginning to feel as if they had slipped or pinched his feet, and all that. His body is beginning to scream. The common-sense thing for him to do, we would say, is to sit down, open his rucksack, eat his lunch, and go home. But there are people who willingly go out for weeks—they even go to Mount Everest—to perform the **extraordinary** feat of a sort of play. "Cold turkey," they resist the common-sense temptation to eat lunch and go back home. These people go **on** climbing the mountain. Why do they do that? Why do people in Zen meditation rooms set through a **seshin,** a six-day retreat, with their legs getting worse and worse, and their minds getting more and more addled, and the guru becoming a more and more terrible and horrible figure, a figure of utter fear and contempt until...well, they go on, and perhaps in the last two days suddenly the whole thing switches over and looks different. A paradigmatic change, of a very deep order, has occurred.[11]

They say play has no purpose, but really its purposes are of a paradigmatic order. Consider Shiva, the **Nataraj** figure, the Dancing Shiva. This is a paradigm, imposed upon the entire world of experience; in which it is assumed that everything that happens, ranging from earthquakes to gossip, to murder, to joy, to love, to laughter, and all the rest, is an incredible ziz-zag of what might seem otherwise to be unclassifiable and disordered experience, but is, in fact, all framed within the Shivaite concept as **The Dance.** Dance is perhaps not quite the same thing as play; it has an aesthetic angle that play doesn't have, but it is, at any rate, an extension of what I used to call the "play frame," wider and wider, until it encloses the whole of existence.

In the present epoch the grown-ups and people in my generation wish

14

we could experience a paradigmatic change, and we are rather envious of the youth engaging in all sorts of lunacy to try and achieve a wisdom for themselves. They do this and they do that in their communes, none of it very sane, **unless** you say, "But the hunt for paradigmatic change is the **only** sanity."

We play, and we try to make the jump. What I'm trying to do is to encourage you to make the jump.

NOTES

[1] **The Keynote Address,** Third Annual Meeting of The Association for the Anthropological Study of Play, San Diego, California, April 8, 1977. Transcribed, edited and annotated by Phillips Stevens, Jr. This paper was revised, with Mr. Bateson's assistance, from an earlier draft which appeared in the TAASP *Newsletter* (1977). With the exception of n. 11, the following notes are my own, added for the reader who may be unfamiliar with Bateson's work. I am grateful to Wendy Seubert and Irene Suhr for their assistance in transcribing the working draft.

[2] Jurgen Ruesch, with whom Bateson wrote "Structure and Process in Social Relations" (1949), and the seminal *Communication: The Social Matrix of Psychiatry* (1951).

[3] In San Francisco.

[4] Referring to Bertrand Russell (d. 1970), known principally as an eminent and pioneering mathematician and philosopher (see his *Principia Mathematica* [1910-13]) and Nobel Laureate, but also interested in paradoxes and logical-type levels. His "barber paradox" (the village barber said that he shaved everyone who did not shave himself, which is a trustworthy statement until it is asked, "Who shaves the barber?") is well known in logic, and this led to what is known as the "Russell Paradox," which has to do with statements about classes which are members of themselves and classes which are not members of themselves. Russell was an early mentor of Norbert Wiener (see n. 7).

[5] *The Nature of Play — Part 1: River Otters.* 16 mm., one reel, 1952.

[6] Cretan prophet and seer of the 6th century B.C., credited with having made the statement, "Cretans always lie," which could not be a true statement, since he himself was a Cretan.

[7] Norbert Wiener (d. 1964), the so-called "father of cybernetics," mathematician and logician (see his *Cybernetics: Or, Control and Communication in the Animal and the Machine* [1948]).

[8] Mathematician and logician (see his *Probability and Scientific Inference* [1957]; and *Laws of Form* [1969]).

[9] For elaboration, see Bateson (1956 and 1972a).

[10] For elaboration, see Bateson (1972b).

[11] For a vivid account of paradigmatic change in Zen *seshin,* see Dass (1977).

REFERENCES

Bateson, Gregory, 1956, The Message 'This is Play'. *In* Group Processes: Transactions of the Second Conference. Bertram Schaffner, Ed. New York: Josiah Macy, Jr. Foundation. Pp. 145-242.

1958, Naven: A survey of the Problems suggested by a Composite Picture of a Culture of a New Guinea Tribe drawn from Three Points of View. Stanford, California: Stanford University Press.

1972a, A Theory of Play and Fantasy. *In* Steps to an Ecology of Mind: Collected Essays in Anthropology, Psychiatry, Evolution and Epistemology. San Francisco: Chandler Publishing Co. Pp. 177-193.

1972b, The Cybernetics of 'Self': A Theory of Alcoholism. *In* Steps to an Ecology of Mind: Collected Essays in Anthropology, Psychiatry, Evolution and Epistemology. San Francisco: Chandler Publishing Co. Pp. 309-337.

1977, Play and Paradigm. TAASP Newsletter 4(1):2-8.

Brown, George Spencer, 1957, Probability and Scientific Inference. New York: Longmans and Green.

1969, Laws of Form. London: George Allen and Unwin.

Dass, Ram, 1977, Grist for the Mill. Santa Cruz, California: Unity Press.

Hampden—Turner, Charles, 1976, Sane Assylum. Delancey Street Foundation. San Francisco: San Francisco Book Co.

Kuhn, Thomas S., 1962, The Structure of Scientific Revolutions. Chicago: University of Chicago Press.

Lorenz, Konrad, 1964, King Solomon's Ring: New Light on Animal Ways. London: Methuen & Co.

Ruesch, Jurgen and Gregory Bateson, 1949, Structure and Process in Social Relations. Psychiatry 12:105-124.

1951, Communication: The Social Matrix of Psychiatry. New York: W. W. Norton.

Russell, Bertrand, and A. N. Whitehead, 1910-13, Principia Mathematica. 3 Vols. Cambridge, England: Cambridge University Press.

Weiner, Norbert, 1948, Cybernetics: Or, Control and Communication in the Animal and the Machine. Cambridge, Mass: M.I.T. Press

## THE STUDY OF PLAY FROM FIVE
## ANTHROPOLOGICAL PERSPECTIVES

Alyce Taylor Cheska, University of Illinois, Urbana

## INTRODUCTION

Play as a social phenomenon worthy of scientific study came into its own during the past century with scholars from different disciplines perceiving play in varied ways. Psychoanalysts regard play as a therapeutic tool (Waelder 1933:208); educationalists see it as simulated skill practice (Piaget 1962:111); sociologists examine play in its modern institutionalized form of sport (Luschen 1975:39); and anthropologists explore play as instrumentally contributing to man as a cultural being (Kroeber 1948:29).

This paper surveys five theoretical perspectives of anthropology and presents representative play studies whose rationales were formulated within these perspectives. Future research directions, based upon current and developing postulations, are proposed.

## THEORETICAL PERSPECTIVES OF ANTHROPOLOGY—FRAMEWORKS FOR THE STUDY OF PLAY

In anthropological study, the play of man has been interpreted within the framework of five theoretical perspectives: 1) antiquarianism, 2) evolutionism, 3) diffusionism, 4) functionalism, and 5) structuralism.

1. **Antiquarianism,** a method of descriptive recording, helped to identify and describe play activities in specific cultures. In many instances these descriptions of games and pastimes preserved information before it disappeared entirely. Numerous accounts by captives, missionaries, entrepreneurs, administrators, teachers, and travelers, provided personalized information about the play participation of particular peoples. Such records were sporadic; they lacked uniformity, completeness and continuity, but did furnish archival reports of cultural activities now vanished. These play activities primarily included rhymes, games and festival play. [1]

2. **Evolutionism,** as an important anthroplogical concept, was first considered in the late 1800's and received revised re-enforcement in the mid-1900's. The earlier evolutionism proposed the following general postulates: 1) culture has developed through stages in a predetermined, uniform way; 2) culture evolved from the simple to the complex; 3) similarities among different societies were explained by the "psychic unity" of man which accounted for parallel development and independent invention.

Edward B. Taylor, the first professional anthropologist to realize the potential of games as a key to understanding culture, observed that: "In the study of civilization, as of so many other branches of natural history, a theory of gradual evolution proves itself a trustworthy guide. But it will not do to assume that culture must always come on by regular unvarying progress. That, on the contrary, the lines of change may be extremely circuitous, the history of games affords instructive proofs" (1879b:747). Tylor considered the ordered stages of culture to be savagery, barbarism and civilization. He first concluded that a "psychic unity" among mankind explained parallel invention of cultural traits and produced similar evolutionary histories. Tylor came to realize that cultures borrowed traits through contact with each other. His analysis of similar attributes of the Aztec game of 'patolli' and the Indian game 'pachisi' concluded that the Mexican civilization, in large measure, was the result of Asian influence (1879a:129). In Tylor's classic book, **Anthropology** (1881), games were classified as: imitative games and toys, such as the Eskimo tiny oil-lamp; practical sports, such as Indian bow and arrows; diffused games, such as kites; games of survival of ancient times, such as hoops; and indoor games, such as chess and cards (1881:174-176). In analyzing the function of play in culture, Tylor stated: "Games which exercise either body or mind have been of high value in civilization as trainers of man's faculties" (1881:176).

Proponents of the evolutionary theory of play categorized children's play in development classifications. Hall's (1906) recapitulation theory proposed that children's play-stages were the reflections of the cultural stages in the development of cultures. One such play-stage scheme was Mabel Reany's (1916) age-stages: animal, savage, nomad, pastoral, tribal.

Scholars have long been searching for the origin (s) of play. Huizinga, in his provocative volume, **Homo Ludens** (Playing Man), observed that: "the apparently quite simple question of what play really is leads us deep into the problem of the nature and origin of religious concepts" (1955:25). Observing the similarity of Asian and native American games, Stewart Culin, early American ethnologist, proposed that games of the North American Indians originated in religious ceremonial traditions of the Orient. He contended: "Games must be regarded not as conscious inventions, but as survivals from primitive conditions, under which they originated in magical rites and chiefly as a means of divination" (1895:XVIII). The systematic association of ball games with religion and magic has been proposed by Krickenberg (1948), Mendner (1956), Glassford (1969), and Simri (1975). Krickenberg (1948), in analyzing the Mayan and Aztec rubber ball court game, believed it to be an expressive part of religious ritual; Glassford (1969) reviewed the change of the game from its sacred to profane orientation. Damm (1960:10), in examining the question of the origin of sportive games, separated sport and cultive games, affirming that primitive people knew and celebrated sportive physical activities, while similar games during cultive events were derived from magic motives. Damm maintained that in the process of mankind's longer development the cultive games would be transformed into games with playful character.

By the mid-1900's, neo-evolutionism was promoted by White's (1969:368) premise that culture evolved and increased as the means of efficient uses of energy were increased; this assumed that cultural evolution was determined mostly be technological conditions within culture. Sahlins and Service (1960:12) proposed two kinds of evolution—specific and general—pointing out that sequence of change occurred in a specific culture in a specific environment, while there was also a universal progress of man's culture from lower to higher forms.

Neo-evolutionism currently has advocates in the study of play. A progression from simple to complex structure is indicated in the change from play to games to sports by Edwards (1973). Ibrahim (1975:40) proposed that sporting is an evolutionary step from kinetic play and games, and that certain social conditions need to be present in a society for sporting to exist. Luschen (1970:9) regarded sport and games in primitive societies as part of other institutions like religion; but in modern societies a form of linear evolution is found in institutional separation as seen in the delineation of sports as a societal sub-system.

3. **Diffusionism** as a general theoretical perspective considered that: 1; independent invention was rare (British school); 2) culture traits diffused from a geographical center outward (German-Austrian Kulturkreis school); and 3) culture traits diffused over wide geographical areas (American school).

Culin was the first American to propose the study of games as a science (Cheska 1975). He (1898:246) advocated the comparative study of games, feeling that two kinds of evidence afforded promise: linguistics and morphology. Using these methods in developing his compendium, **Games of the North American Indians** (1907), he provided ample evidence of the diffusion of dexterity and chance games throughout the North American continent. British anthropologist, A. C. Haddon's interest in play activities was crystallized in his book, **The Study of Man** (1898), a major portion of which was devoted to history and diffused patterns of various activities, e.g. top, kite, bull roarer. Nordenskiold, a Swedish ethnologist, primarily interested in the historical distribution of South American culture elements, reported game play of various tribes of the Gran Chaco. He (1910) found similarities between the South and North American Indians' versions of the two-sided lot game and the dart-throwing contest. In his cultural-traits studies, Kroeber (1920, 1925) included descriptions of dexterity and chance games of the many Indian tribes of California. His (1931:149-151) interest in diffusion prompted his analysis of Tylor's evidence of diffusion of patolli-pachisi. Kroeber concluded that it was extremely unlikely that the people who brought pachisi from India to Mexico would have brought nothing else; therefore, the context probability was against connection (1948:551).

Erasmus (1950) explained the similarities of patolli and pachisi by the limitation of possible variations within the concept of a game. Brewster, folklorist (1953, 1956), described games from many regions of the earth. He pointed out that the comparative studies of games provided clues regarding general contact between cultures. Brewster's studies are significant because he was among the few scholars recording the actual content of games cross-culturally. Raum (1953:104-121) examined the wide distribution of the rolling target (hoop-and-pole) game in Africa, Oceania, South American and North America. The rich symbolic ritualistic possibility of the game was given as the reason for its world-wide distribution.

The concept of change by diffusion, acculturation and innovation is a viable, perplexing issue among anthropologists today. As shall be discussed under "functionalism," current hologeistic studies reflect these concerns.

4. **Functionalism** (functional analysis) became widely accepted during the first part of the twentieth century. The basic premise that customs have purpose or social function was pointed out by the French sociologist Emile Durkheim (1933), whose writing greatly influenced British anthropologists, Radcliffe-Brown and Malinowski, strong advocates of functionalism. It was Malinowski (1922), by the participant-observation approach to his Trobriand Islands study, who popularized the concept of anthropological field work.

The crucial ideas of functionalism were: 1) each culture is to be treated as a functionally interrelated system; 2) social behavior exists to maintain society's social structure (Radcliffe-Brown 1952); 3) a society is the total network of social relationships (Radcliffe-Brown 1952); 4) cultural traits are useful parts of the society in which they occur (Malinowski 1939); and 5) a cultural trait's function is to satisfy some basic and/or derived need of the individuals in a society (Malinowski 1939). Within functionalism were the universal concepts of functional consistency, institutions and differentiation of social roles.

Many studies of play are based on the theoretical approach of functionalism, and several functions of play in culture have been advocated. A major function as perceived by some scholars was enculturation, the adaptation of an individual to a culture.[2] The pre-exercise theory was proposed by the German biologist Groos (1901), who considered play as practice for adult activities. These activities helped to perpetuate the social order. The cathartic function of play was introduced by Freud in his classic book, **Beyond the Pleasure Principle** (1922). Freud suggested that children in play re-enact situations which they wish to master. Waelder (1933) synthesized the contributions of the psychoanalytic orientation to play as follows: instinct of mastery, wish fulfillment, assimilation of overpowering experiences by repetition or compulsion, transformation of participant from passive to active state, and level of absence from reality of super-ego fantasies about real objects. Erikson (1950) proposed that play was the function of "ego" attempting to synchronize the body and social processes. He suggested that play unfolded in three stages: 1) autocosmic play—beginning with and centering in the child's own body; 2) microsphere play—learning the laws of the thingworld by playing with manageable toys; and 3) macrosphere play—playing with others as their world is shared (1950:220-221). Psychoanalysts have utilized the method of play therapy as a major tool for remediation of an individual's deficiencies in mastering real life situations (Schaefer 1976). Little consideration has been given to the practice by the 'average' person in utilizing the play activities as a technique for power over unmanageable situations of real life (Szasz 1961; Berne 1964).

Game participation as practice for interpreting social roles in life was proposed by the American social psychologist George Mead (1934:224). Herron and Sutton-Smith (1971) pointed out that games with rules were based on status positions and provided access to and experience in handling them.

Within **developmental studies,** Piaget (1962) considered play as the primacy of assimilation (adjustment of objects into a child's schemata) over accommodation (adaptation of the child to objects), both aspects of cognition. Within intellectual development, the child moved through stages of cognition: pre-conceptual, representational and concrete operational, as preparation for the mature, formal operational period. Correspondingly, characteristic play types were: sensory-motor practice games, symbolic games and games-with-rules. Piaget stated: "We have seen that they [games with rules] mark the decline of children's games and the transition to adult play, which ceases to be a vital function of the mind when the individual is socialised. In games with rules there is a subtle equilibrium between assimilation to the ego—the principle of all play—and social life" (1962:168).

An important thrust within the theoretical framework of functionalism in the United States has been the study of interrelationships between the individual personality and the cultural pattern. Through the work of anthropologists, such as Ruth Benedict, Margaret Mead, Alfred L. Kroeber, and Ralph Linton (1945), has evolved **psychological anthroplogy.** Mead's early ethnography, **Coming of Age in Samoa** (1928), showed that there were tracable relationships between childhood experiences and adult personality. Other studies also showed that child-training patterns appeared to be congruent with other variables in the culture (Benedict 1934; Roberts and Sutton-Smith 1962, 1964; J. and B. Whiting 1963; Sutton-Smith 1969). Child-training scholars projected that distinct modal personalities existed in societies (Mead 1928; Benedict 1934); the study of culture-themes opened the possibility that all elements of a particular culture were reflections of that culture's dominant theme. Among correlative variables studied were ceremonies, games, social organization and belief in the supernatural (Roberts, Arth, and Bush 1959; Roberts and Sutton-Smith 1962; Roberts, Sutton-Smith, and Kendon 1963; Ball 1972, 1974; Barry, Josephson, Lauer, and Marshall 1976).

**Ethnography**, the descriptive study of human societies, utilized the functionalist perspective that cultural traits are necessary to a society. To do justice to the number of play studies within this rubric, a separate paper would be necessary. A selection of ethnographic papers read at recent TAASP (The Association for the Anthropological Study of Play) conferences (1975-1977) will serve as examples: Ager (1976), "The reflection of cultural values in Eskimo children's games;" Jackson (in this volume), "The conveyance of social beliefs and values through aesthetic sport: the case of Kendo;" Heider (1977), "From Javanese to Dani: The Translation of a Game"; Lancy (1976), "The play behavior of Kpelle children during rapid cultural change"; Miracle (1977), "Some functions of Aymara games and play"; Rich (in this volume), "Values and games in Iceland"; Robinson, (in this volume), "Social adaptation of Vietnamese refugee children through play"; Rosentiel (1976), "The role of traditional games in the process of socialization among the Motu of Papua New Guinea"; Scheffler (1976) "Wake games from the state of Tlaxcala, Mexico"; and Steven (1976), "Social and judical functions of Bachama song-contests."[3]

Implicit in functionalism was the **comparative method.** This was the comparison of particular cultures by searching for the general functional inter-relationships which apply to the whole of human society. Available ethnographic materials for hologeistic or pan-cultural work were concentrated in the Human Relations Area File (HRAF), Yale University (Murdock 1957); Society Research Archives System, University of Minnesota (Naroll and Cohen 1970); and the Cross Cultural Cumulative Code Center, University of Pittsburgh (Murdock and White 1969). Using the HRAF, Roberts, Arth and Bush (1959) delineated three major types of games (physical skill, strategy and chance), determined their distribution patterns and examined their association within and between societies. They indicated that games of physical skill, strategy, and chance, respectively, might be exercises in the mastery of environment or of self, of the social system, and of the supernatural (1959:604). Games have provided projective indicators of group attitudes and interests (Roberts and Sutton-Smith 1962, 1966; Roberts, Sutton-Smith and Kendon 1963; Sipes 1973; Textor 1967).

Roberts and Sutton-Smith have been major contributors in cross-cultural game research. A general summary of their findings showed that: 1) in cross-cultural studies there are hundreds of statistically significant associations between the presence of games and other cultural variables; 2) these patterns are associated with different types, absence and presence of games; and 3) games are associated with child training, economic, technological, political, and sociological variables (Sutton-Smith 1974:10).

Frederickson (1960), in an examination of the meaning of sport in American culture, reviewed and suggested ritual and spectator behavior studies of other cultures. Luschen (1970) summarized the function of sport for a socio-cultural system as mainly for pattern maintenance and integration and, in modern polity dominated societies, for goal attainment. In primitive cultures he felt that the sport's function was universal and thus functioned for adaptation.

Inherent in functionalism was the ability of cultural customs and institutions to reduce conflicts and tensions. However, conflict origins and resolutions in culture have not been clarified in functionalism. Even more imperative has been functionalism's lack of accommodation of culture change. How play may provide mechanisms for expressing conflict and change has increasingly become the subject of play theorists' attention. Norbeck (1974) examined forms of symbolic inversion as rites of reversal; he saw in play the potential novelty for the larger society. Various ways in which role inversions in play situations could occur were suggested by Sutton-Smith (1974:10); thus 1) the player was provided with a novel experience rather than with replication of cultural experience; 2) each player gets a turn at roles he may not normally assume; 3) games of order and disorder model the system only to destroy it; 4) all games provide much leeway within any given role for tactical variations and innovations. In the question of novelty and its relation between playfulness and creativity, he (1975, 1976) suggested that play, defined in the evolutionary sense, could be regarded as adaptive potentiation. This would be possible by changing the habitual relations between means and goals, for if the direction of habitual activities were changed, as in play, then non-habitual responses would have been created.

5. **Structuralism** and functionalism in many ways resembled two sides of the same theoretical perspective, one being a system's component and the other being its relationships; however, each has led to differing research directions.

The crucial concepts of structuralism are: 1) structure is an ordered arrangement of parts or components; 2) social structure is manifest in the functioning of elements as a system (Radcliffe-Brown 1952:9); 3) these elements or particular features are parts of an organized whole (Radcliffe-Brown 1941:17). Radcliffe-Brown and other British structuralists studied social structure holistically and examined its mutual interdependence to rules of society and environment. The social person's actions were fully defined by the rules which pertained to his social situation.

It must be noted that structuralism has been modified from Radcliffe-Brown's conceptions in several divergent perspectives. One modification has been the separation of social structure from social relations. Fortes (1949:56) made the distinction between the concrete 'reality' of social relations and the social structure or 'model' which is not immediately visible. Firth (1963) pointed out the discrepancy between what actually happened in reality and what a formal study of the rules might lead one to expect. In his article on the dart match in Tikopia, Firth (1930) pointed out that the organization and factors of this long established game carried clear, defined procedures and rules of strong sanction, yet the game seemingly carried little behavioral significance.

Levi-Strauss, French anthropologist, proposed a greatly different structuralism from Radcliffe-Brown. Levi-Strauss (1953, 1963, 1966) perceived man's culture as a surface representation of the underlying structure of the human mind. Malefijt contended that "Levi-Strauss does not maintain that structures of thought determine culture, but holds instead that they operate within a cultural context" (1974:325). Levi-Strauss believed that each human group had its own contingent history and its own physical and social environment which interact with structured modes of thought. There was in this a coherence which transcended all utility and function; and the principles of this logic could be accounted for only in terms of the inherent and unconscious structure of the human mind itself. The ways in which primitive peoples perceived and classified things in the world around them had been studied by Levi-Strauss. In comparing the structure of social games and ritual games, he perceived that in the former, the pre-game symmetry of participants is rendered assymetrical by taking part in the structure or rules of the event in relation to the participants' will, chance or skill. In ritual games, the pre-event assymmetry of participants is structurally changed by participation in the event, rendering each symmetrical or equal in condition (1966:32-33).

**Linguistics,** a discipline based on human speech, offered to anthropology a structural model for understanding social structure and social relations. Linguistics attempted to reconstruct the underlying thought patterns of human speech, examining every sentence for both surface and deep structures. Structural linguistics was concerned with syntax or with rules which determine how sounds and words were put together, and semantics or the relationship or meanings of these words. The playful use of language in humor, joking and folk tales is not discussed in this paper; however, these are of much interest to ethnolinguists and folklorists.

The structural grammar of play, games and sports has been explored by several scholars. Bateson (1955) proposed that play is a signaled message denoting what the actions in which the players are engaging stands for, rather like a frame demarking a class of behaviors from the surrounding context. He argued that the message "this is play" enabled the receiver to discriminate between mood-signs and other signs which resemble them. Goffman (1961) identified gaming encounters as focused gatherings concerned with the fun in them. The joint engrossment in something with others, reinforced the immediate reality of the interaction. The game rules governed the game moves, but the structure of gaming encounters governed the individual's execution of the game moves. To sustain the situation, a socially organized set of 'irrelevant' behavior rules had to be followed, otherwise the character of the external world intervened, destroying the gaming encounter.

The structural elements of games helped Von Neumann and Morgenstern (1947:186-219) in developing their economic theory of games. These elements were: 1) number of players; 2) rules or procedures; 3) results or pay offs, and 4) strategies employed in game play (Avedon and Sutton-Smith 1971:420). Von Neumann and Morgenstern showed that the economic transaction, like a game, was simply a totality of rules which described it. In their economic theory of games they depended heavily on the mechanical model of cooperation and competition through rational choices and the use of the psychological strategy of bluffing.

Redl, Gump and Sutton-Smith (1971) identified thirty basic game dimensions which they though elicited behavior and whose presence or absence determined the game's suitability to differing groups. Sutton-Smith (1972) examined in a chase-and-catch game ("Bar the Door"), the player interaction with the game's structural features: game challenge, player roles, player performances, space, and time. Vernes (1965) considered the major role that the temporal element held in competitive games. He proposed that games were temporally separated into succescive moves to provide opponents time to resolve problems and surmount difficulties in the immediate future of the game, thus constructing the necessary relationship between the logical structure of the game and the psychological reactions of the players.

Renick (1977) analyzed the deep intrastructure of a game as a system consisting of two basic structural elements: 1) state (constant relationships between player-units and game constraints), and 2) sequence (repeatable patterns of particular relationships between player-units and game constraints in a given state). Sutton-Smith (1975) divided games into three social interaction levels which parallel differential organizational complexity, moving from unity to dyadic to quadratic organization of players. Game levels of interaction were delineated as moving from pastimes to competitive games to sport. In analyzing the structure of ludic (play) action, Ingham and Loy (1974) pointed out that ludic activities served as socialization situations for individual stability by providing appropriate behaviors ranging from assimilation to accommodation. The ludic domain consisted of the ludic frame or situation, the institutionalized ludic activities or forms, and their institutionalized role behavior or fronts. A limited frame of reality was constructed, maintained and transformed by the ludic domain.

## CURRENT RESEARCH STATUS OF THE STUDY OF PLAY

Theoretical paradigms in anthropology have continually been developed and refined. Each of these perspectives provides a benchmark from which to view man as a social being. Several such current orientations have provided rationales for research in the area of play: 1) psychobiological orientation; 2) cultural ecology; 3) structural analysis.

1. **The psychobiological orientation** assumes that play is partly an expression of the basic biological nature of man. That this parallel is found in other animals has been purported in ethology with increasing momentum. Primate studies have furnished exciting data on the dichotomy of instinctive vs. social play (Groos 1898; Beach 1945; Walker 1961; Loizos

1967; Van Lawick-Goodall 1967; Dolhinow and Bishop 1945; Suomi and Harlow 1971; Chevalier-Skonikoff 1974; Aldis 1975; Oakley and Reynolds 1976; Baldwin 1977).

Examination of play's neurophysiological correlates and its evolutionarily selective aspects are currently being investigated by Parman (1977) who proposed that play is evolutionarily homologous to dreaming as survival adaptation. De Rios and Schroeder (1977) are examining the brain hemisphere dominance (left brain serving symbolic function and right brain serving manipulation function) in relation to occupation and play activity selection.

2. **Cultural ecology** as an overarching paradigm examines the ecological adaptation of man and environment. Glassford (1970) applied the economic theory of games to the traditional Eskimo culture.

3. **Structural analysis,** as an extension of structuralism, focused upon semantic structural analysis and ethnoscience in which native ideas and concepts have been analyzed. Geertz in his classic article, "The Balinese Cockfight," points out that: "In the cockfight, then, the Balinese forms and discovers his temperament and his society's temper at the same time. Societies, like lives, contain their own interpretations. One has only to learn how to gain access to them" (1972:29).

The current status of the anthropological study of play can be gained from the excellent reviews of research by Malina, Norbeck, Sutton-Smith, Schwartzman, and Stevens. Malina (1969), physical anthropologist, reviewed studies emphasizing the importance of physical activity perception and performance within the cultural context. He called for a joint effort in understanding the intra-cultural as well as the cross-cultural significance of physical activities.

Norbeck (1974), social anthropologist, indicated the relevance to anthropology of the study of play as a biological and a cultural universal and as specific forms and aspects of human play. He (1974:7-8) offered the following subjects for research: 1) play as a mirror of pervasive values and attitudes (motivation, achievement); 2) play and social control (inter- and intra-societal conflict, social sanctions of wit and humor, safety valve, index of tensions); 3) play and social psychological problems of Western society; 4) play and linguistics (communication); 5) cognition and symbolism; 6) religion and play. Also listed by Norbeck was the relation of play to: ecstasy, art, game theory, politics, law, aggression, creativity or cultural innovation, and the didactic and socializing value of play among children and adults.

Sutton-Smith (1974), psychologist, insightfully viewed past play studies as stressing either "text" or "context." Textual play has been examined as content behavior isolated from situation, such as a player's response to game rules; contextual play has been the analyses of situations in which play occurred, not the play itself, such as in play therapy. Sutton-Smith summarized cross-cultural findings and proposed that the antecedents and postcedents of play's innovative function in culture be stressed.

Schwartzman (1976), anthropologist, presented a thorough review of children's play studies. This included ethnographic, anthropological, sociological, cross-cultural, ethological, ecological, and psychological oriented studies. Schwartzman recommended that attention be especially directed to cross cultural ethnographies of children's play with both text and context orientation. Also proposed was the ethnographic testing of various theories of play stages, e.g. Erikson's ego synchrony and Piaget's cognitive development theories.

Stevens (1976), cultural anthropologist, reviewed the classical, psychological and anthropological approaches to play. He (1976:11-12) stressed the necessity to accept the previously tested 'givens': 1) play is reflective of, and expressive of, cultural values; 2) play is instructive of social roles; 3) play facilitates the development of motor control; and 4) play is a release mechanism. He felt that play should be studied as a biosocial phenomenon, dividing it into the pre-cultural dimension (biological process) and the cultural dimension (socio-cultural process).

## FUTURE RESEARCH DIRECTIONS IN THE STUDY OF PLAY

In addition to research proposed by Malina, Norbeck, Schwartzman, and Stevens, play study in the near future could take many viable investigative directions. This author suggests the following general research topics: 1) play as an equivalent for 'reality;' 2) work and play as expressions of a universal phenomenological construct; 3) importance of the mental construct of dualism in play structure; 4) exploratory behavior correlates of play; 5) play as creative behavior; 6) play as individual symbolic perception vs. socially conceived action; 7) play as sacred and profane ritual; 8) ramifications of correlations between play and other cultural variables; 9) cross-cultural significance of competition, cooperation, and equivalency in game means and goals; 10) verification of etic and theoric (cross-cultural) themes of human play; 11) transmigrant evidence of homologous play activities; 12) bias of socioeconomic class play in ethnological analysis; 13) meaning of reversal or role inversion in play; 14) effect of behavior imperative in play structure on acculturation; 15) effect of game and sport structure on participant behavior; 16) linguistic analyses of play, games and sports language (structural relations and meanings, origins, distributions, diachronic changes); 17) exploration of the neurophysiological correlates of social play; 18) commonalities between primate and human developmental play patterns and expressions; 19) relationship of constance/change in play forms throughout the life cycle.

An over-riding theoretical perspective could provide an integrating model for the study of the play of man. Various disciplines could then pursue specific research in concert with, not in isolation from, other disciplines. The topical survey and interpretation of play studies within each discipline could be a beginning step. A synthesis of proposed hypotheses, findings, and needed investigations would help clarify the digms of theoretical structures and investigations would help clarify the collective research stance. The development of suggested priorities in play research could advance the collective endeavor. In addition, the current procedure of each scholar pursuing his or her own interests could be reinforced by a national and international projection of potential projects. Institutes of play research might provide leadership in information, coordination, financing and dissemination. The Association for the Anthropological Study of Play could serve to motivate foci in future directions of play research.

## SUMMARY

Five theoretical perspectives of anthropology, antiquarianism, evolutionism, diffusionism, functionalism, and structuralism, have provided the backdrop for perception, reporting, and interpretation of play in the past century.

Within antiquarianism, archival accounts of specific play, game and pastime activities in particular cultures have been identified. Within evolutionism, play studies have stressed progressive complexity of play forms and transformation over time from a sacred to a secular character. Within diffusionism, play as a transmittable culture trait was reviewed. Within functionalism, play's multiple purposes were purported to be: role practice, remediation, integration, maintenance, and potentiation. Also described have been dominant intra- and inter-culture themes. Within structuralism, situational elements and meanings have been advanced; specifically the structural elements of games have been studied as interactive factors determining player behavior.

Current play research has been noted within developing theoretical paradigms of anthropology: psychobiological orientation, cultural ecology, and structural analysis. Future play research may polarize around symbolism and structure, bio-cultural phenomenon, and adaptive potentiation.

NOTES

[1]Examples of antiquarianism include the following books: Alfonso I, King of Castile. *Libro de Juegos* (Book of Games) (1283); Strutt, Joseph. *Sports and Pastimes of the People of England* (1801); Falkener, Edward. *Games Ancient and Oriental* (1892); Culin, Stewart. *Korean Games, with Notes on the Corresponding Games of China and Japan* (1895); Newell, William W. *Games and Songs of American Children* (1883); Spence, Lewis. *Myth and Ritual in Dance, Game, and Rhyme* (1947); Brewster, Paul. *American Nonsinging Games* (1953); Opie, Peter and Iona. *Children's Games in Street and Playground* (1969); Knapp, M. and H. *One Potato, Two Potato* (1976).

[2]For a comprehensive review of the anthropological study of children's play, see Schwartzman (1976).

[3]Some of the ethnographic papers read at TAASP (The Association for the Anthropological Study of Play) conferences from 1975-1977 appear in the published Proceedings of the Association: 1) *The Anthropological Study of Play: Problems and Prospects.* D. Lancy and B. A. Tindall, Eds. Cornwall, N.Y.: Leisure Press, 1976; 2) *Studies in the Anthropology of Play: Papers in Memory of B. Allan Tindall.* P. Stevens, Jr., Ed. Cornwall, N.Y.: Leisure Press, 1977; 3) *Play: Anthropological Perspectives.* Michael A. Salter, Ed. Cornwall, N.Y.: Leisure Press, 1978.

REFERENCES

Ager, L. P., 1976, The Reflection of Cultural Values in Eskimo Children's Games. *In* The Anthropological Study of Play: Problems and Prospects. D. Lancy and B. A. Tindall, Eds. Cornwall, N.Y.: Leisure Press. Pp. 79-86.

Aldis, O., 1975, Play Fighting. New York: Academic Press.

Alfonso I, King of Castile, 1283, Libro de Juegos.

Avedon, E. and B. Sutton-Smith, 1971, The Study of Games. New York: John Wiley & Sons.

Baldwin, J. D., and J. I. Baldwin, 1977, The Primate Contribution to the Study of Play. Paper at The Association for the Anthropological Study of Play Conference, San Diego (in this volume).

Ball, D. W., 1972, The Scaling of Gaming: Skill, Strategy, and Chance. Pacific Sociological Review 15:277-294.
1974, Control versus Complexity: Continuities in the Scaling of Gaming. Pacific Sociological Review 17:167-184.

Barry, H., Josephson, L., Lauer, E., and C. Marshall, 1976, Traits Inculcated in Childhood: Cross-Cultural Code. Ethnology 51:83-114.

Bateson, G., 1955, A Theory of Play and Fantasy. Psychiatric Research Reports, American Psychiatric Association 2:39-51.

Beach, F., 1945, Current Concepts of Play in Animals. The American Naturalist 70:523-541.

Benedict, R., 1934, Patterns of Culture. Boston: Houghton Mifflin.

Berne, E., 1964, Games People Play. New York: Grove Press, Inc.

Brewster, P., 1953, American Nonsinging Games. Norman: University of Oklahoma Press.
1956, The Importance of the Collecting and Study of Games. Eastern Anthropologist 10:5-12.

Cheska, A., 1975, Stewart Culin: An Early Ethnologist of Games. Newsletter, The Association for the Anthropological Study of Play 2(3):4-13.

Chevalier-Skolnikoff, S., 1974, The Primate Play Face: A Possible Key to the Determinants and Evolution of Play. Rice University Studies 60(3):9-29.

Culin, S., 1895, Korean Games, with Notes on the Corresponding Games of China and Japan. Philadelphia: University of Pennsylvania Press.
1898, American Indian Games. Journal of American Folklore 11(43):245-252.
1907, Games of the North American Indians. Twenty-fourth Annual Report to the Bureau of Ethnology. Washington, D.C.: Government Printing Office.

Damm, H., 1960, To So-Called Sport Activities of Primitive People: A Contribution Towards the Genesis of Sport. G. Luschen and F. Keenan, Trans. Studium Generale 13:1-10.

De Rois, M. D. and R. Schroeder, 1977, American occupations, leisure time use and left brain/right brain balance: some explorations. Paper at the American Ethnological Society Annual Meeting, San Diego.

Dolhinow, P. and N. Bishop, 1970, The Development of Motor Skills and Social Relationships among Primates Through Play. Minnesota Symposia on Child Psychology 4:141-198.

Durkheim, E., 1933, The Division of Labor in Society. G. Simpson, Trans. New York: The Free Press. (Originally published 1893 in French.)

Edwards, H., 1973, Sociology of Sport. Homewood, Illinois: The Dorsey Press.

Erasmus, C. J., 1950, Patolli, Pachisi, and the Limitation of Possibilities. Southwestern Journal of Anthropology 6:369-387.

Erikson, E., 1950, Childhood and Society. New York: W. W. Norton & Company.

Firth, R., 1930, A Dart Match in Tikopia. Oceania 1:64-96.
1963, Elements of Social Organization. Boston: Beacon Press.

Falkener, E., 1961, Games Ancient and Oriental. New York: Dover Publications Inc. (Originally published 1892.)

Fortes, M., 1949, Social Structure: Studies Presented to A. R. Radcliffe-Brown. Oxford: Clarendon Press.

Frederickson, F. S., 1960, Sports and the Cultures of Man. In Science and Medicine of Exercise and Sports. W. R. Johnson, Ed. New York: Harper & Brothers. Pp. 633-646.

Freud, S., 1922, Beyond the Pleasure Principle. C. J. M. Hubback, Trans. Vienna: The International Psycho-analytical Press.

Geertz, Clifford, 1972, Deep Play: Notes on the Balinese Cockfight. Daedalus 101(1):1-37.

Glassford, R. G., 1969, The Mesoamerican Rubber Ball Game. In Proceedings of the First International Seminar on the History of Physical Education and Sport. U. Simri, Ed. Neyanta, Israel: Wingate Institute for Physical Education. Lecture No. 22.
1970, Application of a Theory of Games to the Transitional Eskimo Culture. Ph.D. dissertation, University of Illinois, Urbana, Illinois.

Goffman, E., 1961, Encounters: Two studies in the sociology of interaction. New York: The Bobbs-Merrill Company, Inc.

Gomme, A. B., 1964, The Traditional Games of England, Scotland, and Ireland, Vol. 1. New York: Dover Publications. (Originally published 1894.)
1964, The Traditional Games of England, Scotland, and Ireland. Vol. 2. New York: Dover Publications. (Originally published 1898.)

Groos, K., 1898, The Play of Animals. E. L. Baldwin, Trans. New York: D. Appleton and Company.
1901, The Play of Man. E. L. Baldwin, Trans. New York: D. Appleton and Company.

Haddon, A. C., 1898, The Study of Man. New York: G. P. Putman's Sons.

Hall, G. S., 1906, Youth. New York: D. Appleton & Company.

Heider, K., 1977, From Javanese to Dani: The Translation of a Game. *In* Studies in the Anthropology of Play: Papers in Memory of B. Allan Tindall. P. Stevens, Jr., Ed. Cornwall, N.Y.: Leisure Press. Pp. 72-81.

Henderson, R. W., 1947, Ball, Bat and Bishop. New York: Rockport Press, Inc.

Herron, R. E. and B. Sutton-Smith, 1971, Child's Play. New York: John Wiley & Sons, Inc.

Huizinga, J., 1955, Homo Ludens: A Study of the Play Element in Culture. Boston: The Beacon Press. (Originally published 1944.)

Ibrahim, H., 1975, Sport and Society. Long Beach, California: Hwong Publishing Company, Inc.

Ingham, A. and J. W. Loy, 1974, The Structure of Ludic Action. International Review of Sport Sociology 10(9):23-60.

Knapp, M. and H. Knapp, 1976, One Potato, Two Potato...New York: W. W. Norton & Company, Inc.

Krickeberg, W., 1948, Das mittelamerikanische Ballspiel und seine religiose Symbolik. Paideuma 3:118-190.

Kroeber, A. L., 1920, Games of the California Indians. American Anthropologist 22:273-277.
1925, Handbook of Indians of California. Bureau of American Ethnology, Bulletin 28. Washington, D.C.: Government Printing Office.
1931, Historical Reconstruction of Culture Growths and Organic Evolution. American Anthropologist 33:149-156.
1948, Anthropology. New York: Harcourt and Company.

Lancy, D. F., 1976, The Play Behavior of Kpelle Children During Rapid Cultural Change. *In* The Anthropological Study of Play: Problems and Prospects, D. Lancy and B. A. Tindall, Eds. Cornwall, N.Y.: Leisure Press. Pp. 72-79.

Levi-Strauss, C., 1953, Social Structure. *In* Anthropology Today. A. L. Kroeber, Ed. Chicago: The University of Chicago Press. Pp. 524-553.
1963, Structural Anthropology. C. Jacobson and B. G. Schoepf, Trans. New York: Basic Books, Inc.
1966, The Savage Mind. G. Weidenfeld, Trans. Chicago: The University of Chicago Press.

Linton, R., 1945, The Cultural Background of Personality. New York: Appleton-Century-Crofts.

Loizos, C., 1967, Play Behavior in Higher Primates: A Review. *In* Primate Ethology. D. Morris, Ed. Chicago: Aldine. Pp. 176-218.

Luschen, G., 1970, The Cross-Cultural Analysis of Sport and Games. Champaign, Illinois:

Stipes Publishing Company.
1975, The Development and Scope of a Sociology of Sport. American Corrective Therapy Journal 29:39-43.

Malefijt, A. deWaal, 1974, Images of Man: A History of Anthropological Thought. New York: Alfred A. Knopf.

Malina, R., 1969, An Anthropological Perspective of Man in Action. In New Perspectives of Man in Action. R. C. Brown, Jr. and B. J. Cratty, Eds. Englewood Cliffs, New Jersey: Prentice Hall, Inc. Pp. 147-162.

Malinowski, Bronislaw, 1922, Argonauts of the Western Pacific. New York: E. P. Dutton and Company.
1939, The Group and the Individual in Functional Analysis. American Journal of Sociology 4:938-964.

Mead, G., 1934, Mind, Self and Society. Chicago: The University of Chicago Press.

Mead, M., 1928, Coming of Age in Samoa. New York: William Morrow & Sons.

Mendner, S., 1956, Das Ballspiel im Leben der Voelker. Muenster: Aschendorff.

Miracle, A. W., 1977, Some Functions of Aymara Games and Play. In Studies in the Anthropology of Play: Papers in Memory of B. Allan Tindall. P. Stevens, Jr., Ed. Cornwall, N.Y.: Leisure Press. Pp. 98-105.

Murdock, G. P., 1957, World Ethnographic Sample. American Anthropologist 59:664-687.
1969, Standard Cross-cultural Sample. Ethnology 8:329-369.

Naroll, R. and R. Cohen, 1970, A Handbook of Method in Cultural Anthropology. New York: Columbia University Press.

Newell, W. W., 1883, Games and Songs of American Children. New York: Harper Brothers.

Norbeck, E., 1971, Man at Play. Play: A Natural History Magazine Special Supplement December:48-53.
1974, The Anthropological Study of Human Play. Rice University Studies 60(3):1-93.

Nordenskiold, E., 1910, Spiele und Spielsachen im Gran Chaco und in Nordamerika. Zeitschrift fur Ethnologie 42:427-433.

Oakley, F. B. and P. C. Reynolds, 1976, Differing Responses to Social Play Deprivation in Two Species of Macaque. In The Anthropological Study of Play: Problems and Prospects. D. F. Lancy and B. A. Tindall, Eds. Cornwall, New York: Leisure Press. Pp. 179-188.

Opie, P. and I., 1969, Children's Games in Street and Playground. London: Oxford University Press.

Parman, S., 1977, An evolutionary theory of dreaming and play. Paper at the American Ethnological Society Annual Meeting, San Diego.

Piaget, J., 1962, Play, Dreams and Imitation in Childhood. C. Cattegno and F. M. Hodgson, Trans. New York: W. W. Norton & Company, Inc.

Radcliffe-Brown, A. R., 1941, The Study of Kinship Systems. Journal of the Royal Anthropological Institute 70:1-18.
1952, Structure and Function in Primitive Society. New York: The Free Press.

Raum, O. F., 1953, The Rolling Target (Hoop-and-Pole) Game in Africa. African Studies 12:104-121.

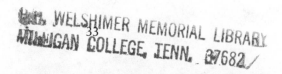

Reany, M. J., 1916, The Psychology of the Organized Group Game. Cambridge: Cambridge University Press.

Redl, F., Gump, P., and B. Sutton-Smith, 1971, The Dimensions of Games. In The Study of Games. E. Avedon and B. Sutton-Smith, Eds. New York: John Wiley & Sons, Inc. Pp. 408-418.

Renick, J., 1977, The Structure of Games. Seattle, Washington: University of Washington, mimeographed paper.

Roberts, J.; Arth, M.; and R. Bush, 1959, Games in Culture. American Anthropologist 61:597-605.

Roberts, J. and B. Sutton-Smith, 1962, Child Training and Game Involvement. Ethnology 1:166-185.
1964, Rubrics of Competitive Behavior. Journal of Genetic Psychology 105:13-37.
1966, Cross-Cultural Correlates of Games of Chance. Behavior Science Notes 3:131-144.

Roberts, J., Sutton-Smith, B., and A. Kendon, 1963, Strategy in Games and Folk Tales. Journal of Social Psychology 61:185-199.

Rosenstiel, A., 1976, The Role of Traditional Games in the Process of Socialization among the Motu of Papua New Guinea. In The Anthropological Study of Play: Problems and Prospects. D. F. Lancy and B. A. Tindall, Eds. Cornwall, N.Y.: Leisure Press. Pp. 52-58.

Sahlins, M. D., 1960, Evolution: Specific and General. In Evolution and Culture. M. Sahlins and E. R. Service, Eds. Ann Arbor: University of Michigan Press. Pp. 12-44.

Schaefer, C., 1976, Therapeutic Use of Child's Play. New York: Jason Aronson, Inc.

Scheffler, L., 1976, Wake Games from the State of Tlaxcala, Mexico. Paper at the Association for the Anthropological Study of Play Conference, Atlanta.

Schwartzman, H. B., 1976, The Anthropological Study of Children's Play. Annual Review of Anthropology. Vol. 5. Palo Alto, California: Annual Reviews, Inc.

Simri, U., 1968, Religious and Magical Functions of Ball Games in Various Cultures. In Proceedings of the First International Seminar on the History of Physical Education and Sport. Neyanta, Israel: Wingate Institute for Physical Education. Lecture No. 2.
1975, The Religious and Magical Dimensions of Play Involving Physical Activities. In Proceedings of an International Seminar, Neyanta, Israel: Wingate Institute for Physical Education and Sport. Pp. 121-127.

Sipes, R. G., 1973, War, Sports and Aggression: An Empirical Test of Two Rival Theories. American Anthropologist 75:64-86.

Spence, L., 1947, Myth and Ritual in Dance, Game and Rhyme. London: Watts & Co.

Stevens, P. Jr., 1976a, Laying the Groundwork for an Anthropology of Play. Newsletter, The Association for the Anthropological Study of Play 3(2):2-14.
1976b, Social and Judicial Functions of Bachama Song-Contests. In The Anthropological Study of Play: Problems and Prospects. D. F. Lancy and B. A. Tindall, Eds. Cornwall, N.Y.: Leisure Press. Pp. 164-171.

Strutt, J., 1876, The Sports and Pastimes of the People of England from the Earliest Period to the Present Time. London: Chatto & Windus. (Originally published 1801.)

Suomi, S. J. and H. F. Harlow, 1971, Monkeys at Play. Play: A Natural History Magazine Special Supplement December: 72-75.

Sutton-Smith, B., 1969, The Two Cultures of Games. *In* Aspects of Contemporary Sport Sociology. Gerald Kenyon, Ed. Chicago: Athletic Institute. Pp. 135-147.

1972, The Folkgames of Children. Austin: University of Texas Press.

1973, Games, the Socialization of Conflict. Canadian Journal of History of Sport and Physical Education 4(1):1-7.

1974, Toward an Anthropology of Play. Newsletter, The Association for the Anthropological Study of Play 1(2):8-15.

1975, Play as Adaptive Potentiation. Sporwissenschaft 5:103-118.

1976, Footnotes to TAASP Keynote Address in Atlanta, 1976. Newsletter, The Association for the Anthropological Study of Play 3(2):15-21.

Sutton-Smith, B., Roberts, J. M. and R. M. Kozelka, 1963, Game Involvement in Adults. Journal of Social Psychology 60:15-30.

Szasz, T. S., 1961, The Myth of Mental Illness. New York: Hoeber Medical Division, Harper & Row.

Textor, R. B., 1967, A Cross-cultural Summary. New Haven: Princeton University Press.

Tylor, E. B., 1879a, On the Game of Patolli in Ancient Mexico. Journal of the Royal Anthropological Institute of Great Britain and North Ireland 8:116-131.

1879b, The History of Games. The Fortnightly Review 25:735-747.

1881, Anthropology. New York: Appleton and Company.

1896, On American Lot-Games, as Evidence of Asiatic Intercourse Before the Time of Columbus. International Archives for Ethnographie, Supplement 9:56-66.

Van-Lawick-Goodall, J., 1967, My Friends the Wild Chimpanzees. Washington, D.C.: National Geographic Society.

Vernes, J. R., 1965, The Element of Time in Competitive Games. Diogenes 50:25-42.

Von Neuman, J. and O. Morgenstern, 1947, Theory of Games and Economic Behavior. New York: Wiley & Sons.

Waelder, R. R., 1933, The Psychoanalytic Theory of Play. Psychoanalytic Quarterly 2:208-224.

Welker, W. J., 1961, An Analysis of Exploratory and Play Behavior in Animals. *In* Functions of Varied Experience. D. W. Fiske and S. K. Maddi, Eds. Homewood, Illinois: Dorsey. Pp. 175-226.

White, D. R., 1970, Societal Research Archives System: Retrieval, Quality Control and Analysis of Comparative Data. *In* A Handbook of Method in Cultural Anthropology. R. Naroll and R. Cohen, Eds. Garden City, New York: Natural History Press. Pp. 676-688.

White, L. A., 1969, The Science of Culture: A Study of Man and Civilization. Garden City, New York: Doubleday.

Whiting, J. and I. Child, 1953, Child Training and Personality. New Haven: Yale University Press.

Whiting, J. and B. Whiting, 1963, Six Cultures: Studies of Child Rearing. New York: Wiley & Sons.

## PIAGET'S THEORY OF PLAY:
## A REVIEW OF THE CRITICAL LITERATURE

David L. Post, Pacific Graduate School of Psychology

The book, **Play, Dreams and Imitation in Childhood,** by Jean Piaget (1951) includes an elaborate theoretical account of the behavior known as play. Piaget focuses on play from a cognitive orientation. Through careful observation he has incorporated his findings on play into a larger theoretical framework of child development. This paper reviews and evaluates the literature which has come forth in criticism of Piaget's concepts. The papers examined vary in their intensity of criticism, some seeking to merely refine and suggest changes in emphasis, while others have mounted full scale attacks. An attempt has been made here to evaluate these works in their own right, taking note of those that make a particular contribution while suggesting to others a different interpretation or a need for more complete evidence.

The first paper is by Sutton-Smith (1966) and concentrates on Piaget's (1951, 1954, 1960) categorization of imitation as accommodation on the one hand, and play as assimilation on the other. Sutton-Smith notes that Piaget appears on the surface to form a Hegelian dialectic of opposites which through a higher synthesis becomes reconciled into more adaptive structures of logic. In fact, however, it is maintained that Piaget does not assign the equal role of thesis and antithesis to imitation and play. Instead, only imitation is given a major part in the origin of concepts. Sutton-Smith claims that by providing imitation or, more accurately, accommodation with such a major role, Piaget has implicitly incorporated a copyist theory of knowledge about the environment into his theory. It is observed (Sutton-Smith 1966) that it was this very copy-theory of knowledge which Piaget had previously denounced and replaced with the concepts of accommodation and assimilation. The implicit copyist notion of imitation which gives accommodation the role of initiating and sustaining representative activity, "leaves play intellectually functionless" (Sutton-Smith 1966:106) within Piaget's system. Quoting from Piaget (1951), Sutton-Smith shows that play in Piaget's theory makes no intrinsic contribution to the development of thought. Instead it is suggested that play is given a number of definitions while imitation is given only one. With no role in the development of though, Piaget (1951) assigns as the positivie contribution of play the role of ego continuity, a function quite distinct from thought. Assigning this lone function to play leads to the serious problem of a disjunction between cognitive functions and affective functions which Piaget has already stated are inseparable. As Sutton-Smith says, "If play has a constitutive affective function of this sort (ensuring ego continuity), Piaget's general position of affective-cognitive relations requires that it should also have a constitutive intellective function" (1966:106).

Sutton-Smith also finds it unfortunate that Piaget (1957) is concerned with only logical directed thinking and does not consider forms of less directed thought, such as reverie, creative imagination, and other divergent thinking. With the concentration on directed thinking, Piaget finds a relative disequilibrium between the young child and adults; again seen by Sutton-Smith as implying a copyist theory of knowledge. Further, it is maintained that a serious semantic confusion results when Piaget refers to the relative ontogenetic disequilibrium in the developing organism and then maintains that each stage of development has an equilibrium of its own. Sutton-Smith notes the logical difficulties which arise when there is equilibration of early stages which are, however, less in equilibrium than later stages. The reader thus is forced to grapple with such entities as "disequilibrial equilibriums."

This unfortunate semantic situation leads to a more serious problem with Piaget's theory. The disequilibrial ontogenetic state of the child compared to the adult, based on directed thinking, leads to play as a means of an "affective holding action" when the intellectual structure is disrupted by intractable environmental data. Again, play is deprived of any cognitive function and yet is expected somehow to reestablish equilibrium at every cognitive stage. This leads to a further step in which Sutton-Smith sees Piaget as making as disjunction between the operations of adult thought and childhood thought. Thus, it is found that "childhood thinking is bolstered by the affective operations of play, but the thinking of adults is not" (Sutton-Smith 1966:107).

Sutton-Smith objects to Piaget's view that play for adults "ceases to be a vital function of the mind when the individual is socialized, and that with age the symbolic games of childhood are replaced by realism" (Piaget 1951:168). Instead of a decrease in symbolic play with age, examples are given which show a shift in the application of the symbolic function, such as determining the outcomes of games. Evidence is also cited (Sutton-Smith, Roberts and Kozelka 1963) which support the view that games of adulthood are highly symbolic and have little to do with what is rational or real. Other authors (Huizinger 1949; Roberts, Arth and Bush 1959; Roberts and Sutton-Smith 1962; Sutton-Smith and Roberts 1964) are shown to disagree with Piaget (1951) and maintain that play is a vital function of the mind in socialized adults and indeed permeates their activities. "Without such a point of view it is difficult to understand the verbal play of adults, their social and sexual play, their rituals and their carnivals, their festivals and fairs, and their widespread and diversified playfulness" (Sutton-Smith 1966:109).

In considering Sutton-Smith's critique of Piaget it becomes clear that certain of the criticisms are of greater validity than others. To begin with, Sutton-Smith's attempt to show that Piaget's theory involves an implicit copyist theory of knowledge, because Piaget does not assign an equal role to imitation and play, would appear to be somewhat inaccurate. It would seem that Sutton-Smith is unaware of the fact that according to Piaget (1952) accomodation (imitation) and assimilation (play) are really sub-categories of the invariant function called adaptation and as such are not required to be of equal potency, but rather available to the organism when needed. Even of greater importance, Piaget (1966) replies that in play assimilation is primary over accommodation in that it allows the transformation of reality-states without having to submit the action to a standard of objective fact. Thus, play is able to exercise action scheme so that the child can understand the transformations involved between reality-states (Piaget 1966). In this way, play has a definite cognitive component which is not subordinate to imitation.

Sutton-Smith appears to be on much firmer ground when citing Piaget's disjunction between directed and undirected thinking. Shortcomings of Piaget are also rightly pointed to, as the illogical nature of the discussion on equilibrium and the semantic mess which exist in Piaget's writings on the subject. All of this, in turn, justifies the criticism that Piaget has created a disjunction between childhood and adult thinking. Finally, the criticism of Piaget in his concepts of symbolic play becoming more realistic, while the depreciated function which play serves in adults should be taken seriously.

Although complimenting Piaget on his close observations and his highly developed theory of play, Singer (1966) nevertheless notes that serious gaps exist. Singer rightly maintains that Piaget has neglected the very important interaction patterns which are established between the parents and the child. It is omissions of this sort that make it very difficult to accept Piaget's account without serious reservations. Because of its properties of exclusion it is also very difficult to establish connections between Piaget's theory and the work of others, such as Sullivan (1953), in the case of parent-child interactions. This, of course, does not invalidate what Piaget says, but rather forces caution until such gaps are filled. To illustrate another example of a critical gap, it is suggested that Piaget does not really work the emotional component of play directly into the theoretical structure. Thus, while observing the considerable joy children manifest while engaging in make-believe games, for instance, nothing is developed out of such important and widespread data (Singer 1973). This criticism is both accurate and yet limited. Piaget (1951) does indeed incorporate joy into his theory of play. However, Piaget sees joy as being only a by-product of play behavior which developes automatically from the realization of the inherent potential of the organism. According to Piaget, it is the nature of the child's cognitive structure that leads to play. It is this subordinate role as a by-product assigned to the emotion of joy that Singer would be correct in criticizing. Certainly the failure to include, as a stimulus, the emotion of joy in a theory of the behavior known as play is a grievous omission which any child would be quick to point out.

Eiferman (1971) has studied the play of children both in different cultures, using Arab and Jewish schools, and between different economic and social classes within a culture. Eiferman's data show first, that contrary to Piaget's "games with rules" increasing "in number both absolutely and relatively with age" (1951:146), they actually decrease in percentage of play participants with age. The decline in rule-governed games is both relative and absolute. Piaget defines "games with rules" as those games involving sensori-motor or intellectual combinations "in which there is competition between individuals" (1951:144). Eiferman (1971) disagrees noting that there are also individual and cooperative "games with rules." This data holds true whether all rule-governed games are considered or only those which Piaget defines as "games with rules". These results are particularly impressive since the sample is so large (with N = 65,000 children when rule-governed games of all types are considered and N = 56,560 when only including competitive rule (governed games). The data hold true, not only for children's play in school, but also for children observed at play out of school. Further, partial data revealed that the decline in "games with rules" continues beyond school age. It is interesting to note that the data shows that the absolute decline in "games with rules" sets in at about age 11, while the relative decline in such games begins to occur somewhat later at about age 13.

Eiferman (1971) also considered the collected data in terms of Piaget's contention that both symbolic and practice play forms decline while games with rules increase. Since the latter was not supported by the data, it seemed possible that the former would also be shown as inconsistent with the observations. In fact, the results were not as clear cut. Eiferman reported that the analysis of collective symbolic play supported Piaget's thesis that there is a decline in such play with age. It was also found that children from a school for "high" achievers reached the peak of symbolic play at an earlier age than did children from a school for "low" achievers. With regard to practice play, however, Eiferman reports data that contradicts Piaget's (1951) claim that there is a necessary decline with age. Indeed, the data shows that after an initial decline there is again an increase in practice play corresponding to the decrease reported earlier in games with rules. The timing of the decline and subsequent increase in practice play varies according to "high" or "low" school with the changes occurring sooner among children from the "high" school.

A note of caution should be sounded here. While Eiferman's data contradicts Piaget it also flies in the face of what is considered common knowledge about play, a fact which Eiferman (1971) also acknowledges. Thus the results, while impressive, must be interpreted carefully at this time. Certainly more studies are needed to see if the results can be replicated. Also, experimental designs need to be compared to determine what differences, if any, could account for inconsistent results.

Gilmore (1966) begins with a very clear overview of Piaget's theory. In this overview it is observed that Piaget (1951) sees a close link between the play of children and the process of dreaming. Gilmore shows that Piaget simply accepts the process underlying both play and dreaming and makes no attempt to explain it. Rather, Piaget is content to label and describe the important aspects of the process. This is a good beginning (Gilmore 1966) to help organize information about both, but must eventually give way to a more complete understanding.

Gilmore then proceeds to report on a series of experiments in which categories developed by Piaget to identify play are tested. The first category is termed "compensatory combinations" and refers to behavior that distorts reality to make it fit more agreeable and desired thoughts. The second category is known as "liquidating combinations" and refers to behavior released "from a need to allow for the presence of strong affect that, originally, came connected with the play-provoking situation" (Gilmore 1966:350). He reports that the studies fit Piaget's theory without providing great support for it. In fact, an interaction effect between "compensatory combinations" and "liquidating combinations" which was hypothesized was not supported at all. Gilmore leaves the question of the validity of Piaget's theory open. Instead, he goes on to give an excellent description of the problems involved in empirically testing the various theories of play and suggests possible solutions.

In conclusion, the importance of Piaget to the theories of play has been made obvious in this review of his critics. Such a review would not be possible unless other researchers found his theory worthy of serious consideration. It does appear, however, that as these authors have shown, the theory of play which Piaget presents is not complete. There are omissions of data, inconsistencies within the system, and concepts which are not supported by experimental evidence. Some of the criticisms are small as to be almost trifling, while others have major implications. The critics have done themselves proud by sticking to facts and objectivity while avoiding polemics and distortion. It is hoped that by this paper a clearer understanding of the contentious aspects of Piaget's theory has been provided so that further progress will be enhanced.

REFERENCES

Eiferman, R. R., 1971, Social play in childhood. *In* Child's Play. R. E. Herron and B. Sutton-Smith, Eds. New York: John Wiley and Sons Inc. Pp. 270-297.

Gilmore, J. B., 1966, Play: A Special Behavior. *In* Current Research in Motivation. R. N. Haber, Ed. New York: Holt, Rinehart and Winston. Pp. 343-354.

Huizinga, J., 1949, Homo Ludens: The Play Element in Culture. London: Routledge and Kagan Paul.

Piaget, J., 1951, Play, Dreams, and Imitation in Childhood. C. Gattegno and F. M. Hodgson, Trans. New York: W. W. Norton and Co. Inc.
1952, The Origins of Intelligence in Children. M. Worden, Trans. New York: International Universities Press.
1954, The Construction of Reality in the Child. M. Cook, Trans. New York: Basic Books, Inc.
1957, Logic and Psychology. New York: Basic Books, Inc.
1960, The Psychology of Intelligence. Paterson, N.J.: Littlefield and Adams.
1966, Response to Brian Sutton-Smith. Psychological Review 73:111-112.

Roberts, J. M., Arth, M. J. and R. R. Bush, 1959, Games in Culture. American Anthropologist 61:597-605.

Roberts, J. M. and B. Sutton-Smith, 1962, Child Training and Game Involvement. Ethnology 1:166-185.

Singer, J. L., 1966, Daydreaming: An Introduction to the Experimental Study of Inner Experience. New York: Random House.
1973, The Child's World of Make-Believe: Experimental Studies of Imaginative Play. New York: Academic Press.

Sullivan, H. S., 1953, The Interpersonal Theory of Psychiatry. New York: Norton.

Sutton-Smith, B., Roberts, J. M. and R. Kozelka, 1963, Game Involvement in adults. Journal of Social Psychology 60:15-30.

Sutton-Smith, B. and J. M. Roberts, 1964, Rubrics of Competitive Behavior. Journal of Genetic Psychology 105:13-37.

Sutton-Smith, B., 1966, Piaget on Play: A Critique. Psychological Review 73:104-110.

## INFORMATION MANAGEMENT: A SYSTEM MODEL
## OF RITUAL AND PLAY[1]

Reed D. Riner, University of Northern Arizona

Ethologists have for several decades watched primates scurrying, clambering, cantering, brachiating, and even walking about, intent on satisfying their vital needs. They acquire food and produce offspring. They defend the synergetic advantage of troop from external predation and from internal disorder and discoordinate behavior. They maintain a niche sufficient to these activities. Ethologists have also reported numerous incidents of recurrent, though neither immediately nor directly effective, behavior. These performances are usually referred to the polar, if sometimes overlapping catagories of ritual and play.

Ethologists explain the effective behaviors efficiently in terms of gross physiological survival and the immediate adaptation of the organism and the troop, but ritual and play have eluded a general and efficient explanation. An explanation is possible in the paradigm of General System Theory; it proposes that ritual and play behaviors are polar expressions of a single behavioral process whose objective is to keep informational inputs within an optimum range.

The examples for this model, which is intended to apply to all adapting systems, have been drawn from the field of primate ethology to provide examples of sufficient complexity. Examples drawn from the human realm would entail elaborate symbolic and self-referrential behaviors that would be inordinately complex for the minimum essential model intended here.

## THE SYSTEM PARADIGM

A system is defined as any set of interacting variables abstracted from reality, be that the general eco-system, a species population, a single organism, or a man-made mechanical or social system. Obviously the potential number of variables and resultant systems is without limit. The designation of the boundary of the system is arbitrary and those variables which fall outside the boundary are called parameters. They constitute the effective environment for the system variables. Distinguishing between system variables and parameters is not difficult for systems which have conspicuous boundary structures, such as shells and skins, or man-made boundaries, such as city limits.

The behavior of natural systems is dominated by entropy—the universal tendency of material elements to disorder and of energy differentials to equalize. All of the living and some of the more complex man-made systems are anti-entropic; they impose order on material elements and build up energy differentials. The members of this class are all to some extent self-regulating.

Each of these systems has a certain number of variables which it strives to keep within optimum ranges. The system achieves its goal conditions by controlling its output of products and directed energies in order to get optimal or satisfying inputs (Powers 1973:47). In this way a system satisfies its needs and develops an adaptive relationship with its environment. This relationship is dynamic. Both the environment and the parts of the system are continually changing. As these changes effect the whole system, moving one or more variables away from optimum satisfaction, the system experiences hunger, discomfort, frustration, fatigue, boredom or pain. The system seeks to establish a new adaptive relationship, in part by eliminating from consideration the less effective variables, and by locating and extending control to the more

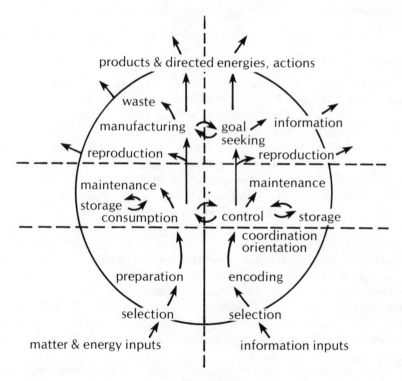

Figure 1

Essential Processes of a Living System

effective variables (Stucki 1970). Need satisfaction is self-rewarding (the General Effectance Motive identified by White [1959] and by Byrne and Clore [1967:4]) as the system establishes its new adaptive relationship. When effective memory is present in the system, this dynamic homeostatic process includes learning among its component processes.

Figure 1 identifies essential processes for a living system, treating its environment very simply as matter and energy on one hand, and as information on the other. There are corresponding forms of management for the two kinds of inputs.

This diagram suggests why lines of behavior relevant to physical survival and adaptation have received their descriptions first. Their events, messages and products are in greater part material (e.g. chemical compounds) which persist in time, are more obvious and are easily measured. Fully complementary informational events do not persist in time, are more subtle, and are not easily measured.

## ETHOGRAPHIC FOUNDATIONS

Previous explanations of ritual and play appeal particularly to the more material lines of behavior, such as subsistence, defense and reproduction. To illustrate: Kortlandt (1955) and Loizos (1967) contend that play and ritual are the release of individual tensions as a physiological safety valve. Wickler (1967), after an exhaustive study of the presenting ritual of over thirty species, concludes that this ritual arises initially and directly from sexual functions and is later partially displaced into the service of social coordination. Observing the same phenomenon, Gartlan (1968) notes its service within the dominence hierarchy, argues for more, though not complete, independence from sexual functions and supports a multi-factorial view. Lorenz (1963), Ardrey (1961, 1966) and Morris (1968) view play and ritual as a coordination imposed on conflicting drives within the "parliament of instincts". In sum, there are proposals relating ritual and play behaviors to aggressive, dominence, territorial, sexual, investigatory and communicative behavior. Each argument lends insight, yet no one of them, nor all of them taken together, presents an integrated and efficient explanation for the observed behaviors.

The complexity of these observed behaviors is exemplified by the following three cases: the presenting ritual of the hamadryas baboon, the threat ritual of the gorilla and the rain dance of the chimpanzee.

1. The presenting ritual of the hamadryas baboon:

In the presenting ritual one baboon places her, or his, genital area in demonstrative proximity to the face of another. It serves as an invitation to mating and is the major preoccupation of the female baboon in oesterous. But such behavior is exhibited by all members of the troop regardless of sex or maturity.

Presenting is employed when one baboon approaches another, especially one more dominant who could be expected to attack to enforce his status. Generally when any baboon is threatened he will invariably present—and as invariable avert attack.

Presenting occurs when a baboon encounters a new acquaintance whose status in unknown and the frequency of presenting greatly increases during the period of troop formation.

Yet baboons, present regularly even to old friends and frequently, especially in this context, presenting serves as an invitation of grooming.

Finally one observes that the frequency and intensity of presenting increases markedly among confined baboons. It continues to increase as the area of confinement is diminished until destructively antisocial behavior erupts. (Washburn and DeVore 1961; Kummer and Kurt 1963; and Wickler 1967.)

2. The threat ritual of the gorilla:

Gorillas can exhibit strong feelings, especially when they are threatened. They scream in alarm and as a warning to the other members of the troop. They toss leaves in the air. They also beat their chests. All gorillas, even young ones, do this, rising up on two legs on the ground, or popping up from amid the foliage of a tree to give a few brief slaps before fading out of sight.

The full performance is put on by the silver-back males, and is as formalized as the entrance of a fighter into the ring. It begins inconspicuously with a series of soft clear hoots that gradually quicken. Already the silver-back male apparently expects to command attention, because, if interrupted, he is liable to look around in annoyance. As he continues to hoot, he may stop, pluck a leaf from a nearby plant and place it to his lips. This curiously incongruous and delicate gesture is a prelude to coming violence, and when they see it the other gorillas get out of his way. The violence is not immediate. First the gorilla rises to his full height and slaps his hands on his chest or belly, on his thighs or on another gorilla, producing a booming sound that can be heard a mile away. The chest beating over, the violence erupts. He walks sideways for a few steps, then drops down on all fours and breaks into a full-speed dash, wrenching branches from trees and slapping violently at everything in his way, including other members of the troop who haven't the wit to keep clear. Finally there comes the last gesture; the silver-back thumps the palm of his hand violently on the ground, and then sits back, looking as if he were now ready to hear the applause. (Schaller 1963; illustration after Eimerl and DeVore 1965:66-67.)

3. The rain dance of the chimpanzee:

The active chimpanzee travels through the forest in loose bands which at intervals devote themselve to choruses of shrill calls accompanied by drumming on the butresses of trees. This is particularly focused about the meeting of groups, moving in or out of feeding places, when groups divide, and at nesting and waking.

These displays can be accompanied by stamping on the ground, shaking saplings, waving branches, slapping trees and swinging wildly about.

There is a positive correlation between the size of the group and the frequency of these outbursts (Reynolds 1963).

On occasion these outburst will occur in the night and continue for hours, giving rise to the forest legend of Chimpanzee Carnivals.

But probably the most curious of all these displays is the rain dance reported by Goodall (1963).

When the rain started falling, they came down from the trees and started walking up the slope in two groups. At the skyline the females and juveniles climbed high into the trees. As the rain turned into a violent tropical deluge, the males, amid crashes of thunder, began their spectacular display. One, turning suddenly, charged diagonally down the slope, slapping the ground as it went, and as though this were a signal all other males joined in. Some charged down hitting at vegetation, other sprang into the trees, tore off great branches, hurled themselves to the ground and raced down the hill at break-neck speed dragging the branches behind them. At the bottom, each chimpanzee swung up into a tree to break its headlong flight. There it sat for a moment before climbing down and plodding up the hill again to resume, with wild cries, its downward rush. Then, as suddenly as it had begun, the show was over; the spectators climbed down from the trees and the whole group disappeared over the horizon.

## ANALYSIS AND MODEL

These various primate behaviors share a common set of processes; elements are selected from the animal's repertoire of effective behaviors and are operated upon. These selected elements are templates for action stored as information in the system. Morris (1967) gives a summary of the operations; once lifted from their normal context, the elements of daily behavior may be:

| | |
|---|---|
| 1) reordered | 7) recombined |
| 2) exaggerated | 8) intensified |
| 3) repeated | 9) intent altered |
| 4) fragmented | 10) tempo altered |
| 5) abstracted | 11) pattern altered |
| 6) incompleted | |

Morris was discussing the behaviors as ritual. Loizos (1967) offers semantically identical criteria for the recognition of play as a performance in which effective elements of behavior are altered by:

| | |
|---|---|
| 1) rythmic repetition | 5) change in coordination |
| 2) differential exaggeration | 6) differential speed |
| 3) omission | 7) change in vigor |
| 4) change in sequence | |

The equivalence of these two lists suggest that ritual and play behaviors have a common origin. The lists provide an operational definition for the recognition of the general process. A cybernetic model must first account for these component processes then provide for meaningful distinction between ritual and play behaviors as they are observed in adapting systems generally.

The development of this model must first consider a single variable initially at optimum satisfaction. A change occurs in the relevant parameter. Sensed by the system, a proportional change is registered into the system, moving the variable away from its optimum. This generates a degree of disequilibrium. This is always a negative value because it is a difference from optimum satisfaction, regardless of whether the disturbing input is excessive or deficient. Discomforted, the system seeks a new value for the variable that will decrease the error signal towards zero. To achieve this more adaptive state the system generates a new value for the variable; this is represented in Figure 2 by the angle at 0, and the vector represents the consequent signal. This new value may be drawn either from memory, if one is present, or generated at random. The new vector and its consequent error signal are generated. The new signal is evaluated and the process is repeated until the variable is brought to satisfaction. This is the simplest sort of corrective feedback mechanism, operating to reduce deviation (Maruyama 1963). The process may be executed continuously or in a step-wise progression.

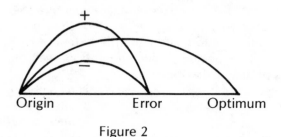

Figure 2

Single Variable Satisfaction Model

System efficiency is greatly improved when the system is sensitive to the results of its own performance. The most important sensitivities are to a) the value of the correction, b & c) the direction and the amount of the error signal and d & e) the direction and amount of the correction; indeed one or more of these sensitivities must be present if the mechanism is to function at all. On the other hand, provisions for all five sensitivities would be both redundant and excessively complex. Figure 3 illustrates lines of behavior generated by four possible combinations. This small sample illustrates both a part of the hierarch of efficiency among the various combinations and how simple homeostats can generate divers behaviors.

In figure 3, line A illustrates the situation in which both the optimum (a) and the direction of the correction (d) are known; the variable proceeds to satisfaction directly and continuously. Line B illustrates the situation in which the direction of the correction but not the optimum is known; here the absolute error decreases steadily, but there is marked oscillation as the variable proceeds towards its goal. Line C illustrates the situation in which the optimum but not the direction of the correction is known; here the error may increase with the initial try, but will thereafter decrease from the initial error. This, and the following line of behavior, is depicted as a step-wise process in Figure 3. Line D illustrates the situation in which neither of the above sensitivities are present. Here the variable may wobble out of its field at any time and satisfaction is achieved only by accident. All of these examples assume that the homeostat is sensitive to the amount of the correction (e); the opposite condition is so unstable that it defies graphic representation.

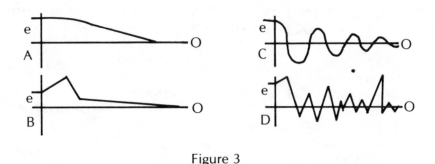

Figure 3

Possible Routes to Satisfaction

Two additional sensitivities should now be considered for the single variable model. Superior sensors may operate to achieve a) an optimum **rate** at which satisfaction is achieved and b) an optimum **unit of correction,** so that corrections are neither so small as to be imperceptible, nor so large and erratic as to be incomprehensible. The design of these superior sensors could be identical in structure to the subject homeostat, receiving their input from it.

The preceding model accounts for how a single variable may be brought to satisfaction. In the encounter between a natural system and its environment a very large number of variables and parameters are involved. These are often linked together into sets or sub-systems and may be supposed to have differential effects on one another. Much more complex behaviors are permitted. For example, the system may adjust the optimum to meet the altered variable in some instances, or may sacrifice maximum satisfaction for one variable in order to achieve greater whole-system satisfaction in other cases.

Three kinds of information are now at work within the model: 1) the input signals about changes in the environment and in parts of the system, 2) stored information representing the repertiore of behaviors available to the system and 3) the referential signals about the conduct of processes ongoing in the system. Information in the second catagory may be generated either at random, drawn from memory, or both in some combination. In systems with effective memory, the stored information may include sets of selection criteria that provide for alternate solutions to a single problem and for the assembly of sequential activities which may be called routines.

The model described above could be build as an electronic-mechanical homeostat; many of the more complex man-made systems already include similar components. The behavior of this kind of homeostat exhibits the following characteristics from the Morris-Loizos lists; the actions at its disposal are:

| | |
|---|---|
| 1) reordered | 1) rythmically repeated |
| 3) repeated | 3) omitted |
| 4) fragmented | 4) changed in sequence |
| 5) abstracted | 5) changed in coordination |
| 6) incompleted | |
| 7) recombined | |
| 10) tempo altered | |

These criteria can be further reduced to selective repetition and partial-to-complete omission.

Six of the initial criteria for the recognition of play and ritual behavior remain to be explained. Their absence in typical machine performance is due to the uniform rate of activity of machines. Natural systems employ a variety of rates of activity simultaneously. Much of this is due to differential rates of entropic decay in the different sub-systems. Introduction of differential rates of activity into the model accounts for the remaining variables:

| | |
|---|---|
| 2) exaggeration | 2) differential exaggeration |
| 8) altered intensity | 6) differential speed |
| 9) altered intent | 7) change in vigor |
| 11) altered pattern | |

To summarize the model, ritual and play behavior are distinguished from other need satisfaction behaviors as a method of information management. This general process is characterized by a set of distinctive features or operations. These operations are implemented to maintain informational inputs at optimum levels for the system. As those inputs become deficient, the system acts to generate more input; as they become excessive the system acts to reduce those inputs.

The reduction of informational inputs has been identified as the distinguishing feature of ritual:

> . . . each ritual is a particular sequence of signals which, once announced, allows no uncertainty, no choice, and hence, in the statistical sense of information theory, conveys no information from sender to receiver. . . by reducing the information content of experience below the often bewildering level of complexity and disorder with which reality confronts him, [it] permits adaptive response. (Wallace 1966:233, 239)

The complementary process of input enrichment operationally defines play.

## IMPLICATIONS

This systems approach to play and ritual behaviors emphasizes adequate information as an autonomous basic need for all adapting systems. It argues for pre-cultural, indeed pre-homonoid, origins of play and ritual, and for the trans-human and trans-cultural expression of the same process.

The model contradicts many common usages of the labels "play" and "ritual"; rather it groups performances and parts of performances according to common processes and common ends. It asserts that the only play in music and theater is the virtuosity permitted the performers and that many solemn rites included episodes of play. Virtually all performances are mixtures of play and ritual, the enrichment of some informational inputs and the simultaneous reduction of others.

The model, thus, underscores the importance of theoretical positions such as : Dance is not a medium; it is an imperative—a universal deep-structure activity which requires a medium for its expression (Keali'inohomoku 1976).

The model provides a means for distinguishing between the deep structure activity and the surface structure medium of its expression. It also facilitates discrimination as to which system the performance serves, the individual or the group; it discriminates between the services to both, which may be mostly play for one system and mostly ritual for the other.

Finally, the model suggests that play and ritual in their more moderate forms underlie all creative problem solving activity, and that in their more extreme forms they may drive the system to transcent its normal limits, to stretch its horizons, and to provide for opportunities for system growth.

## NOTES

[1]A draft of this paper appeared in the *Newsletter* of The Association for the Anthropological Study of Play (1976). The author is indebted to students, correspondents and collegues, especially Dr. Joann M.W. Keali'inohomoku, for their constructive criticisms toward this version.

## REFERENCES

Ardrey, Robert, 1961, African Genesis. New York: Dell Publishing Co.
    1966, The Territorial Imperative. New York: Dell Publishing Co.

Byrne, D. and G. L. Clore, 1967, Effectance Arousal and Attraction. Journal of Personality and Social Psychology 6(4):Whole No. 638, Monograph Supplement.

Eimerl, S. and I. DeVore, 1965, The Primates. New York: Time Life Books.

Gartlan, J. S., 1968, Structure and Function in Primate Society. Folia Primatologica 8:89-120.

Goodall, Jane, 1963, My Life among Wild Chimpanzees. National Geographic 124(2): 272-308.

Keali'inohomoku, Joann M. W., 1976, Theory and Methods for an Anthropological Study of Dance. Doctoral dissertation, Indiana University, Bloomington, Indiana.

Kortlandt, A., 1955, Chimpanzees in the Wild. Scientific American 206(5):128-138.

Kummer, H. and F. Kurt, 1963, Social Units in a Population of Free-living Hamadryas Baboons. Folia Primatologica 1:4-19.

Loizos, C., 1967, Play Behavior in the Higher Primates. In Primate Ethology. D. Morris, Ed. Chicago: Aldine. Pp. 176-218.

Lorenz, K., 1963, On Aggression. New York: Harcourt & Brace, World, Inc.

Maruyama, M., 1963, The Second Cybernetics: Deviation Amplifying Mutual Causal Processes. American Scientist 51:164-179.

Morris, D., 1967, Primate Ethology. Chicago: Aldine.
    1968, The Naked Ape. New York: Dell Publishing Co.

Powers, W. T., 1973, Behavior: The Control of Perception. Chicago: Aldine.

Reynolds, V., 1963, Outline of Behavior and Social Organization of Forest Living Chimpanzees. Folia Primatologica 2:247-263.

Riner, Reed D., 1976, A Homeostatic System Model for Play. TAASP Newsletter 3(3):5-9.

Schaller, G., 1963, The Mountain Gorilla. Chicago: University of Chicago Press.

Stucki, L., 1970, The Entrophy Theory of Human Behavior: Indian Miners in Search of the Ultrastable State during a Prolonged Copper Strike. Doctoral dissertation, University of Colorado, Boulder, Colorado.

Wallace, A. F. C., 1966, Religion: An Anthropological Approach. New York: Random House.

Washburn, S. and I. DeVore, 1961, Social Life of Baboons. Scientific American 204:62-71.

White, R. W., 1959, Motivation reconsidered: the concept of competence. Psychological Review 66:297-333.

Wickler, W., 1967, Socio-Sexual Signals and their Intra-specific Imitation among Primates. In Primate Ethology. D. Morris, Ed. Chicago: Aldine. Pp. 69-147.

# THE PRIMATE CONTRIBUTION
# TO THE STUDY OF PLAY

John D. Baldwin and Janice I. Baldwin,
University of Caifornia, Santa Barbara

Research on primates and other mammals has led to the synthesis of a multifactor theory of play which may have far-reaching implications for the study of human play and the encouragement of playfulness in people of all ages. In this paper we outline the basic features of this primate theory, then present data from humans that suggest that the theory holds, with certain modifications, for humans, too.

## WHY DO PRIMATES PLAY?

A large body of data (summarized in Baldwin and Baldwin 1977) is now accumulating to demonstrate that primate play is a learned behavior which is acquired through operant conditioning due to sensory stimulation reinforcement. Sensory stimulation (**SS**) consists of the total stimulus input through the five extroceptive sense modalities and the introceptive sensory system. When a primate (**P**) tumbles or chases a peer up a liana vine in play, the **P**'s actions generate a great deal more **SS** than sitting passively does. The world of visual input spins and changes with great speed. Hands and feet alternate between impact and free flight, producing rapid changes in tactile stimulation. Movements of the muscles and viscera create introceptive stimuli, while the vestibular apparatus registers complex balance changes. This is multi-modal sensory input, typical of active play. Play can focus on any combination of sense modalities, even one single modality.

Under certain circumstances, the **SS** created by play activity serves as a reinforcer that strengthens the habits of play. The reason that **SS** is a reinforcer is that it can induce optimal levels of arousal in the central nervous system (**CNS**). **SS** entering the **CNS** causes activity or "arousal" in the **CNS**[1]. Generally, the greater the **SS** input, especially novel **SS**, the greater the arousal that is produced. Figure 1 shows how arousal is related to behavior. When an infant **P** first wakes up, the arousal in its **CNS** is low since little **SS** enters during sleep (A in Figure 1). For the waking infant, low levels of arousal are aversive, or "boring" in human-

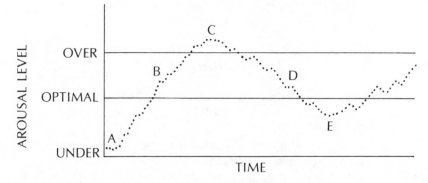

Fig. 1

When an individual first awakens, arousal is generally low (A). During arousal-inducing activities, such as **e&p**, a **P** may become increasingly aroused, gaining the reinforcers of optimal arousal (B). Continued **e&p** can, however, lead to overarousal (C), at which time the **P** usually seeks arousal-reducing activities, such as clinging to its mother. After calming down into the optimal arousal zone (D) or the underarousal zone (E), the **P** will again find arousal-inducing activities such as **e&p** positively reinforcing.

terms. Nothing is going on. Things are dull. Under these circumstances, any behavior that the infant happens to generate which allows it to escape this aversive condition will be reinforced. If the infant crawls off the mother's body to play in the vines, branches and palm fronds near her, the multimodal sensory inputs of watching the forest canopy and moving through the trees impinge on the infant's sense organs and stimulate activity in the **CNS** arousal systems. As the infant continues to explore and play in the trees, the continued **SS** drives the **CNS** arousal level out of the aversive underarousal zone and into an optimal zone (B in Figure 1). The arousal level rises slowly due to the inertia in the arousal systems; the summation of repeated inputs is needed to induce widespread activity in the **CNS.**

Optimal arousal occurs when the brain is actively processing inputs, and is neither underloaded (by boring inactivity) nor overloaded (by overstimulation). Optimal arousal produces a state of positive affect that serves as a reinforcer for those behaviors which produced it. Thus, once the infant's arousal level reaches B (in Figure 1), its exploration and play are rewarded by pleasant sensations and not merely by the escape of boredom.

As the infant continues to explore and play, venturing further from the mother's body to tumble with some nearby players, the continuing bombardment of **SS** can eventually cause the infant's arousal level to rise above the optimal zone into the overarousal zone. Under conditions of excessive sensory input, the brain's ability to process the inputs is overloaded and sensory overload induces an aversive state of stress (C in Figure 1). At this point, continued exposure to **SS** only worsens the aversive sensory overload; but a hasty retreat to the comfort of mother's body can serve to terminate the overly arousing **SS**. Mother's warm, soft fur and gently movements provide a low level of sensory input. Clinging passively to her further lowers the input. In addition, mother's body is familiar and familiar stimuli (as opposed to novel ones) also minimize arousal induction. With **SS** reduced significantly, the arousal level of the infant's **CNS** begins to drop from the overarousal zone down to the optimal zone (D in Figure 1). The drop is not instantaneous, again due to the inertia in the **CNS** arousal systems. The **CNS** does not stop functioning the instant stimuli cease coming in. Nerve circuits may continue to reverberate for several seconds or minutes before the low levels of **SS** have their calming effect on the infant's **CNS.**

As the infant is calmed down into the optimal zone, it escapes the aversive state of overarousal and obtains the positive reinforcers of optimal arousal. Both of these events reinforce the habits of running to mother when the infant is overaroused. Mason (1965, 1968, 1970) and Mason and Kenney (1974) have shown that the arousal-reducing qualities of the mother (or surrogate mother) are the primary qualities that cause the infant to fall in love with its mother and to feel security when with her.

If the infant continues to cling to mother after the arousal level has descended to the optimal level, the mother's arousal-reducing qualities can lower the infant's arousal even further, into the underarousal zone (E in Figure 1). If the infant is fatigued or sleepy, this low arousal state is compatible with drowsiness and the onset of sleep. However, for the well-rested infant, underarousal is aversive and the infant is again in a position where arousal-inducing levels of **SS** are more reinforcing. If the infant leaves the mother's body to explore and play at point E in Figure 1, the **SS** that results from exploration and play will again induce optimal arousal and the positive reinforcers of optimal arousal will further strengthen the habits of exploration and play. Thus, exploration and play are both operant activities which are reinforced by the optimal arousal they generate.

It is common to see young primates pass through a period when they alternate between bouts of arousal-inducing exploration and play and bouts of arousal-reducing contact with mother. This pattern has been observed in human infants, too (Ainsworth 1964; Ainsworth and Wittig 1969; Rheingold and Eckerman 1970). When bored, the infant explores away from mother, but when these ventures expose the infant to strange, unexpected, overarousing stimuli, the infant returns to mother for arousal-reduction and security.

As infants grow older they come to tolerate higher levels of sensory input, and stimuli that would have overaroused a young infant become boring to a juvenile. This transition occurs due to **familiarization** and **habituation**. Novelty is a key feature of stimuli that elicit startle, surprise and cause arousal-induction in the **CNS**. After repeated exposure to a stimulus, the novelty of the stimulus is lost as the observer gains familiarity with the stimulus and habituates to its arousal-induction properties.

For the newborn infant, the whole world is novel, hence the neonate is easily overstimulated and in great need of a mother (or surrogate) for arousal-reduction. The neonate need only open its eyes or move its body to experience novel input. However, as familiarization and habituation rob the nearby world of novelty, the infant ceases to find passive looking, listening, or simple body movements sufficiently arousal-inducing to escape boredom. It is gradually reinforced for venturing forth, widening its horizons and locating new **SS**. Figure 2 shows how infant monkeys turn to ever more novel, complex and rowdy activities as they exhaust the novelty and excitement of earlier activities. This escalating trend carries the infant away from infantile activities and from its mother in search of new experience.

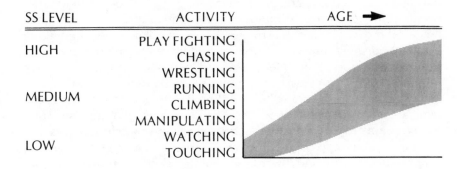

| SS LEVEL | ACTIVITY | AGE ➡ |
|---|---|---|
| HIGH | PLAY FIGHTING<br>CHASING<br>WRESTLING | |
| MEDIUM | RUNNING<br>CLIMBING<br>MANIPULATING | |
| LOW | WATCHING<br>TOUCHING | |

Fig. 2

After repeated experience with arousal-inducing stimuli, familiarization and habituation operate to raise a **P**'s optimal sensory input level. **SS** above and below this optimal zone are aversive; **SS** within this zone is a positive reinforcer. The figure shows the general trend in the awake **P**'s optimal input zone, averaging out the hourly and daily fluctuations (due to diurnal cycles, fatigue, differences in current behavior patterns, etc.) in order to focus on broader developmental patterns.

SIX PHASES OF EXPLORATION AND PLAY

Exploration is one mode of activity that allows a **P** to locate novel **SS**; play is another. When watching a monkey interact with a novel stimulus, we can observe how both exploration and play serve to provide **SS**, though in different ways. The relationship between **SS** reinforcers and **e&p** can be seen in the behavioral changes that occur from a **P**'s initial exploration of a highly novel target stimulus to the termination of **e&p** with that same stimulus. The typical pattern can be divided into 6 general phases, based on 6 different reinforcement contingencies, though much variance can occur within each phase and finer discriminations are possible. (Not all the following phases appear if the stimulus is not sufficiently novel, if the **P** is too young, too old, or too inhibited to play, or if competing responses interfere with the typical pattern.) All 6 phases can appear in both social and nonsocial forms of **e&p**.

1) **Early exploration**. When a **P** (who has already learned a repertoire of **e&p** behaviors) first encounters a highly novel stimulus, proximity to the stimulus can easily overarouse the **P**, which would reinforce the **P** for moving away. At larger distances, the novel stimulus displaces a smaller

portion of the **P**'s total perceptual field and, if the rest of the field is not overarousing, the novel stimulus is less frightening at this "safe" distance. (If the whole field is extremely novel, the **P** may flee the field or break into distress responses, such as, huddling, rocking or vocalizing. Extreme overarousal and fear can produce such strong avoidance responses that the **P** never familiarizes or habituates to the stimulus and never proceeds to the next phase.) As the **P**'s arousal level drops due to familiarization and habituation, the **P** will find looking at the stimulus a source of novelty and may approach for closer examination. In phase 1, there are often approach-withdrawal responses as the **P** vacillates between overarousal and lower arousal states. As the **P** further familiarizes and habituates to the stimulus, the **P** may scamper up to briefly touch the stimulus, then jump away after making contact. With repeated contacts, the stimulus continues to lose some of its extreme novelty, the **P** ceases to be so easily overaroused by it and contacts become more lengthy, though still tentative and interrupted by bouts of withdrawal.

Early contact with peers at the period before **P**s discover social play has this same approach-avoidance quality with tentative, interrupted contacts.

2) **Intermediate exploration**. As the **P** becomes familiar with the stimulus, the stimulus ceases to overarouse and begins to produce optimal arousal. The **P** is reinforced for directing its full attention to the stimulus and for examining it from all different directions if it presents new stimulation from different angles. As a consequence of the **P**'s investigations and inspection, the **P** learns what the properties of the stimulus are and furthers the processes of familiarization and habituation. As the novelty and arousal-induction potential of the stimulus decline, there are diminishing reinforcers for exploration and gradually the **P** will show a declining number of exploratory responses, while phasing into either of the next two phases (Figure 3).

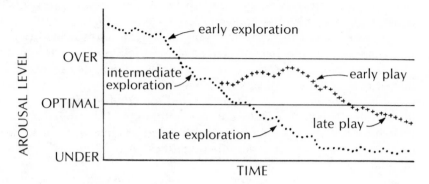

Fig. 3
The six phases of **e&p** are determined by the arousal-induction properties of the stimulus and by the **P**'s response to the stimulus: during
exploration the **P** is focusing on **what** the stimulus is or does; during
play, the **P** is **doing** things with or to the stimulus and thus creating
heightened stimulus impact.

3) **Late exploration.** Once the target stimulus can no longer induce
optimal arousal levels, the **P** is most likely to avoid the stimulus and
seek **SS** elsewhere. However, if, a) there are no alternative stimuli with
more impact than the target stimulus and, b) the **P** can no longer
succeed in increasing the impact of the target stimulus with its present
repertoire of play or creative behavior, then the **P** may explore the target
stimulus as the best source of **SS** among even worse alternatives. Caged
**P**s are often forced into this type of exploration. Late exploration tends
to be low-key, halfhearted and easily interrupted by distractions. Also,
the **P** may not look at the target stimulus as intently as it did in early and
intermediate exploration.

4) **Early play**. As the target stimulus loses its novelty, the **P** can create
increased **SS** by **doing** things with or to the stimulus; rolling it, dropping
it, hitting it, chasing it, etc. The **P**'s behavior elicits more **SS** from the
stimulus than is available during much of exploration, in which the **P**
merely attended to the properties of the stimulus. Naturally, a playful
swat may cause the stimulus to generate overarousing levels of **SS** (if the
stimulus is an object that crashes to the ground or a larger animal that
startles, jumps up and chases the **P**) and this may inhibit the development of playful responses to the particular stimulus.

The **P** may spend more time in phase 4 with other animals, especially peers, than with inanimate objects. The **P**'s repertoire of playful behavior may be able to elicit several dozen new sights and sounds from an inanimate object; but because animals, especially peers, often return play, animals may generate much more **SS** than inanimate objects when played with. Animate objects are usually more complex, more unpredictable and hence a less easily exhausted source of **SS**. Still, access to the **SS** they produce is usually contingent upon the **P**'s generating playful behavior; hence the general rule still obtains: in phase 4, the **P** must combine its own behavior with the properties of the stimulus to obtain optimal arousal.

Thus, early play tends to be a more active process than exploration, which fits with Welker's (1961) definition. And compatible with Hutt's (1966) observations on children, play involves using or doing something with the stimulus; whereas exploration is the prior period which is focused on "learning the properties" of the stimulus. The **P** at play learns behaviors or games that combine the stimulus with other stimuli, behaviors and play patterns to create more **SS** than the stimulus alone gives off.

5) **Late play**. After the **P** has explored and tried a variety of play behaviors on the target stimulus, the novelty is eventually exhausted. If novel stimuli in the environment, the **P** may leave the first stimulus and never reach phase 5. However, if there are no alternatives more novel than the target stimulus, the **P** may continue halfhearted, low-key play with the stimulus merely because it offers at least some **SS**, which is better than nothing. Older juveniles and adults often play in this manner. They have exhausted most of the readily available **SS** in the environment, yet are habituated to relatively high levels of **SS**. They are bored doing nothing but excited by progressively fewer alternatives in their environment. As they wait for something new to happen, they put some minimal effort in the old familiar play patterns. The **SS** of having a young juvenile jumping around at arm's length can be maintained with a few swats or incipient chases by older **P**. The game is not novel, but the **SS** it generates is better than nothing.

6) **End of e&p**. As the target stimulus loses all novelty and arousal-induction capacity, the **P** will cease both **e&p** with it, except for possible rebounds of **e&p** after recovery periods.

When children explore and play, their stimulus-seeking activities often follow the same general pattern. For example, Hutt (1966) observed thirty 3 to 5 year old nursery-school children explore and play with a red metal box which had a 4-way lever that could be programmed to activate various combinations of counters, bells and buzzers. When the box was adjusted to give both visual and auditory feedback, it reinforced higher levels and longer periods of **e&p** than when the box was adjusted to give **SS** through fewer modalities. Exploration was the first response the children showed, as they focused their attention on the box and learned all the properties of the 4-way lever along with the sensory effects associated with each mode of manipulation. After discovering the properties of the box, exploration began to extinguish while playful responses increased. Finally, the children created novel games that incorporated the lever-box as part of their play props. For example, one child sat on the box with the lever located at her side and drove her imaginary omnibus using the lever as a gear-shifter and a source of sound effects. The lever was no longer the target of exploration, but its **SS** reinforcers made it a rewarding addition to a broader set of play activities.

## Supporting Evidence

Data from research on human infants show that **SS** can serve as a reinforcer from the first weeks of life and that **e&p** are among those behaviors reinforced by **SS**. Bower (1966) found that infants as young as 2 weeks old learned operant head turning responses if the responses were followed by a "peek-a-boo" from the experimenter. Given the quiet nature of the testing room, the "peek-a-boo" was a novel and multimodal source of **SS** and head turning was the behavior that allowed the infants to explore the **SS**. Older infants learned in a similar manner. Watson (1966) reported that a 10 week old infant selectively hit at a swinging toy when the toy was stationary rather than when it was moving, indicating that the hitting was most likely when **SS** reinforcers coming from the toy's movement were contingent upon the behavior. Berlyne (1958) observed that infants begin targeted "looking" after several weeks of life. Instead of merely having the early reflex-like response of a randomly wandering gaze, "looking" consists of focusing on a selected stimulus. Using test cards with different stimulus patterns, Berlyne found that infants, who were 3 to 9 months old, focused most attention on cards with the greatest internal contours and stimulus complexity. Rheingold **et al.** (1962) studied 6 month old infants in a special seat equipped with a metal sphere within easy reach. The infants learned to manipulate the sphere when it activated a motion picture display of moving colored geometric forms (**SS**) on a screen in front of them. When the **SS** was given "free" (i.e., not contingent on the infants' manipulation) the explorative touching responses did not become more frequent, showing that the lights did not elicit reflexive manipulation, but rather reinforced responses contingent upon the **SS** presentation. Leuba and Friedlander (1968) studied 20 children, 7 to 11 months of age, to see which knob they would learn to explore when presented with 2 knobs, associated with different **SS** effects. After an initial period of handling both knobs, the infants focused most of their exploration on, and established a preference for, touching the knob that activated a door chime and lights rather than the one without audiovisual effects.

The fact that people will push for access to novel flashing lights, sounds, views of outside events or pictures, and so forth, indicates that novel or varied sensory input can serve as a reinforcer. However, extremely high levels of **SS** are overarousing and aversive while very low levels of **SS** are underarousing, boring and hence also aversive. **SS** is a positive reinforcer only at intermediate levels (Ellis 1973).

Vitz (1966) presented subjects with sequences of tones of intermediate volume but varying levels of pattern complexity. The patterns with least variance and least unpredictability were ranked as most aversive. With increasing pattern complexity, the subjects ranked the tones progressively more pleasant, up to a point. As the pattern complexity and unpredictability rose beyond that point, there was a decline in pleasantness, eventually reaching aversiveness. Vitz's experiment also demonstrates the interaction of stimulus and past learning; people with musical backgrounds found higher levels of tone complexity to be optimal, whereas the other subjects preferred lower levels of complexity. Switzky **et al** (1974) found that children underselected toys that were overly complex. Scholtz and Ellis (1975) studied 4 and 5 year olds in an environment that could be arranged to provide high or low levels of background **SS**. They found that when the environmental **SS** was high, the children selected toys that provided less complex, less unpredictable sources of **SS**; but when the environmental input was low, the children selected more complex, stimulating targets of play. Thus, when background conditions provided ample **SS**, the person selects activities that do not add much more stimulation (and hence avoids overarousal); but when the background conditions are underarousing, the person selects more stimulating activities to avoid underarousal. There is an inverse relation between the amount of **SS** the environment brings to the person without his having to create it and the amount of **SS** the person will create for himself.

Chronic exposure to overstimulation is capable of inducing a variety of stress-related symptoms: anxiety, nightmares, insomnia, poor appetite, irritability, headaches, hypertension and ulcers (Martindale 1977). On the other hand, chronic understimulation is aversive and interferes with several behavioral processes. The sensory deprivation literature (see, Zubek 1969) shows that people generally find low levels of **SS** to be aversive and disruptive of normal cognitive function. Smith **et al.** (1962) observed 25 early release and 23 successful subjects in a 96-hour sensory deprivation experiment. Sensing devices under the bed measured restlessness and activity. There was a -.62 correlation between restless-ness and length of endurance, suggesting that the subjects who have habituated to higher optimal **SS** zones generated more self-stimulation via restless activity and terminated earlier than other subjects due to the greater discrepancy between their optimal **SS** zone and the experimental environment. Vernon and McGill (1960) also found that subjects who needed access to "something to do" dropped out of a 72-hour depri-vation experiment sooner than ones who did not. Bexton (1953) found that subjects in deprivation experiments are in such great need of **any** kind of stimulus input that they will repeatedly request access to tedious and boring inputs (such as 8 repetitions of the 16 bar chorus of "Home on the Range") in order to counteract the sensory deprivation. Thus, even in the suboptimal zone some stimulation is better than none and a person will be motivated to do stimulus-seeking behavior even if the input level does not bring the person completely up to the optimal zone. Jones **et al.** (1961) showed that subjects, given the choice among four levels of information in the patterning of incoming light stimuli, selected the light patterns with the highest information content.

The process of familiarization and habituation also takes place in humans, causing an escalation in **SS** needs to generate optimal arousal. The inevitable loss of impact that accompanies experience with any given stimulus normally serves to motivate further exploration and broadening of horizons (up to a limit). As the stimuli in the person's im-mediate environment become familiar and boring, the individual is negatively reinforced for venturing out into larger spheres of the environ-ment; then, if new sources of **SS** are found out there, the individual is positively reinforced for the new habits of venturing forth. Thus, the process of familiarization plays a key role in motivating the individual to explore and expand his experiential world. Without familiarization, peo-ple would always find their neonatal environment and activities novel, hence would miss a major motivation for giving them up and would be retarded at leaving behind their infantile ways. Neonatal activities would remain reinforcing all through life, and serve to hold the individual in an infant stage of psychosocial development, or at least, to serve as com-peting responses that retarded the broadening of horizons.

The processes of familiarization and habituation can be seen in a variety of studies on stimulus-seeking behaviors in humans. White and Castle (1964) studied 28 infants raised in a state hospital without mothers. An experimental group of 10 infants received 20 minutes a day of extra handling from day 6 to 36. The control group received only the standard care—with little handling. The experimental group began **e&p** at a significantly earlier time than the control group. Early **SS** had hastened their accommodating to higher input and accelerated their progress in the acquisition of stimulus-seeking behavior. Barnes (1971) discovered that 3 and 4 year old children engaged in more lone play than 5 year olds, who engaged in more social play. Social play generates higher levels of **SS** and unpredictability and the 3 to 4 year olds preferred the less stimulating forms of lone play. Iwanaga (1973) found a progressive increase in the frequency of social play when comparing children of three age groups (3, 4, and 5 years old), though there was a considerable amount of lone play in all three of these age groups. In addition, girls spent more time than boys in social play in all three age groups. Boys favored play with toys and building materials, though there was a significant rise in social play around 5 years of age. Koch (1966) found that twins spent more time in solitary play than singletons, which correlates with the fact that twins are slower than singletons in learning social skills. This is due to each twin's having less contact with older, more skillful socializing agents from whom to learn advanced skills and more time with the same aged, similar skilled twin than singletons.

## SOCIAL LEARNING THEORY

Learning in humans is more complex than in nonhuman primates, in large part due to language and increased cognitive capacity. Observational learning and learning from rules are two features of human learning that have an important impact on play above and beyond the reinforcement mechanisms described above. Observational learning is likely to occur when an observer sees or hears about a model, either real (e.g., a parent or sibling) or symbolic (e.g., a movie, TV, or storybook character), performing a behavior. Rules facilitate learning by providing verbally encoded instructions—either explicit ("No peeking,") or implicity ("It's no fun when you peek,")—that guide the recipient's actions. Both observational learning and rules are more likely to cause a change in behavior if they are coupled with reinforcers that reward the relevant behavior (Bandura and Walters 1963).

Each culture provides its own unique pattern of reinforcers, models and rules which, in conjunction with the nonsocial reinforcers of the physical environment, shape the behavioral patterns seen in that culture. Several studies focusing on children's cultural learning experiences shed light on the enculturation of play.

Griffing (1974) found that children from families of higher socioeconomic status (**SES**) were more playful (especially in the areas of make-believe, acting out their make-believe thoughts, sociodrama and verbalizing) than children of lower **SES**. There is good evidence that these class differences can be traced to differences in the patterns of models, rules, prompts and social reinforcers found in the homes of the different **SES**. Hess and Shipman (1965) found that mothers from lower **SES** families used fewer words and fewer rules in interactions with their children than higher **SES** mothers did; also they provided fewer instructions and prompts on how to proact in problem solving—how to weigh alternative solutions and think out complex patterns of behavior. Gray and Klaus (1965) found similar patterns. Thus, one would predict that the children of low **SES** families would have fewer skills for solving problems, generating complex behavior patterns and locating **SS**. In fact, Lovinger (1974) found that children from disadvantaged backgrounds had fragmented and repetitious play patterns compared with the more innovative play of less handicapped children. Lovinger devised an experiment to provide disadvantaged children with models who used complex play patterns and talked (providing rules for how to do what they were doing) while playing. Under these advantageous learning conditions, the children showed a significant increase in verbal expression and complex, innovative play. Beitelson and Ross (1973) had similar results in an experiment on play tutoring. The tutors served as models of innovative play, talking about their activities as they played. The children in the experiment showed significant increases in creative play; and in addition they showed a significant increase in performance on conventional tests of originality, creativity and innovation.

Meichenbaum and Cameron (1974) stress the fact that the internal monologue that people carry on verbally in their heads (talking to themselves as they behave) can significantly affect their creative behavior, if that monologue contains useful rules for effective, creative action. Children raised in verbally rich environments hear more complex verbal behavior from their parents, siblings and peers; hence, they learn more sophisticated internal monologues. When approaching a task that permits creative solutions or demands problem solving, the children with effective internal monologues have an advantage over children with fewer monologue skills (holding other factors constant).

Much of human play—sports, puzzles, board games, etc.—is highly rule-oriented. People with rule-using skills, who are experienced in evaluating different strategies before acting, often have an advantage at these games. In fact, Vacha (1976) observed that when children find games too easy, they often invent new rules to make the game more complex, hence more stimulating to play. More people change from checkers to chess than vice-versa, which again reflects the fact that as people gain skills, more challenge and stimulus variety can be found in games of increasing complexity. People are rule inventors. Some of this can be traced to the pragmatic value of rules for effectively passing on information;

but some is due to the extra game complexity and **SS** that rules introduce into the play of life. As the world tends to become familiar and dull, we spice it up by complicating matters with extra rules.

## CONCLUSIONS

Many sociological and anthropological studies of play have focused on the descriptive level. The learning approach described in this paper allows the descriptive level to be tied to immediate causal factors in the current environment. Scott (1971) states that the proper study of the social sciences is to focus on the environmental reinforcers and contingencies that are responsible for producing the behavioral patterns we observe. Social learning theory provides the tools for tracing cultural patterns of play to the environmental factors that shape and support those patterns. Williams (1972) has demonstrated the use of learning theory in anthropological work, showing how socialization ties an individual to his culture. We believe that learning theory opens a new horizon in the study of play and has important humanistic implications for increasing playfulness in people of all ages (Baldwin and Baldwin in press).

## ACKNOWLEDGEMENTS

We thank Howard Goldstein for his aid in researching the literature on play in humans.

### NOTES

1. For a discussion of the methodological problems involved with measuring arousal, see Baldwin and Baldwin (1977:350-351).

### REFERENCES

Ainsworth, Mary D., 1964, Patterns of Attachment Behavior Shown by the Infant in Interaction with His Mother. Merrill-Palmer Quarterly 10:51-88.

Ainsworth, Mary D. and Barbara A. Wittig, 1969, Attachment and Exploratory Behavior of One-year-olds in a Strange Situation. In Determinants of Infant Behavior IV. B. M. Foss, Ed. London: Metheun. Pp. 111-136.

Baldwin, John D. and Janice I. Baldwin, 1977, The Role of Learning Phenomena in the Ontogeny of Exploration and Play. In Primate Bio-Social Development: Biological, Social, and Ecological Determinants. Suzanne Chevalier-Skolnikoff and Frank E. Poirier, Eds. New York: Garland Press. Pp. 343-406.
In Press, Reinforcement Theories of Exploration, Play, Creativity and Psychosocial Growth. In Social Play in Primates. Euclid O. Smith, Ed. New York: Academic Press.

Bandura, Albert and Richard H. Walters, 1963, Social Learning and Personality Development. New York: Holt, Rinehart and Winston.

Barnes, Keith E., 1971, Preschool Play Norms: A Replication. Developmental Psychology 5:99-103.

Berlyne, Daniel E., 1958, The Influence of Albedo and Complexity of Stimuli on Visual Fixation in the Human Infant. British Journal of Psychology 49:315-318.

Bexton, W., 1953, Some Effects of Perceptual Isolation on Human Subjects. Doctoral Dissertation, McGill University, Montreal, Quebec.

Bower, T. G. R., 1966, The Visual World of Infants. Scientific American 215(6):80-92.

Ellis, Michael J., 1973, Why People Play. Englewood Cliffs, N.J.: Prentice-Hall.

Feitelson, Dina and Gail S. Ross, 1973, The Neglected Factor—Play. Human Development 16:202-223.

Gray, Susan W. and Rupert A. Klaus, 1965, An Experimental Preschool Program for Culturally Deprived Children. Child Development 36:887-889.

Griffing, Penelope, 1974, Sociodramatic Play among Young Black Children. Theory into Practice 13:257-265.

Hess, Robert D. and Virginia C. Shipman, 1965, Early Experience and the Socialization of Cognitive Modes in Children. Child Development 36:869-886.

Hutt, C., 1966, Exploration and Play in Children. Symposium of the Zoological Society of London 18:61-81.

Iwanaga, Margaret, 1973, Development of Interpersonal Play Structure in Three, Four, and Five Year-old Children. Journal of Research and Development in Education 6(3): 71-82.

Jones, Austin, H. Jean Wilkinson, and Ina Braden, 1961, Information Deprivation as a Motivational Variable. Journal of Experimental Psychology 62:126-137.

Koch, Helen L., 1966, Twins and Twin Relations. Chicago: University of Chicago Press.

Leuba, Clarence and Bernard Z. Friedlander, 1968, Effects of Controlled Audio-Visual Reinforcement on Infants' Manipulative Play in the Home. Journal of Experimental Child Psychology 6:87-99.

Lovinger, Sophie L., 1974, Socio-Dramatic Play and Language Development in Preschool Disadvantaged Children. Psychology in the Schools 11:313-320.

Martindale, David, 1977, Sweaty Palms in the Control Tower. Psychology Today 10(9): 70-75.

Mason, William A., 1965, The Social Development of Monkeys and Apes. In Primate Behavior: Field Studies of Monkeys and Apes. Irven DeVore, Ed. New York: Holt, Rhinehart and Winston. Pp. 514-543.
1968, Early Social Deprivation in the Nonhuman Primates: Implications for Human Behavior. In Environmental Influences. David Glass, Ed. New York: Russell Sage Foundation. Pp. 70-101.
1970, Motivational Factors in Psychosocial Development. In Nebraska Symposium on Motivation. William J. Arnold and Monte M. Page, Eds. Lincoln: University of Nebraska Press. Pp. 35-67.

Mason, William A. and M. D. Kenney, 1974, Redirection of Filial Attachments in Rhesus Monkeys: Dogs as Mother Surrogates. Science 183:1209-1211.

Meichenbaum, Donald and Roy Cameron, 1974, The Clinical Potential of Modifying What Clients Say to Themselves. *In* Self-Control: Power to the Person. Michael J. Mahoney and Carl E. Thoreson, Eds. Monterey, California: Brooks/Cole. Pp. 263-290.

Rheingold, Harriet L. and Carol O. Eckerman, 1970, The Infant Separates Himself from His Mother. Science 168:78-90.

Rheingold, Harriet L., Walter C. Stanley, and John A. Cooley, 1962, Method for Studying Exploratory Behavior in Infants. Science 136:1054-1055.

Scholtz, Gert J. L. and Michael J. Ellis, 1975, Repeated Exposure to Objects and Peers in a Play Setting. Journal of Experimental Child Psychology 19:448-455.

Scott, John F., 1971, Internalization of Norms: A Sociological Theory of Moral Commitment. Englewood Cliffs, N.J.: Prentice-Hall.

Smith, S., T. Myers, and D. Murphy, 1962, Activity Pattern and Restlessness During Sustained Sensory Deprivation. Paper at American Psychological Association, St. Louis.

Switzky, Harvey N., H. Carl Haywood, and Robert Isett, 1974, Exploration, Curiosity, and Play in Young Children: Effects of Stimulus Complexity. Developmental Psychology 10:321-329.

Vacha, Edward F., 1976, Children's Culture and Child Socialization. Doctoral Dissertation. University of California, Santa Barbara.

Vernon, Jack A. and T. Lomas E. McGill, 1960, Utilization of Visual Stimulation During Sensory Deprivation. Perceptual and Motor Skills 11:214.

Vitz, Paul C., 1966, Affect as a Function of Stimulus Variation. Journal of Experimental Psychology 71:74-79.

Watson, John S., 1966, The Development and Generalization of "Contingency Awareness" in Early Infancy: Some Hypotheses. Merrill-Palmer Quarterly 12:123-135.

Welker, W. I., 1961, An Analysis of Exploratory and Play Behavior in Animals. *In* Functions of Varied Experience. Donald W. Fiske and Salvatore R. Maddi, Eds. Chicago: Dorsey. Pp. 175-226.

White, Burton L. and Peter W. Castle, 1964, Visual Exploratory Behavior Following Postnatal Handling of Human Infants. Perceptual and Motor Skills 18:497-502.

Williams, Thomas R., 1972, Introduction to Socialization: Human Culture Transmitted. St. Louis: C. V. Mosby.

Zubek, John P., 1969, Sensory Deprivation: Fifteen Years of Research. New York: Appleton Century Crofts.

# CHAPTER II

# Play and Cultural Values

## HOPLOLOGY: THE CASE OF JAPANESE MARTIAL CULTURE AND COMBATIVE SYSTEMS

### Part I
### "Martial Arts": Definitions and Approaches.
### An Introduction to the Concept of Combative Culture.

Donn F. Draeger, East-West Center, University of Hawaii

This paper deals with one specific segment of the Japanese national ethos and culture that to some extent includes the play concept, but at the same time also rejects it. I am referring to the well-advertised but grossly misrepresented so-called "martial arts."

This may be the first anthropological paper written on the subject of Japanese combative culture, an event in itself that leads to the question of why anthropologists have heretofore given so little attention to this conspicuous and important subject.

Combat in Japan has been an inescapable facet of human life ever since man's first appearance on the archipelago, and Japanese in every age have given a great deal of time and effort to devising ways of improving their combative image and effect. Yet the neglect of this area of study, and the present day academic opinions about human combativeness in general, suffer the condemning attitude that has much in common with a Victorian attitude on sex.

There is an undeniable relevance of the study of martial and combative culture to the overall anthropological aims of achieving a better understanding of man. Moreover, the relevance of anthropology to the study ot combative culture is not to be questioned. Nevertheless, this paper implies no pre-eminence for anthropology in this study; rather, it would leave such highly specialized study of martial and combative culture to a discipline, the name of which will most likely be a first exposure for the majority of readers. That discipline is hoplology.

Hoplology is a term derived from the Greek root, **hoplos**, referring to a tool or weapon. In this context, hoplology is an interdisciplinary field that seeks to examine and understand man's combative nature and endeavors. It is not appropriate here to fully discuss the nature, scope and methods of hoplology, for to do so would take us away from the major purposes of this paper. However, because hoplology is relatively unknown, a short digression is in order.

The hoplologist proceeds on the qualified assumption that weapons are man's oldest technology. Weapons and combative culture throughout man's history have been a central area of concern and importance. The hoplologist seeks to make detailed analyses of weapons and combative disciplines, studying them in terms of their genetic histories, creating typologies and assessing their roles and meanings within and between cultures.

The hoplologist is trained in such academic studies as anthropology, archaeology, art history, ethology, history, metallurgy, psychology and sociology. Equally important, he is trained in a wide variety of combative arts. Thus, the hoplologist operates from an "inside" or emic position that is an absolute prerequisite for his study inasmuch as all combative culture is based upon experiential models of learning.

Because combative cultures represent deep and significant human expressions, the study of such disciplines reveals certain depths of man, areas of emotion that are equally as significant to the understanding of man as are his arts and emotions of peace. The study of man's combative arts is not all to do with the "impassioned drama" — war — and its attendant acts of violence and bloodshed. Some of man's greatest peacetime achievements have derived from his spirit and techniques of combat. Martial culture has indelibly influenced language, graphic arts, literature, music and drama, as well as the philosophical and religious systems of thought in virtually every culture known to man. Hoplological study is, moreover, a key to understanding the racial and ethnic identities of different peoples.

How well we understand the content and expression of combative culture and emotion, in all its many and varied aspects, bears directly on how thoroughly we understand ourselves, not to mention the peoples whom we study.

The anthropological concept of culture, in the sense of Tylor's classic definition, is fundamental to the hoplologist's study. However, we must define the combative and martial aspects of culture in a more precise manner. Combative culture is defined as the sum total of man's spirit, thoughts and actions in relation to the production of weapons and the associated ways of using them within a specific cultural context. This includes empty-handed systems, for they use the body as a weapon. The popular dictionary definition of "combative" is highly unsatisfactory to the hoplologist, for it treats only of the pugnacious, wrongly assuming that man can conveniently operate in a tidy emotional compartment that is characterized by offensive thoughts and actions that make no concessions to a non-belligerent state.

The hoplologist's concept of "martial" is strictly interpreted, limiting it to a description of the qualities and attributes of classical warriors in a traditional pre-modern sense. Classical warriors are a special hereditary social class of persons within a specific cultural context who are educated to engage in a lifetime of training, such as concerns all aspects of combative disciplines, for the establishment and maintenance of a specific social order.

With regard to the Japanese ethos, these definitions enable the hoplologist to demonstrate the various and important differences that lie between social types of people and the systems of combat associated with them. These are the classical warrior (**bujin**), the modern counterpart soldier (**gunjin**), and the civilian (**heimin**), all of whom may have recourse to combat at some time in life. Each of these distinct social types exists today in Japan.

Martial arts are the province of both the classical warrior and the modern soldier types of fighting man, while civil arts of personal self-defense pertain to the civilian. Just as we clearly set apart martial law and civil law, so we must distinguish between martial arts and civil arts of combat. Only when this distinction is made is it possible to identify the many technical and ethical differences that lie between these two major categories of combat, and only then is it possible to appreciate the social impacts that each of these categories has had, and will continue to have, on Japanese society. For the hoplologist, then, not all fighting arts are martial arts and not all martial arts are fighting arts.

## THE DEVELOPMENT OF JAPANESE COMBATIVE SYSTEMS

The origins, historical development, techniques, and socio-cultural significances of Japanese combative disciplines are dealt with in my trilogy (Draeger 1973a, 1973b, 1974). It is only important here to provide the basic outlines of my typology of combative systems. The emergence of classical Japanese martial arts (**ko-bujutsu**) was due to the efforts of the classical warriors (**bujin**) who began their rise to power in the eighth century A.D. These martial arts were developed under conditins of almost constant warfare and, therewith, proliferated into over seven thousand **ryu** (martial traditions), many of which are today extant. Classical martial arts are combatively oriented systems that are substantially the monopoly of warrior familes (**buke**) even in our present time. One major purpose for which the classical martial arts were created was to identify and preserve different, but ethnically related, socio-political groups. These arts provided the primary means for battlefiebat combat by warriors until 1877 when, with the defeat of the Satsuma warriors at the hand of the imperial Meiji government armies, the last defense of a closed social nexus by means of classical martial arts came to an end.

About fifty different component systems comprise the classical martial arts and both military and naval matters are subsumed by them. Hoplologists classify these systems according to the weapon/principle/agent used: bladed, stick/staff, projectile, composite and auxiliary systems. Major weapons systems include **kenjutsu** (swordsmanship performed with a drawn blade), **iai-jutsu** (swordsmanship performed from a beginning position with the blade at rest in its scabbard), **sojutsu** (spear art), **naginata-jutsu** (halberd art), **kyujutsu** (bow and arrow art), **bojutsu** (staff art), and **yoroi kumi-uchi** (an art of grappling while armored and armed). But not all martial arts are fighting arts. Those called **chikujo-jutsu** (field fortification art), **noroshi-jutsu** (signal-fire art), **hojo-jutsu** (art of the tying cord), **bajutsu** (battlefield horsemanship), and **karumi-jutsu** (the art of devising methods by which to lighten and prepare the body for jumping high and far), and others, are auxiliary systems that function in support of the actual methods of combat already mentioned.

Long before the reduction of the Satsuma warriors during the Meiji Restoration there developed what is today called **ko budo** or classical martial ways. Though martial ways stem from the classical martial arts (**ko bujutsu**) forms, they are not intended for battlefield use. They are instead spiritual disciplines that purport to lead the advocate in accord with the **do** (michi), the "Way" to an "enlightened" state of mind represented by the "perfected" person.

The first component systems in this category to appear did so in the peaceful Tokugawa times of the seventeenth century. Many of these classical systems are extant today. Exponents of classical martial ways include warrior, soldier and ordinary civilian types.

Typical of the component classical martial ways systems are: **kyudo** (the Way of the bow), **kendo** (the Way of the sword), **iai-do** (the Way of sword drawing), **naginata-do** (the Way of the halberd), and **jodo** (the Way of the stick). It is essential to realize that none of the classical martial ways (**ko-budo**) are identical to modern disciplines that operate under the same generic rubric, but which are formulated and conducted under the aegis of national federations (**renmei**); for example, the All Japan Kyudo Federation **kyudo**, the All Japan Judo Federation **judo**, the All Japan Kendo Federation **kendo**, and so on. Genuine classical disciplines of the martial ways (**ko budo**) category always function as autonomous units — the **ryu** — that are tied to local, regional and ancestral traditions, though some may have varying degrees of liaison and cooperation with the national federations instituted by their modern counterparts. Some examples of classical martial ways are: Heijo Muteki Ryu **kendo**; Heiki Ryu **kyudo**; Jikishin Ryu **judo**; Tendo Ryu **naginata-do**; Mugai Ryu **iaido**; and Imai Ryu **jodo**.

The classical martial ways (**ko budo**) are less broad in scope and also fewer in number than are the classical martial arts (**ko bujutsu**). Hoplologists classify the martial ways according to the weapon/principle/agent that characterizes their mode of performance, as is the case with their ancestral battlefield forms (**ko bujutsu**).

The rapid modernization of Japan, beginning with the Meiji era (post 1868), and down to our modern times, brought with it an amazing growth of what I classify as modern martial arts (**shin bujutsu**) and modern martial ways (**shin budo**). The former category of disciplines is largely the province of modern military and naval personnel, civil defense, law enforcement and private security agencies; while the latter category of modern disciplines is popular among people from all walks of life. The component systems of both of these modern disciplines are founded in the post-classical period (post 1877) and do not necessarily have any direct connections with the classical **ryu** (**ko bujutsu** and **ko budo**), though the influences of these ancestral forms on the modern ones is undeniably great.

**Shin bujutsu**, the modern martial arts, have combative applications that range from those useful on the battlefield to those that are useful in civil life. They differ considerably from their classical forerunners (**ko bujutsu**) in that the majority of the modern arts are not only defensively oriented toward restraining, not killing an enemy, but also operate to protect the individual, not the group. Included in this category are:

**taiho-jutsu** (police art of restraint), **toshu kakuto-jutsu** (military art of unarmed personal self-defense), **jujutsu** (flexible art), **karate-jutsu** (sparring art), and **juken-jutsu** (bayonet art).

The **shin budo**, or modern martial ways, have no affiliations with (but may have liaison with) the classical **ryu**. These modern disciplines are characterized by the existence of national federations that act to supervise all standards and conduct of their respective disciplines. The modern martial ways differ in training methods, ranking system, purpose and social organization from the classical combative systems mentioned. Their purposes reveal a remarkably wide spectrum of applications in spiritual and physical training curricula, cultism, personal civil self-defense and competitive sport contests or trials of skill. Best known among the **shin budo** are **kendo** of the All Japan Kendo Federation, **judo** of the All Japan Judo Federation, **karate-do** of the All Japan Karate-do Federation, and so on.

Inasmuch as the majority of the Japanese people are engaged either directly or indirectly in one or more of the facets of combative disciplines within the educational, social or industrial institutions, or with the symbolic associations of the traditional martial culture, these disciplines constitute an important social phenomenon. Moreover, because many of the modern disciplines are practiced to an international scale, some of them included in international and Olympic sport agenda, the nature of the "game" and "play" naturally attaches to them and therewith brings them within the purview of the study of play.

All Japanese combative disciplines have deep significant meanings in terms of group and personal needs, and are to some extent a form of typically Japanese behavior that is recognized by a combination of specific traits. We may see and describe these disciplines on the basis of being institutionalized channels for the expression and resolution of inter- and intra-societal conflict and hostility, or as functions of play conducted in the manner of a safety valve that is expected to ensure harmonious social relations, or as play in the form of an indicator of social and psychological tensions, but this is to view combative disciplines more in the light of their goals or ancillary functions rather than to examine their vital processes.

The classical disciplines, either the martial arts (**ko bujutsu**) or the martial ways (**ko budo**) and to a lesser extent the modern martial ways (**shin budo**), are first and foremost exercises in ethnic identity and preservation, a series of processes and goals keynoted by the factor of readiness for hand-to-hand combat. It is here that the Japanese presaged Kant (1939) with their belief that combative action, in the long run, tends to unite the human race because grouping lessens the incidence of conflict. Thus, when we come to examine closely the combative disciplines, nowhere, either in spirit or in action, do we find the idea of "play" associated with these disciplines. Moreover, these disciplines clearly lack traits that are normally assigned to human play: voluntary activity; distinctly pleasurable and temporary from other "normal" behavior; a make-believe or transcendental quality; amoral function, non-utilitarian and having a definite beginning and ending in time. All evidence militates against these traits of human play having a bearing on the classical disciplines.

Exponents of classical Japanese combative disciplines scrupulously refrain from referring to their participation in combative disciplines as "play." The word "play," however, is sometimes voiced by the exponents of modern disciplines themselves who "play **kendo**" or "play **judo**." Thus; it might be supposed by an etic observer that, inasmuch as many of the modern disciplines are centered on the sports contest or part-time recreational activity, and because exponents demonstrate behavioral attitudes during practice that are not normally typical of their daily lives, that the modern disciplines are in fact "played" and, therefore, the word "play" is relevant to them.

But the use of the word "play" as it is sometimes applied to modern combative disciplines is only an unfortunate choice of an English word. It originated with the general inability of the Japanese to correctly translate their expression **renshu o suru**, meaning to undertake, perform or practice. **Keiko o suru** is yet another proper expression that is sometimes mistranslated as "play." It refers to engaging in training, practice or lessons, and originally meant to meditate on things of the past.

I would warn those persons who insist on visiting the realm of Japanese combatives (and it is only "visiting" that one can do unless his experience is an emic one) that if one fails to grasp and accept the significance of the variability in the Japanese combative sphere, one misses the fact that these combative disciplines are an exceedingly complex cultural entity over which no one generalization can validly prevail. Whereas the relevance of these disciplines to the subject of human play may provide a profitable course of investigation, this analogy must not be carried too far.

The case of Japanese combative systems suggests that a full critique of Huizinga and the concept of play is much needed. This cannot be done here. However, since Huizinga does mention the Japanese notion of play in his studies, a brief comment is in order.

While Huizinga admits that the concept of play, **asobu**, does not pertain to the Japanese conception of contest (1950: 33-34), he fails to elaborate to even the slightest degree on this very important matter: the

75

Japanese traditionally draw a distinct line between **asobi**, "play," the **shiai**, a game-like contest of skill, and the **shinken shobu**, a real fight to the death. The overall spectrum expressed by these words reflects a deep-seated sociological and psychological difference in Japanese culture between play and competition of any kind and at any level of seriousness. Therefore, only the last two expressions are admissible for use in connection with the Japanese combative disciplines.

Nowhere in the realm of these disciplines is the verb **asobu** or its substantive **asobi** applied in a constructive sense to indicate that these disciplines are forms of play. In fact, the only use of the word **asobu** is found in its negative sense, **asobi ja nai**, which is a warning or criticism that any state of idleness or breech of proper mental or physical attitude is disruptive to serious training ("don't play around").

The classical Japanese combative disciplines (**ko bujutsu** and **ko budo**), as well as the modern martial arts (**shin bujutsu**), are rarely seen outside of Japan. The so-called martial arts known in foreign lands are almost always modern martial ways (**shin budo**). Given the fact that the Japanese combative sphere is generally misunderstood by foreign observers, research based on **shin budo** in other cultures may lead to the superficial view that classical arts as anachronistic technologies are no longer extant, and that the modern disciplines are not only their logical and more desirable replacements, but also that the modern disciplines operate in an extension of the identical spirit and technique of their classical ancestral forerunners.

The hoplologist's work in Japanese combative culture, as well as that of many other cultures, is only beginning, and the success of this exciting venture depends entirely upon recognition of the need for the researcher to be properly trained as a hoplologist. To be so, not only must the researcher be proficient in a number of academic fields, but he must also be proficient in a number of combative disciplines, for past investigations have made it clear that proper classification and description of weapons and combative arts are not self-evident to those who lack an emic experience or who hold an etic orientation that is not shaped by substantial practical experience.

## Part II
## Japanese Martial Culture and Styles of Swordsmanship

Jeffrey Dann, University of Washington

Martial culture and combative systems, particularly those involving the use of the sword, have long been at the core of Japanese culture.

They provide a cultural referent for Japanese cognitive, emotional, and somatic associations and are an experiential learning model that has indelibly shaped all aspects of Japanese life. It is paradoxical that while commentators on Japanese culture have found the symbolic ramifications of martial culture so obvious, no one has thought to examine in detail the actual systems of combative training that have forged the generations of men who created Japanese culture. Despite the seminal ideas of Ruth Benedict's **Chrysanthemum and the Sword** (1946), and the exciting leads developed by Thomas Rohlen (1973, 1974, 1976) in understanding the basis of Japanese "spiritual education" (**seishin kyoiku**), the key role of combative systems as the dominant model for Japanese education or self-cultivation have hardly been touched upon.

The work of Draeger (1969, 1973a, 1973b, 1974) stands alone in the literature on Japan in seeking to classify these combative traditions, to understand their role and development over time, to assess their knowledge about the nature of man, and to study the processes of training and self-growth.

The Japanese combative arts have endured over time, but they have not remained static institutions. They reveal a great variety of forms, evidence of a dynamic character highly responsive to the changing needs of society. At every juncture significant in Japanese history, the combative disciplines show an adaptation to the new circumstances.

Research in Japanese combative systems, even when limited to a single component system such as the sword arts, indicates differences in social organization, purpose and training methods that not only preclude facile generalizations about Japanese culture in general, but also cast doubt upon statements of the cultural meanings of swordsmanship and the martial tradition when these statements are not grounded in specific cultural contexts. My research suggests that for all areas of martial and combative study, the individual **dojo**, or training hall, be the basic unit of analysis. Through the interpretation and organization of training by the headmaster and other members, the **dojo** is the medium of transmission of tradition in the local community over time.

Contemporary **kendo** (The Way of the Sword) belongs to Draeger's category of the **shin budo** or modern martial ways. Even within this one particular discipline, however, significant variations in training and meaning may be found among different **dojo**. These variations, based upon specific criteria in the organization of training methods, are of relevance for our understanding of the question as to whether or not the **budo** are to be understood by Western notions of sport and play.

I suggest that three styles of types of contemporary **kendo** exist and that, furthermore, they provide a developmental model of the Japanese response to the martial tradition as it has been adapted to the three major periods of social change that have occurred in Japan over the past one hundred and fifty years.

Briefly formulated, the three types are (1) classical **kendo**, (2) cultural **kendo**, and (3) sports **kendo**. These may be conceived as a continuum with classical **kendo** and sports **kendo** in polar opposition, and with cultural **kendo** in an intermediate or transitional position. The exponents of classical and cultural **kendo** are emphatic in their insistence that their disciplines are not a sport, and further, that their ways lack any of the characteristics associated with play, a concept which is highly developed in other segments of Japanese culture.

## CLASSICAL KENDO

Classical **kendo** seeks to preserve the training methods and traditions of the pre-modern combative systems as a system of self-cultivation that is grounded in combat realistic training. The classical **kendo dojo** will often have an affiliation with a classical martial way (**ko budo**) and has, as a central element of training, practice of the **kata** (pre-arranged sequences of attack and defense), of the **ryu**, or classical tradition with the **bokken** (hardwood sword). **Iaido kata** with the live sword will also be practiced. While the majority of training may be with the bamboo sword (**shinai**) in a free-style exercise, all actions with it are referred back to the combat-effective fundamentals of the **kata**.

In addition, the symbolic and expressive training procedures derived from the traditional martial culture will also be included. Examples of this are special practice sessions during the climatic extremes of winter and summer and the use of traditional martial poetry and songs as teaching devices. Furthermore, the classical **kendo dojo** and its members will maintain a deep relationship with the native Shinto religion. Indicative of this relationship is the presence of the Shinto altar (**kamidana**) as the central feature of the **dojo**, as well as the participation of members in shrine festivals devoted to martial dieties and traditions. Classical **kendo** is seen by its practitioners as a unique expression of the essence of Japanese culture, a path of spiritual self-cultivation based upon the traditional model of warrior combat effectiveness and readiness with the sword.

## CULTURAL KENDO

Cultural **kendo** represents the adaptation of classical swordsmanship to the modern social conditions of Japan after the Meiji Restoration. The main features of cultural **kendo** were systematized at the turn of the twentieth century and designed for the physical and mental development of the entire citizenry, particularly for male youths in the new public education system. Cultural **kendo** may be seen as an adaptation of traditional values and techniques to the modernizing needs of the new nation-state through the public school system which gave it a more sports-like cast.

The **dojo** of this type is less concerned with combat effectiveness than classical **kendo** and de-emphasizes **kata** training and the use of the hardwood sword. However, the abbreviated ten forms of the All-Japan Kendo Kata, created in 1912, serve as the proper model to real sword usage. Training centers around the use of the bamboo **shinai** as a physical culture regimen derived from the heritage of the idealized warrior class. Competitive contest (**shiai**) is considered a useful device for motivating school age members, but it is the idea of contest or trial of skill that is important, not that of sport or play.

SPORTS KENDO

Sports **kendo** is distinguished from cultural **kendo** by its de-emphasis on the symbolic and expressive elements in the traditional martial culture. Whereas the cultural **kendo dojo** will have a Shinto affiliation and use song and dance in training, the sports **kendo dojo** will lack these features. Essentially a post-war phenomenon, this style of **kendo** is considered by its practitioners and by the Ministry of Education to be a pure sports form; that is, an activity for recreation, health and enjoyment, albeit a sport that springs from the Japanese cultural heritage. Competition and success in tournament are considered as end-goals in themselves. Combat-effective techniques, being banned by tournament rules, are shunned in practice and participants strive for speed and light hitting actions that "take points" according to the aesthetic canons of the art.

With the overwhelming emphasis on proficiency with the bamboo **shinai**, there is an increasing tendency to view the All-Japan Kendo Kata as irrelevant and non-essential to competition skills. Finally, the presentation of instruction tends to be more verbal and rationalized as containing "packaged sequences", which are the result of modern physical education theories. Classical **kendo** instruction tends to be more non-verbal, intuitive and individualized, while the pedagogy of cultural **kendo**, because of its affiliation with the pre-war school system, shares features of both.

CONCLUSION

These three types of **kendo** reveal significant differences in purpose, training methodology, weapon's use, social organization and even symbolic content. Space has precluded the full discussion of these types of **kendo**, the criteria used to determine them and their relationship to the modernization process. There are, despite their numerous differences, important similarities among these styles of **kendo** and I offer here as an example their shared features of underlying psycho-kinesthetic concepts.

The three styles of **kendo** share concepts of the nature of mind and body and of the utilization of energy and strength, in which, it is posited, the psychic and somatic unity of the individual is located in the central torso region. This is characteristic of a larger pattern of Japanese psycho-kinesthetic concepts as described by Durckheim (1962), Rohlen (1976), and others. The characteristics of the "forging process" (**shin shin tanren**) found in **kendo** and all Japanese spiritual disciplines derive from these concepts.

Awareness of, and training in cultivating these psycho-kinesthetic experiences are a fundamental aspect of Japanese combative systems and are clearly related to the combative complexes of other Asian martial traditions, such as those of China and Korea. A fuller description of the psycho-kinesthetic dimensions of training in Japanese swordsmanship is contained in Dann (1977) and it is suggested that the cross-cultural study of psycho-kinesthetics in combative systems including derivative sport forms is an untapped area of research. The point here, however, is that despite shared cultural concepts, we cannot say that the combative systems are all the same. Even where a common ideational structure is shared by related systems, the particular use of different training methods causes the types and purposes of the disciplines to significantly vary. Therefore, research must be grounded in specific behavioral contexts, as well as in the cultural or ideational order.

In conclusion, I should like to make several recommendations for further research in combative systems, particularly for researchers who may base their studies on those combative disciplines that have achieved a modicum of popularity or recognition in America or Europe.

First, combative traditions, even within related weapons or fighting systems in a particular culture, are highly dynamic and exhibit variations in purpose, content and structure. At this stage of research, therefore, it is difficult to speak with great confidence about the general nature, processes and meanings of the combative arts in different cultures. Moreover, if the research is based upon systems that have found acceptance in cultures outside the country of their origin, it must be realized that they may represent highly variant forms and that they are probably in a dynamic state of change as they adapt to new cultural contexts. In all likelihood, these disciplines will represent post-classic developments in combative systems in the original culture, already having been modified to modernizing conditions in the home country.

Second, individual teachers who are bringing these disciplines into different cultural contexts may be actively changing the systems, sloughing off features embedded in the original cultural context or adding new elements that are believed to be more in accord with the values and customs of the recipient culture. This is particularly true if the combative art is being commercialized. The developments of **karate** and other empty-handed systems in America offer a fertile field of research in this regard. However, it is doubtful that an accurate assessment of any combative system as a whole can be made through research conducted in America or Europe without baseline studies first being made in the culture of its origin.

Third, hoplological analysis suggests that research be conducted by individuals trained in combative arts. Although the anthropological concept of participant-observation finds solid support here, the researcher must strive more for in-depth proficiency and breadth of experience rather than for brief participation or observation. Most combative systems state that understanding can come only through "doing" and through accumulated experience. Among and within related systems, numerous techniques may either look the same and be quite different, or they may look different and yet be strongly related. In many cases, the effectiveness of techniques and their relationships would be noticeable only to the researcher who is trained in combative systems and hoplological analysis. In addition, shared symbolic referents based upon martial hero imagery may mask, to the untrained observor, crucial differences in training and effectiveness.

Finally, it is hoped that this brief glimpse at the study of hoplology and combative systems will promote dialogue and future research to help clarify our conceptions of sports, contest, play, and combative systems.

REFERENCES

Benedict, Ruth, 1946, The Chrysanthemum and the Sword. New York: Houghton, Mifflin Co.

Dann, Jeffrey, 1977, Japanese Martial Culture: Learning in Swordsmanship, The Case of Kendo. Doctoral dissertation, University of Washington, Seattle, Washington.

Draeger, Donn F., 1973a, Classical Bujutsu. Tokyo: Weatherhill.
1973b, Classical Budo. Tokyo: Weatherhill.
1974, Modern Bujutsu and Budo. Tokyo: Weatherhill.

Draeger, Donn F. and Robert Smith, 1969, Asian Fighting Arts. Tokyo: Kodansha International.

Durckheim, Karlfried von, 1962, Hara: The Vital Center of Man. London: Methuen and Co.

Huizinga, Johan, 1950, Homo Ludens. Boston: Beacon Press.

Kant, Immanuel, 1939, Perpetual Peace. New York: Columbia University Press.

Rohlen, Thomas, 1973, Spiritual Education in a Japanese Bank. American Anthropologist 75(5):1542-1562.
    1974, For Harmony and Strength: Japanese White-Collar Organization in Anthropological Perspective. Los Angeles: University of California Press.
    1976, The Promise of Adulthood in Japanese Spiritualism. Daedalus Summer: 125-143.

## THE CONVEYANCE OF SOCIAL BELIEFS AND VALUES THROUGH AESTHETIC SPORT: THE CASE OF KENDO

Gary B. Jackson, University of Redlands

Since their earliest efforts, anthropologists have demonstrated a concern over expressive culture. Collectively, they have compiled a literature which traverses cultural traditions such as painting, ceramics, literature, music, theatre and dance as well as a host of other related fine and expressive arts. The list of those anthropologists contributing in this endeavor are numerous and include renowned scholars, such as Frans Boas, Douglas Fraser, Alfred Kroeber, Gertrude Kurath, Margaret Mead, Bruno Nettl, Stith Thompson and Ruth Bunzel. Their works have given theoretical shape to the ethnographic study of expressive institutions throughout the world and have lent, in a motivational sense, to the development of specialized departments offering advanced degrees in areas such as ethnomusicology, dance ethnology, folklore and semiology.

While at first inspection the overall magnitude of this concern may seem applaudable, further reconnaissance indicates a serious level of professional apathy. Unfortunately, there exists an astounding methodological and theoretical schism between the study of expressive culture and the more "reputable" concerns of contemporary anthropology. For example, when compared to the "thickly" treated areas of "Language and Culture" or "Kinship and Social Organization", it is strikingly apparent that expressive culture is a relatively non-treated anthropological concern in recent times. In addition, it becomes glaringly obvious that the basic theoretical premises upon which anthropologists rely, when analyzing expressive institutions, are primarily derived from non-anthropological sources and are therefore not always appropriate to ethnographic analysis. That is, the concerns of the art historian or the philosopher may not run concurrently with the concerns of the anthropologist.

Fortunately, this lack of professional enthusiasm and subsequently non-serious treatment by anthropologists, is currently under re-assessment. The most exciting and promising aspect of this turnabout is that no longer need the social scientist be satisfied with the redundant cataloging of art for art's sake, but now, under the critical gaze of a more supportive discipline, can develop a scientific dialogue around which a more comprehensive theory of expressive culture may evolve.

In the hope of contributing to this dialogue, the present paper, speculative in nature yet theoretical in intent, examines a traditional Japanese expressive institution. The example I refer to is a tightly structured and refined tradition that falls within the **bujutsu** or martial arts. It is the practice and way of the sword known as **Kendo** (Ken: sword; do: the way of), and considered by many as the grandfather of Japanese martial practices.

My examination places emphasis on **Kendo** as an expressive institution that has served to preserve and convey traditional values, beliefs and practices over time. In addition, it is argued that **Kendo** has remained socially salient through periods of social re-orientation through a selective form of institutional flexibility, and that the nature of that flexibility is a coalesced feature of social utility.

## A HISTORICAL PERSPECTIVE

According to the earliest historical documentation (i.e., the national anthologies **Kojiki** and the **Nihon-shoki**), the first written evidence of **Kendo** is traced back to the Taika Reform of 645 A.D. (Sasamori and Warner 1967:25-26). At this early point in the development of Japanese martial practices, reference was to sets of skills revolving around the practice of swordsmanship known as **Kenjutsu** (Ken: sword; jutsu: technique) and the rudimentary beginnings of an ethical doctrine later to be known as **Bushido** (Bushi: warrior; do: the way of).[1]

With the fall of the Tenno dynasty and the rise of the Kamakura Bakafu (military ruling faction) in 1185 A.D., Japan passed from a civil monarchy to a centralized government completely controlled by a warrior class known as **Bushi**. This event marks the formal beginnings of feudalism in Japan and was not to end until the fall of the Tokugawa Shogun during the Meiji Restoration of 1868.

The centuries of warrior dominance had substantial effect on Japanese society, much of which is still evident in contemporary times.

It was during this period of warrior predominance that **Bushido** took hold as a national moralistic standard. So socially pervasive was it that its tenets were not only strictly adhered to by the warriors themselves, but acclaimed by the Japanese people as the "highest level of human conduct" (Harrison 1939:45-63). He goes on to state that it was, and is, "one of the greatest molding forces in the development of a national culture and education that the world has observed. A force first observed in the way of life adopted by the Japanese 'samurai' and later carried into daily living by the people."

Although the political power of the warrior class was severely diluted after the Meiji Restoration, their values remained influential as a social exemplar. In this regard, Norbeck notes that, "the customs sketched for Japan a century ago have by no means disappeared without a trace. The long span of the Tokugawa-rea allowed a very firm set. The Meiji era that followed saw many great changes, but these occurred in ways that allowed, even encouraged, the continuation of a social order and supporting values that in many ways did not radically differ from the past" (Norbeck 1965:9).

## AN INFORMATIONAL AND EXPRESSIVE MEDIUM

Human culture is a labyrinth of ways, the complexity of which remains unclear. It is, above all else, an informational system that generates, protects and conveys meaningful aspects of itself over vast periods of time. To this extent, Roberts states that, "every culture may be viewed as an informational system in which information is stored, retrieved and utilized in decision making and other activities" (Roberts 1971:208). Although Roberts primarily concerns himself with the storage and reordering of "outmoded" technology, he concurrently notes the importance of preserving "motorskills, values and beliefs as a total pattern of information conservation" by expressive institutions.

As an expressive institution, **Kendo** serves as an informational system in the preservation and transmission of traditional values, beliefs and practices. Unlike the cases cited by Roberts, where knowledge is conserved as an adaptive measure for possible future use, **Kendo** has retained, throughout it's history, social utility. What at first may appear to be "outmoded" technology, i.e., the skills associated with swordsmanship, retain social importance by affixing to the mastery of **Kendo** technique the attainment of enlightenment. That is, through the continued and methodical practice of **Kendo**, the practitioner will attain a body and mind set which reflects the Japanese idealization of the ultimate level of human awareness.

Such beliefs are evidenced throughout Japanese society. Rohlen's description of a modern Japanese water treatment company's approach to initial employee indoctrination is a good case in point. Here we see a program that is modeled on a pre-war naval officer candidate training system. The rationale for the implementation of such a program centers on the belief that through it the company will be better able to enhance technological development by instilling traditional values regarding group conformity and loyalty (Rohlen 1970). An important note here is that the naval cadet program was not only based upon dictates central to the **Kendo** experience, but incorporated **Kendo** training as the means by which those dictates could be properly learned. Another example is cited in Harris' translation of **Go Rin No Sho** (A Book of Five Rings) written by the most famous of all Kendoists, M. Miyamoto. In it, Miyamoto describes his approach to the mastery of **Kendo** by illustrating the role of strategy. Harris notes that, "Japanese businessmen have used **Go Rin No Sho** as a guide for business practice, making sales campaigns like military operations, using the same energetic methods" (Harris 1974: 22).

The kinds of examples cited by Harris and Rohlen are, as previously stated, not unique. The ring of **Kendo** influence extends not only into the industrial realm, but as well, touches agencies such as government, law enforcement and public education. As such, it is a significant agent in the never ceasing process of socialization. It is an expressive medium whereby the ways of the past are exonerated in the present and preserved for the future.

MIEN TRANSPOSITIONS

**Kendo**'s successful adaptation and contemporary popularization in the face of rapid social change was facilitated by a self-regulated form of institutional flexibility. In itself, institutional flexibility within a highly ritualized institution such as **Kendo** is not an anomalous phenomenon. For example, Fischer illustrates how **Sumo** (a traditional form of Japanese wrestling) was able to overcome internal conflict due to rapid social change by encouraging "individual behavioral differences and by modifying rules in response to pressures from other social institutions" (Fischer 1966:31).

These observations apply equally well to **Kendo**. However, where Fischer places emphasis on the loss of individual conformity and the modification of rules as a consequence of social change, I would like to examine **Kendo**'s ability to retain institutional integrity without significant alteration to important beliefs and practices. This I believe, was accomplished by sequential adjustments to social change through what I term here as mien transpositions. Mien, in the sense of institutional demeanor only, and transposition, in that institutional demeanor changes without substantial effect of dogma.

There appear to be four major mien transpositions in the development of **Kendo**. They are in chronological order: (1) **Kendo** as martial practice with emphasis on style and technique; (2) **Kendo** as metaphysical martial practice; (3) **Kendo** as aesthetic martial practice; and (4) **Kendo** as aesthetic sport.

## KENDO AS MARTIAL PRACTICE WITH EMPHASIS ON TECHNIQUE

The exact date of **Kendo**'s technical beginnings is unfortunately lost to antiquity. The most reliable estimate comes from early Japanese historians who suggest that it occurred with the advent of the **Kashima no tachi** style created by the famous swordsman, Kunimatsu no Mahito, during the period of tribal states in Japan somewhere between 57 and 600 A.D. (Sasamori and Warner 1967). This is apparently based upon what appears to be the first mention of stylistic distinctions and possible preferences. That is, the **Kashima no tachi** was apparently categorized into three styles: (1) the **Joko-ryu** (ancient style); (2) the **Chuko-ryu** (middle style); and (3) the **Shinto-ryu** (new style).

Presumable, from this simple distinction arose a competitive fetish for the complexity of style that culminated by the end of the Edo period, in the establishment of thousands of **dojo** (fencing schools) each with a founding master and each purporting to have attained the ultimate approach to **Kendo** through their own unique **ryu** (style). Collectively, these schools amassed a technical compository the magnitude of which staggers the imagination. It was not until the end of feudalism that this stylistic diversity was standardized. As a result, more than six hundred separate **Kendo ryu** (styles) were converted into seven basic fighting stances (**Kamae**) that were further segmented into six primary attack modes (**Shikakewaza**) with twenty-one variations (**Ooyo**), and four primary counter-attack modes (**Ooji-waza**) with twenty-six variations (**Ooyo**) (Jackson 1975). (See Figure 1.)

As is the case with all Japanese **Do** practices, style and form play a significant role. Within the martial arts this is extremely so since, in a pragmatic sense, it is only through the enactment of technique and style that victory or loss can be measured. And, in the case of **Kendo**, victory and fame are clearly predicated, equally on style and individual prowess. In **Kendo**, this relationship between warrior and style are inseparable. So much so, that they become one in thought and action.

**Figure 1. Kendoo no Kata: Kendoo styles and techniques**

Kendoo no Kata

Shikake-Waza (attack mode) — Konpon no Waza (primary techniques)

| Okori | Harai | Renzoku | Hiki | Katsugi | Katate |
|---|---|---|---|---|---|
| Debana Men | Men | Kote kara Men | Men | Men | Men |
| Debana Kote | Kote | Men kara Doo | Doo | Kote | Tsuki |
| Hikibana Men | Doo | Tsuki kara Men | Kote | | |
| Hikibana Kote | Tsuki | Tsuki kara Kote | | | |
| | | Kote kara Men to Doo | | | |

Ooji-Waza (counter attack mode) — Konpon no Waza (primary techniques)

| Nuki | Kaeshi | Suriage | Uchiotoshi |
|---|---|---|---|
| Men Nuki Men | Men Kae. Migi Doo | Men Sur. Men Hidari Biraki | Men Uchio. Men Kiriotoshi |
| Men Nuki Doo | Men Kae. Hidari Doo | Men Sur. Men Migi Biraki | Men Uchio. Men Migi Biraki |
| Men Nuki Kote | Men Kae. Migi Men | Men Sur. Hidari Doo | Men Uchio. Men Hidari Biraki |
| Kote Nuki Men | Kote Kae. Men | Men Sur. Migi Doo | Kote Uchio. Men |
| Kote Nuki Kote | Do Kote Men | Men Sur. Kote | Doo Uchio. Men |
| | Tsuki Kae. Migi Doo | Kote Sur. Men | |
| | Katate Men Kae. Hidari Doo | Tsuki Sur. Men Migi Biraki | |
| | | Katate Tsuki Sur. Doo | |
| | | Katate Migi Men Sur. Men | |

*The terms in the two boxes represent the different applications (Ooyo).

During the early development of **Kendo**, style and technique remained the essence of the practice. However, with the Kamakura Bakufu, the Japanese warriors were forced to concern themselves with social trends. As a ruling class, they found the need to adjust their social image in a fashion that would sanctify them in the eyes of the populace while simultaneously protecting their ethics and values. This they accomplished in part through religious symbolism — the second mien transposition.

## KENDO AS METAPHYSICAL MARTIAL PRACTICE

Immediately following the establishment of the Kamakura Bakufu began, what Koosaka terms, "the age of religious culture" (Koosaka 1967:248-253). This was a time of social preoccupation with religion and religious idealism. No area within Japanese society was immune. Not even the non-religious warriors of the new Seii-tai Shogun, General Yoritoma, could avoid the intrusion of religious symbolism. However, unlike many other social institutions, the **samurai** were able to adjust religion to fit their specific needs. That is, at all costs it must not alter the philosophical base upon which the way of the warrior was predicated.

As a result, the **samurai** adopted the religious non-religion **Rinzai Zen**. Originally, it was a Chinese tradition stemming from the "Five Houses" of Zen Buddhism and considered, as apposed to other forms, most agreeable to the warrior class since it prescribed to a form of enlightenment attained through beatings and shoutings (Yamaguchi 1969). Even of more importance, it was not a theology or a philosophy, and possessed no dogma. In this regard, it was somewhat neutral and non-threatening. Toshimitsu adds that it is, "...not an ethic, and knows nothing of the question, 'what ought I do?' it does not teach the value of an individual action, but the man of Zen knows without reflection how he ought to act" (Toshimitsu 1962:13). It was, in fact, in perfect harmony with the **samurai** reverence for style and technique, and presented an ideal medium through which **Kendo** could be taught and learned. Its emphasis on discipline and mental training was an essential element in the molding of young warriors. Through meditative practices such as **Shugyo**, it was felt that a more perfect blending of technique, style and spirit could be achieved (Suzuki 1959). Where, to the non-practitioner, it may have seemed mysterious and esoteric, to the initiate it was the path, a systematic method to the mastery of style. Respectfully, Herrigel attested to the methodicalness of the Zen experience in his book **Zen in the Art of Archery** (1953). He states that,

> Mysterious, unfathomable, and unutterable as the mystic experience itself
> is, the road that leads to it should not be. It is meant to be accessible to
> anyone of good will, if only in stretches, as measured out to him by fate.
> There is thus a practicalness about Zen which inspires confidence. So it is
> not surprising if, for the same reason that the way has to be divided up,
> schematically and thematically, into single steps, the learning of these steps
> should turn into a regular routine. There is a rigorous training in Zen which
> strikes one as utterly soulless. Everything must go with clockwork precision
> (Herrigel 1974:23).

The incorporation of **Rinzai Zen** into **Kendo** added many general features attributed to religious institutions. It functioned in an explanatory sense by defining the mystical in meaningful terms (Spiro 1965). It gave validation through religious symbolism. That is, religious symbols function to reinforce with efficacious authorization the basic social institutions, values, practices and goals of a society (Geertz 1965). It provided a form of psychological reinforcement by reducing, through religiously sanctioned practices, such as **zazen**, the extreme levels of anxiety accompanying the **samurai** way of life (Kluckhohn 1942). It served to integrate social and psychological reality (Geertz 1965). And of particular importance, it helped to conserve and pass on **Kendo** knowledge over generations. That is, religious ritual is an important mode by which members of a culture program, store and pass on significant forms of information (Leach 1965).

The importance of Zen in the **Kendo** experience can not be overemphasized. It was a necessary element in the adaptation of tradition to change and set a precedence for the third mien transposition.

## KENDO AS AESTHETIC MARTIAL PRACTICE

Shortly after the ascension of Imperial power, Japanese society underwent a radical re-ordering of its basic social fabric. Feudalism came to an abrupt end placing hundreds of thousands of unwanted warriors in social limbo. Disheartening as this may have been to the once magnanimous warriors of the Tokugawa era, in and of itself, it posed little threat to **Kendo** and the basic values and beliefs of the **samurai**. It was obvious that the new social order would need, as much as ever, the talents and skills associated with martial practices. The greatest threat to **Kendo** came as a result of Japan's end to isolationism and determination to modernize at all costs. As a result, **Kendo** teetered on the brink of becoming an antique of the past, socially impotent, and at the mercy of social whim. As a result of such pressures, **Kendo** threw off its feudal image and renewed itself through the artistic experience. **Kendo** became traditional art and thereby continued as a conveyor and conserver of the way.

As in the case of **Rinzai Zen**, art was a transport and not transmutating. Functionally, art was a perfect fit. Through it, **Kendo** dictates regarding the importance of the mastery of method, addiction to style, the relationship between style and individual and most significantly, the way itself, remained paramount. Where Zen gave method, art provided the medium whereby traditional values and practices not only remained influential in the Japanese experience, but spread throughout the world. The way and art become one. That is, in as much as the way embodied the aesthetics of life, art presented a way.

A new dimension in the **Kendo** experience was achieved through art. It now began to become popularized. While in the past, **Kendo** was a practice reserved for a privileged few, as a Zen art the range of possible practitioners grew in geometric proportions. This trend continued into contemporary times resulting in international appeal. The answer to the question, "how Zen?" — a question that attracted the attention of millions throughout the world — became, "by art." As a consequence, Zen arts, such as **Kendo**, remained the source through which the mysteries and wisdoms of Zen Buddhism could be learned.

The impact Japanese Zen arts has had on peoples throughout the world is not insignificant. One need only look about to witness the signs. There are works, such as Suzuki's, **Zen and Japanese Culture** (1959), for the intellectually minded, or their popular counterparts, such as Pirsig's **Zen in the Art of Motorcycle Maintenance** (1976). There are countless Zen monasteries, such as the renowned Tassajara in Northern California, and even more self-proclaimed Zen gurus, ready to sell you the wisdoms of the east in places like Esalen near Big Sur, California. Even Castaneda's (1969) somewhat invisible "Don Juan" instructs and enlightens in ways queerly similar to Zen. Certainly, such examples stretch far beyond the limits of understanding, and are intended here only as an illustration of the effect art has had on popularizing Zen traditions; and in effect, laid the groundwork through which **Kendo**, in a controversial move, became identified with sport.

KENDO AS AESTHETIC SPORT

The combination of the devastating defeat of the Japanese militarists during World War II, followed by the Allied occupation and subsequent prohibition against any organized form of martial practices in Japan, reduced **Kendo** to a socially stigmatized and secretively practiced militant handicraft. It wasn't until after the occupation that **Kendo** began to re-surface in Japan.

Unfortunately, at least in the eyes of its more traditional and conservative members, the social setting in Japan had drastically altered.

Western influence had taken effect and Japan was undergoing substantial social displacement. Tradition was a thing of the past and seen as passe as opposed to the new and modern pastimes. Buddhism and the traditional religions in general, became ritual vestiges of the past and drew much less attention than the new Soka Gakkai religion. Traditional fine arts such as **Sumi-e** (ink wash painting), **Shodo** (calligraphy), **Ikado** (flower arrangement), fell behind the more appealing "avant-garde" approaches to art. And, the martial practices found themselves struggling against the spectre of Western sport.

Sports, as Snyder and Spreitzer have suggested, are "cultural universals and basic institutions in societies, and are some of the most pervasive aspects of culture in industrialized societies" (Snyder and Spreitzer 1974:467). Like religion and art, sport plays a significant role in the transmission of social beliefs and values (Boyles 1963) and represent a particular society's basic values and norms (Roberts and Sutton-Smith 1962). As Snyder and Spreitzer point out, some observers feel that "sport has a 'conservatizing' effect on youth through its emphasis on hard work, persistence, dilligence, and individual control over social mobility" (1974). (See also, Phillips and Schafer 1970; Rehberg 1971; Schafer 1971; Scott 1971). And, of primary significance, it is an agency of socialization (Piaget 1962; Erickson 1965; Sutton-Smith 1971).

On one hand, the institution of sport presented, to the keepers of **Kendo** traditions, a natural force by which it could re-establish itself in a world fixated on modern progress. Sport had all the superficial qualities needed to justify it in this sense. By its very definition it provided a comfortable fit. This is illustrated quite well in Edwards' definition of sport. He sees sport as "activities having formally recorded histories and traditions, stressing physical exertion through competition within limits sets in explicit formal rules governing role and position relationships, and carried out by actors who represent or who are part of formally organized associations having the goal of achieving valued tangibles or intangibles through defeating opposing groups" (Edwards 1973: 47-48).

As tempting as the institution of sport might seem to **Kendo**, it as well carried a stigma completely inacceptable to the traditionalist within its ranks. Inexplainable, it was not clear where the line between sport and play was drawn. As Luschen (1967) suggests, sport must lie somewhere between work and play and therefore is much too vague a category. Above all else, to the traditionalist, **Kendo** and the way had to remain a serious pursuit and not fall into the meaningless and self-destructive weaknesses they associated with play.

This controversy appears to be fixed, at least at this point in time, as an unresolvable dilemma. However, as an outgrowth, **Kendo** has become bi-functional. On one side, it remains as it always has been—a traditional Zen art that presents, as an essential element of its function, a way of life. On the other, it has become a sport, with all the associated social ramifications. This bi-functional configuration, disregarding the frequent battles carried on by the traditionalists and modernists, has been far more beneficial than harmful. As opposed to similar martial practices such as **Kyudo** (Zen archery), which has resisted identification with sport, and **Judo,** which has lost much of its original intent and purpose through total alliance with sport, **Kendo** is able to remain flexible and benefit from the popularization attained through the identity of sport, thereby continuing to conserve traditional beliefs and practices central to the way and the Japanese experience.

## SUMMARY

In summary, I would like to reiterate the main points presented in this paper. First, **Kendo** is presented as a traditional Japanese expressive institution encompassing fundamental beliefs and values from which Japanese society is predicated on. Secondly, **Kendo** understandings are believed to be learned through the disciplined mastery of style and technique. Thirdly, as a specialized cultural expression, **Kendo** adapted to external pressures due to social change through a form of selective institutional flexibility which infiltrated only those features of religion, art and sport that provided renewed social utility. That is, in all cases, the "mien transpositions" maximized institutional and social viability while minimizing the loss of institutional integrity.

## NOTES

[1]According to Draeger (see previous article), *bujutsu* should be divided into *ko budo* (classical martial ways) and *shin budo* (new martial ways). This distinction between the new and old developed with the founding of the "Dai Nippon Butokukai" in 1895 and the creation of non-style affiliated Kendo clubs in public schools.

## REFERENCES

Boyles, R. H., 1963, Sport: Mirror of American Life. Boston: Little, Brown.

Castaneda, Carlos, 1969, The Teachings of Don Juan: A Yaqui Way to Knowledge. Berkeley: University of California Press.

Edwards, H., 1973, Sociology of Sport. Illinois: Dorsey.

Erickson, Erik H., 1965, Childhood and Society. New York: W. W. Norton.

Fischer, Ann, 1966, Flexibility in an Expressive Distribution: Sumo. Southwestern Journal of Anthropology 22(1):31-42.

Geertz, Clifford, 1965, Religion as a Cultural System. Anthropological Approaches to the Study of Religion. Monography #3. London: Tavistock.

Harris, Victor, 1974, A Book of Five Rings: A Guide to Strategy. New York: Overlook.

Harrison, E. J., 1939, The Fighting Spirit of Japan: An Esoteric Study of the Martial Arts and Way of Life in Japan. London: W. Foulsham.

Herrigel, Eugen, 1960, The Zen Method. New York: Pantheon.

Jackson, Gary B., 1975, Kendo no Gakumon: The Value of Knowledge, Rank and Learning in the Japanese Zen Art of Swordsmanship. Irvine: University of California. Social Science Working Papers No. 77a.

Kluckhohn, Clyde, 1942, Myths and Rituals: A General Theory. Harvard Theological Review 35:45-79.

Koosaka, Masaaki, 1967, The Status and the Role of the Individual in Japanese Society. In The Japanese Mind: Essentials of Japanese Philosophy and Culture. Charles A. Moore, Ed. University of Hawaii: East-West Center Press. Pp. 248-253.

Leach, Edmund, 1965, Ritualization in Man in Relation to Conceptual and Social Development. In Reader in Comparative Religion. W. A. Lessa and E. Z. Vogt, Eds. New York: Harper and Row.

Luschen, Gunther, 1967, The Interdependence of Sport and Culture. International Review of Sport Sociology 2:127-141.

Norbeck, Edward, 1965, Changing Japan. Case Studies in Cultural Anthropology. Stanford University. pp. 9-10.

Phillips, John C. and Walter E. Schafer, 1970, The Athletic Subculture: A Preliminary Study. A paper presented at the American Sociological Association.

Piaget, Jean, 1962, Play, Dreams and Imitation in Childhood. New York: Norton.

Pirsig, Robert, 1976, Zen in the Art of Motorcycle Maintenance. New York: Bantam.

Rehberg, Richard A., 1971, Sport and Political Activism. A paper presented at the Conference on Sport and Social Deviancy. State University New York. Brockport, New York.

Roberts, John M., 1971, I—Expressive Aspects of Technological Development. Philosophical Social Science. Great Britain. pp. 207-219.

Roberts, John M. and Brian Sutton-Smith, 1962, Child Training and Game Involvement. Ethnology 1(April):166-185.

Rohlen, Thomas P., 1970, Sponsorship of Cultural Continuity in Japan: A Company Training Program. Journal of Asian and African Studies 5:184-192.

Sasamori, J. and G. Warner, 1967, This Is Kendo. Tokyo, Japan: Charles E. Tuttle Co.

Schafer, Walter E., 1971, Sport, Socialization and the School: Toward Maturity or Enculturation? Paper presented at the Southern Section California Health, Physical Education and Recreation Conference. San Fernando Valley State College.

Scott, Jack, 1971, The Athletic Revolution. New York: The Free Press.

Snyder, Eldon E. and E. Spreitzer, 1974, Sociology of Sport: An Overview. The Sociological Quarterly 15(Autumn):467-487.

Spiro, Melford E., 1965, Religion: Problems of Definition and Explanation. Anthropological Approaches to the Study of Religion 2:85-126.

Sutton-Smith, Brian, 1971, A Developmental Approach to Play, Games, and Sport. A paper presented at the Second World Symposium on the History of Sport and Physical Education. Banff, Alberta, Canada.

Suzuki, D. T., 1959, Zen and Japanese Culture. Bollinger Series LXIV. Princeton University Press.

Toshimitsu, Hasumi, 1962, Zen in Japanese Art: A Way of Spiritual Experience. Translated from German by John Petrie, New York: Philosophical Library.

Yamaguchi, Minoru, 1969, The Intuition of Zen and Bergson. Herder Agency. Enderle Bookstore.

## THE FUNCTIONS OF PLAY AND THE
## PLAY MOTIF AT A STATE PENITENTIARY

John Aron Grayzel, University of Oregon

INTRODUCTION

It is generally recognized that among humans, as well as among many other species (and even between species), a signal (metacommunication) to the effect that "This is play," often precedes or accompanies actual play activity (Miller 1973: 88-89). To a large extent, such a message seemingly functions as an introduction to, or clarification of, the play behavior itself. However, one characteristic of man is his ability to recognize that ". . . signals are only signals which can be trusted, distrusted, falsified, denied, amplified, corrected, and so forth" (Bateson 1972: 178). Therefore, it would seem reasonable to suspect that, at least among humans, while adults may not play as much as children, they are more consciously aware that the symbols indicative of play are symbols and, consequently, are better able to manipulate them as might suit their purposes.

An example of just such an ability of adults to manipulate the concept of play was presented to me in 1973, while I was engaged in an ethnographic study of a State Penitentiary, a type of institution usually conceived as being somber in nature. There I discovered a population who, both consciously and unconsciously, had become actively engaged in a mass effort to so amplify the metacommunication "This is play", that it became the dominant frame of reference for the majority of their daily activities. To try and explain exactly why and how this occurred, is the purpose of this paper.

RESEARCH SITUATION AND STRATEGY

For approximately nine months in 1973, the author and a colleague,

94

Sam Fujisaka, conducted an ethnographic study of Oregon State Penitentiary, in Salem, Oregon. During this time, we were provided with total freedom to mingle with the prison population in virtually all areas of the institution.[1]

O.S.P., as it is commonly called, is Oregon's only maximum security facility. Its' approximately 1,100 male inmates represent a more diversified spectrum of offenders than is found in many larger states where multiple institutions allow for greater separation of individuals according to the nature of their crimes and their records of behavior. Several characteristics of this population, especially a strong suspicion of outsiders and a highly developed manipulative comportment **vis-a-vis** would-be investigators, soon made it obvious that any attempts at random surveys or standardized questioning were doomed to failure. Instead we settled on a **modus operandi** that we call "partnership research", which involved independent, but coordinated research that stressed naturalistic observation and the concentration by each researcher on selected people, both prisoners and staff, with whom we could form comfortable and trusting relations.[2]

My own observations on play and the function of a play motif at O.S.P. are the result of this approach and not of any **a priori** theoretical interest in the applicability or appropriateness of the concept of play, **per se.** Thus the situation was not one of my seeing "play" in various adult actions, but rather a case of numerous actions that the participants themselves viewed as "play" and so denoted linguistically. That the way they perceived the activities and their denotion of "play" was frought with ambiguities and contradictions, was itself an essential ingredient in determining how the play motif affected their institutional lives.

## HISTORICAL BACKGROUND

Since "the past" as opposed to "the present" was a conscious dichotomy in the minds of the population, which influenced their ideas and actions, some understanding of that past is a necessary prerequisite to discussing the situation as I found it.

For fifteen years, prior to 1968, the prison was ruled by a highly autocratic warden who had previously retired from the federal penitentiary system. In their daily lives prisoners lived under strict authoritarian control. They walked to work in single file, on a red line from which they could not deviate, and which came to be the most powerful symbol of their way of life. They ate at long tables under the eyes of armed guards. The rule stated that a man could take as much food as he wanted, but he had to eat everything on his plate. Almost all decisions were made based on a written directory of 82 "general orders" that were precise, dogmatic and picayune. These covered everything from the correct angle to prop up a man in the gas chamber, to distinguishing permissible cashews and mixed nuts from contraband Almond Roca candy bars. In response to a legislative directive requiring the promulgation of a regulation "allowing a man to visit a dying relative or attend their funeral", an order was written that a prisoner could "either visit the sick relative or attend the funeral, but not both". Printed copies of such rules usually ended with the underlined statement, in captial letters, that: "THERE SHALL BE NO CHANGES, ADDITIONS TO, OR DELETIONS FROM THIS GENERAL ORDER EXCEPT AS AUTHORIZED BY THE WARDEN" (field notes).

While to some people such a regimentation of life might seem unduly hard and border on the grotesque, it was part of a conscious effort to impregnate the institution with an all pervasive atmosphere that was officially denoted as "strict, but just". The administration, itself, was so proud and sure of this philosophy, as to expose and espouse it in a film documentary made in 1957.

Besides the official rules and regulations, there was an accompanying series of unofficial rules that governed general prison life just as strictly as those formally promulgated. Known as the "convicts' code", it was concisely summed up by the expression "Do your own time", meaning "Mind your own business and don't interfere with what another con has going to make his life bearable." It included: "Don't steal from another con"; "Don't welch on debts"; "Keep you word"; and "Don't collaborate with the enemy." This last commandment required a prisoner to refrain from speaking to a guard unless another inmate was present to witness that he wasn't "snitching" (informing).

To a significant extent, this code was shared by all members of the prison community. Thus, a new prisoner would be advised by the staff to "Do his own time". Also shared was the allotted prestige of the convict hierarchy that went along with the code. This placed "hard cons" and "heavy crimes", such as armed robbery, on top, and "snitchers" and sex offenders on the bottom.

Compliance with both the unofficial "convicts' code" and official regulations had definite rewards. As regards the first, its reward was survival; as regards the second, its reward involved the actual length of imprisonment, which was determined largely by the formula, "One third to the Board, two thirds to good time." This meant that after one third of a man's sentence, the parole board decided whether or not to release him. If he were not paroled, and maintained good conduct, he was released at the end of two thirds of his sentence. Bad conduct cases served their full term.

## POST-1968 PRISON LIFE

In 1968, the institution was the scene of a major riot which, if not caused, was encouraged by the absence of the warden, who was dying of cancer. Practices instituted since then to reform many of the major problems have resulted in a significant reorientation of prison life.

## GENERAL CIRCUMSTANCES AND TYPES OF PLAY AT O.S.P.

At the time of this study in 1972, people walked haphazardly around the prison; there was a pass system, but it was often disregarded, and it was common to see guards and prisoners horseplaying with each other, though this was against stated rules. In contrast to the dictatorial nature of the pre-1968 general orders, 1973 written regulations often began with statements such as, "The following instructions for the operation of the post are merely basic and to be used as a guide to assist the officers assigned. They cannot conceivably cover every incident which may occur" (field notes). Such a statement was reflective of a general stress on flexibility rather than rigidity.

Both for purposes of rehabilitation, and perhaps of greater importance, in order to maintain prisoner control, a wide variety of alternative activities and programs had been created. These ranged from vocational training to college education, and from an Alcoholics Anonymous to a "Screaming Eagles Motorcycle Club". An individual's participation in such programs was strongly tied to his obtaining various rewards within the prison, as well as increasing his opportunity for early release either through the work release program, parole, or pardon.

However, it was generally conceded that what was stressed by the administration was not the quality of a man's participation, but his willingness to participate itself, and the implicit cooperation with authority that such participation implied.

Thus a prisoner who was a journeyman, with a long history of employment, was told to enter an educational program, as if lack of education had caused him to commit his crimes. At the same time, a university graduate was programmed for vocational training as an electrician, as if lack of a trade were the cause of his being in prison. What was really being sought was cooperation with the process and a willingness to play a role; and this was precisely the expressed opinion of most prisoners, officers and the treatment staff. As a result, both staff and prisoners viewed "programming", as such activities were called, as basically, "playing a game".

It should be noted, however, that while the concept of "playing" is easily connected with that of "game", the two are not synonymous. Generally speaking, what people in the prison had in mind as "playing" corresponded with the idea of not being serious in what one was doing, such as by presenting a false front, (e.g. making a speech to Alcoholics Anonymous at the same time as fruit was brewing in the speaker's cell). Associated, but different, was the idea of gaming, which involved the serious pursuit of a goal, such as obtaining an early release date by being recommended for parole. Thus "playing the game" was a serious matter at the prison in the sense that valued rewards were to be won or lost.

However, if this stress on playing a role regardless of one's belief in its fundamental value, or one's ultimate commitment to it, were the only form of "play" at the penitentiary, the situation would not really have been that unusual or different from the realities of every day life outside the institution. In fact, it was but the vortex of an atmosphere of play that circulated throughout the institution. In this sense, there was a motif, or theme, of play that colored life in the prison the same way the old standard of "strict, but just" had colored life under the pre-1968 regime. This motif actually had numerous physical embodiments. In addition to two baseball playing fields, basketball courts, and gym facilities—all of which might be justified by the need for healthy recreational diversions—there was a charming eight hole miniature golf course. The entrance to each cell block (e.g. Cell Block A, B, or C) was identified by a gigantic colored square approximately 8x10 feet, in red or blue, with a six foot green or purple letter painted in a block form, reminiscent of modern nursery school architecture. Messages from prisoners to the administration, many of which were "snitch notes" informing on illicit activities, were deposited in a five foot red, white and blue imitation mail box prominantly placed on the way to the dining room. And, in what was perhaps the **piece de resistance,** high on the wall of the hospital ward next to the entrance, looking down on a potted plastic palm tree, was a large electric Howdy Doody clock.

## EMIC EXPLANATIONS FOR THE PREVALENCE OF PLAY

Within the institution, both prisoners and staff had their own explanations of the new (post-1968 riot) situation.

To begin with, prison is a most boring place. In fact, boredom is perhaps the major punishment. It is also the source of much trouble and unrest. Because of this, since 1968, the administration had increased the number of opportunities for prisoners to have something to do and most often this took the form of play. Sometimes this involved game playing, such as pool, baseball, chess, dominoes, cards, or lifting weights, and sometimes it involved imitative playing, such as in activities like the "State Street J.C.'s", a prison version of the Junior Chamber of Commerce that held regular meetings and engaged in local aid projects.

A second interpretation by insiders stressed a more specific relationship between the reality of prison existence and that on the outside, and ascribed a play motif to American life in general. According to this line of reasoning, the prison was merely reflective of outside practices. It is in the outside world that people "play" roles and games. Prison practices were not seen as "play" themselves. Rather, in the prison, people responded to the serious demands of a sometimes subtle, sometimes not, reward-punishment milieu designed to convince them to be willing to "play" as people do on the outside. Thus, a staff member holding this belief claimed: "It's all a question of deceit, a mask. We all wear masks. Nobody wants to be seen for what they really are. Well here they want them to put on more a mask. They don't care what's underneath, just so long as it's covered up better" (field notes).

A third perspective, advanced mainly by staff members, was an expansion of this idea that the prison mirrored outside life, in that it was advocated that such a congruency between reality inside and outside the institution was, and should be, a consciously sought after goal. This view was based on the belief that the differences between classical penitentiary life and normal life in the every-day world, resulted in the enculturation of prisoners to an institutional milieu that made them more unfit for release after their incarceration than before. In response to this, since 1968, the policy at O.S.P. has been to stress the breaking down of barriers between the two worlds through, among other things, the increased participation of volunteers in prison programs, and the participation of prisoners in outside events, (e.g. speeches at schools and community projects). Some results of this policy were such gatherings as the already mentioned Junior Chamber of Commerce meetings within the prison. Here one could see prisoners dressed in prison clothing discussing various projects with J.C.'s from surrounding communities, who were attired in various vests and shirts in blazing colors, with patches advertising local brands of beer, and so on. During such a gathering, it was often difficult to determine just who was acting and who was sincere.

To still others, the question was not only one of preventing prisoners from permanently adapting to institutional life, but of forcing them to accept the mores of that segment of the outside world that they had formerly rejected. This involved the concept of role playing as a tool of enculturation. It was especially found couched in psychological jargon in various group therapy programs in the prison that encouraged the acting out of new patterns of behavior. (In fact, the new color scheme of the prison was seemingly the result of the recommendation of visiting "experts" who were concerned with the psychological atmosphere projected). Among non-psychologically oriented members of the staff, this role playing philosophy was summed up in such vernacular statements as "Let a guy try to fool us long enough and he'll end up fooling himself."

## ETIC ANALYSIS OF PLAY AT O.S.P.

In the end, of course, there is no right or wrong interpretation as to "why" things at O.S.P. were as they were. The different viewpoints expressed by staff members and prisoners were reflective of the combination of factors that existed and their mutual interdependency.[3] However, what struck me as most unusual at O.S.P., and as most in need of explanation was not that there were different types of play fulfilling different specific functions, but that almost everything was perceived, in one way or another, as play, and that there seemed to be an all pervasive atmosphere of play that appeared to exceed any needs of the specific play activities themselves. The question is how to explain that atmosphere itself.

While it may not be the total answer, I wish to suggest that there was a particular situation at the prison that lent itself to the exploitation of the idea of play. It has already been mentioned how, prior to 1968, the prison had an expressed general set of values known as the "convicts' code". This code was the prisoners' contribution to the general milieu that encouraged rigidity of beliefs and actions on the part of both prisoners and staff, and stressed the clear cut separation of the two groups and their inherent antagonism. In such an atmosphere, anything beyond minimal cooperation was virtually taboo. (For example, the fact that a prisoner was never supposed to speak to a guard unless other convicts were present to verify that he was not informing.)

In contrast, in 1973, the prison was alive with activities requiring close fraternization between prisoners and staff. However, this change was not reflective of a change in the composition of the parties themselves. While policy changed in 1968, the participants themselves remained.

The new warden had been the correction training officer under the old system. The head of the activities program—the center of the vortex of play—was a former guard who never let pass an opportunity to express some cynicism as to the very changes he was supervising. Similarly, many of the most active prisoners, and the most successful gamers, were men who had spent years under the old regime, and who still claimed they were ' 'cons" (prisoners who believe in the old code) rather than "inmates" (the new co-operative breed).

The result was a contradiction between former practices, to which some verbal allegiance was still given, and actual behavior. This was pointedly exemplified by the existence of specific joking relationships between prisoners and guards. While prisoners were routinely disciplined for cursing or hitting correction officers, an amazing amount of horseplay continuously occurred. Some prisoners and staff members would routinely exchange punches, shin knicks, and profanities that under other circumstances, or on the part of another party, would have resulted in immediate disciplinary action. As one prisoner said regarding such an interaction: "It's because we both understand each other. He's an old bull (guard) and I'm an old con, and we're both out of place now, like two dinosaurs" (field notes).

What existed, therefore, was a substantial number of "cons" who, as a result of the influx of new "inmate" types, and administrative reorientation, had lost much of the status once afforded them under the old code and hierarchy. Likewise, there were old staffers who sensed their own increasing isolation in the face of change; a feeling amplified by the ever present explanation that much reform had to await the influx of more qualified and better educated employees. Where once the status of each of these groups was largely determined by their domination or defiance of the other, it now rested largely on shared memories of their positions in a rapidly fading past. However, while there remained a certain attraction for many in mythicizing the past to which they had been largely conditioned, new conditions presented them with demands for behavior changes they could not easily avoid. It was in response to this conflict that the desirability of the self-imposition of a "play" motif arose.

Due to the fact that "playing" carries such connotations as "non-serious", "not-real", or "not-permanent", it presents itself as a convenient cover for actions which might not be tolerated if they were meant seriously, or represented permanent standards of behavior. Thus, a "con" or "conservative" correction officer could "play" according to the new rules without acknowledging any fundamental allegiance or agreement to their basic premises. For example, a "con" who felt he had a good chance for a parole if he cooperated might "play" quite actively until that parole was denied, at which time he would become cynical of such "unmanly" behavior. Similarly, a new prisoner might initially reject as childish, activities to which he would later be drawn by boredom, the hope of release, or enculturation to the new prison milieu. Such behavioral permutations were understandable in light of how the prison itself was undergoing rapid change which caused those within it to find themselves in a world of spinning values, circumstances and contingencies. In the face of such a painful psychological experience, the least adaptable found retreating into "play" a useful mechanism for maintaining their mental equilibrium, while the more adaptable found it a valuable aid to prospering within the system and eventually escaping from it.

Of course, there are exceptions to every rule. Newer prisoners and staff who had never been exposed to older prison ways felt less threatened by the ongoing changes. To many of these, the prevalent "play" motif was counter-productive. For example, some newer black inmates, who had no feelings of allegiance to the old value of being "cons" rather than "inmates", felt a paramount need to be recognized as "men", rather than "boys", "Niggers", or "Uncle Toms". To some of these, the play motif connoted behavior appropriate to a child but not a man, and therefore not to be indulged in. In commenting upon the joking relation of a "con" and a guard, one such informant said, "Look at those two playing grab-ass. Now do grown men on the outside do that? You see, I can cooperate just so much before losing my manhood" (field notes).

At the time this study was conducted, since the institution was still largely dominated by old timers—both staff and prisoners—such examples of the negative value of the play motif did not threaten its' functional efficacy for the institution as a whole. However, the existence of these new types suggest that as time passed, and as the composition of the population changed, the motif might well become counter-productive; that in reality it was a temporary adaptation between the demise of an old series of rules and values, and the establishment of new ones;[4] and that it was unwise to propose, (as some people did) it as a valid model for a new penal philosophy. In fact, while no further in-depth study of O.S.P. has been made, indication are that in the years following this study, there has been a significant tightening of rules governing prison policies and prisoner behavior.

## CONCLUSION

The circumstances at Oregon State Penitentiary in 1973 seemed sufficiently intriguing to implicitly warrant their recording and analysis. In pursuit of this, I found the introduction of the concept of play not only invaluable, but virtually indispensable. Consequentially, I was awakened to the need to look for adult play in less obvious situations, and the importance of the study of **adult** play **per se** (Handelman 1974).

As for our understanding of play, itself, I feel that this O.S.P. case study is indicative of the need to recognize that "play", at least adult human play, should not be viewed as existing independent of the cognition of those engaged in it. At Oregon State Penitentiary, the motif of play was not just a way of announcing, or framing, on-going activities. Rather, for many people, seeing, understanding and accepting those activities **as play** was both a mental prerequisite, and a behavioral guide for their participation in them, as well as an important determinant of the structure of events, itself.

## NOTES

[1]The only exception was in regard to prisoners being held in the "security and isolation" unit. Special authorization, which was easily obtained, was required for entrance to this area.

[2]A more detailed account of the methodology of partnership research, its justifications and its rewards, is available in Fujisaka and Grayzel (in press).

[3]Moreover, I feel it can be seen that the varieties of "play" found at the prison corresponded to the varieties existent in the world-at-large. Thus, for example, Piaget has divided types of play into three categories:

(1) Practice play—the exercise of functions or activities simply for the intrinsic pleasure that the exercise gives.

(2) Symbolic play—make-believe, pretense; games that imply representation of an absent object.

(3) Games with rules—rules and regulations imposed by agreement. Their violation carries a sanction (Miller 1973:90).

The various recreational activities at the prison designed to relieve boredom, the play therapy groups and prison facsimiles of outside organizations, such as the Junior Chamber of Commerce, and the entire stress on "programming" as a way to obtain early release, would seem to correspond to each of these three categories, respectively.

[4]Bateson (1972:191) makes some insightful comments on the value of the metacommunication "this is play" in creating a situation condusive to a change in rules. Perhaps one of the most startling examples of just such a use in adult life was the rapid change in Sino-American relations that was ushered in during the Nixon Administration by a Chinese invitation to the United States to send a ping-pong team to China.

## REFERENCES

Bateson, Gregory, 1972, Steps to an Ecology of Mind. New York: Ballantine Books.

Fujisaka, S., and J. Grayzel, In press, Partnership Research: A Case of Divergent Ethographic Styles In Prison Fieldwork. Human Organization

Handelman, Don, 1974, A Note on Play. American Anthropologist. 76(1):66-68

Miller, Stephen, 1973, Ends, Means, and Galumphing: Some Leit Motifs of Play. American Anthropologist 75(1):87-98

## THE BIRDS AND THE BARBER: AN ANTHROPOLOGICAL
## ANALYSIS OF A JOKE IN CHARLES DICKENS' *MARTIN CHUZZLEWIT*

Harold Olofson, Forest Research Institute, Laguna, Philippines

INTRODUCTION

This paper is a small experiment in the bringing together of social anthropology, on the one hand, and English literature and its criticism, on the other, in the context of the anthropology of play. A joking relationship between two characters in **Martin Chuzzlewit** by Charles Dickens[1] is analyzed in terms of anthropological work on the joke. Dickens critics have of late found rich depths for study in the minor characters and in the symbolism of his works. Two recent examples for **Martin Chuzzlewit** are "Mrs. Gamp as the Great Mother: A Dickensian use of the Archetype," by Veronica M.S. Kennedy (1972), and "Dickens and Freedom: Young Bailey in **Martin Chuzzlewit**," by Branwen Bailey Pratt (1975). I will make use particularly of the second piece and also of an analysis of the entire novel by J. Hillis Miller (1968), treating these critics as my ethnographer-guides through much of Chuzzlewit-land.

YOUNG BAILEY

The first character involved in the joke is Young Bailey, who, when first introduced is a porter and servant at Todgers' boarding house; later he becomes a dandified groom in the stables of the villainous Montague Tigg. Two things stand out in Dicken's construction of him: (1) Bailey is a **bricolage** and as such is symbolic of the unclassifiable, and (2) there is a suggestion of the bird in him, as a symbol of free play.

The young men at Todgers' boarding-house know him by a series of nicknames which they apply to him from the ranks of notorious, evil or otherwise famous persons. Miller (1968:150) finds these names inappropriate to Bailey and dissimilar to each other. But in Levi-Strauss' thought (1966:16-22) he is a **bricolage,** a heterogeneous mixture of oddments from within a set—in this case, of historical figures. It is clear that his friends at Todgers' have difficulty therefore in classifying him. They have a psychological need to do so, since the personality of each one of **them** is limited to a certain "turn" in life by which they stereotype and know themselves. But his final name, Bailey Junior, suggests that such a "capture" cannot be easily achieved, for as Pratt (1975) notes, this name is in contradistinction to the Old Bailey, a famous London prison (NO:142-143; Pratt 1975:188). Bailey's nature as **bricolage,** his probable illegitimacy (his parents or true kin are unknown), and his name suggest that he cannot be easily stereotyped. Mrs. Gamp, struck by his youthful looks but great affability and self-assurance, asks whether he is a "man or boy" (NO: 423). Even Dickens has trouble, referring to him as a "something in top-boots" (NO:813) and an "inexplicable creature" (NO:423).

There are also hints that he is a bird-like personage of playful freedom. Mrs. Gamp, amazed at his boldness, calls him "a imperent young sparrow" (NO:461). Twice he is seen going around in circles like a bird, once to show off his costume (NO:420) and once when wounded (NO:813). And he is undaunted by the vertiginous roof-tops in the neighborhood of Todgers', for after accompanying the Misses Pecksniff to the top of the house for a view of the·city he "being of playful temperament...lingered behind to walk on the parapet" (NO:131).

His playful daring, freedom from vertigo and bird-like actions suggest that he is a free-flying bird, a puzzling and unclassifiable one. Pratt sees him as Freudian jokework which "restores sources of pleasure previously made inaccessible by inhibition" (1975:191). His **bricolage** is essentially one of anti-structural freedom.

### POLL SWEEDLEPIPE

Poll is Mrs. Gamp's landlord and an easy-shaver and bird-fancier. He is another piece of **bricolage** and the closest Dickens ever came to depicting a character as an animal, for he is more concretely a bird than Bailey is. His name, Poll, is both a nickname for a parrot and a term for the hair on the head, thus it is an ideal one for a person who combines barbering with the raising and selling of birds.[2] The name Sweedlepipe invokes an idea of the sound of the bird as a musical instrument. His voice is bird-like (NO:419) and in his various aspects of disposition, mood and gesture he is a combination of several species of birds (NO:419). His clothing reminds us of brightly-colored ornithological plumage (NO:419). In short, as Kennedy notes, "he is one with the birds he sells" (1972:3), a small-scale metonym for the entire captive bird-kingdom.

Poll's identification with birds extends to his very dwelling. It is "one great bird's nest" and different species of birds reside in different parts of the house. Moreover, there are "hutches of all shapes and kinds" on the staircase, which is "sacred to rabbits" and in them these creatures "increased in a prodigious degree" (NO:418). The compartmentalization of his house into bird species and the abundance and variety of rabbit containers, leads us to see Poll as a symbol of classification, and the sheer numbers of animals and their variety suggests a fecundity which seems at first quite at variance with Kennedy's view of Poll as "eunochoid" (1972:3). Moreover, Poll identifies **himself** closely with his shop, for he is never able to leave it upon closing up and stepping outside until the shop bell ceases to ring: " 'It's the greediest little bell to ring,' said Poll, 'that ever was. But it's quiet at last.' " (NO:419-420). The bell, that's like a hungry bird chirping to be fed, seems to hold Poll enthralled.

The fertility of the Sweedlepipe establishment is balanced off by the ever-lingering presence of death. It is this aspect of Poll's ambience that Dickens constructs to imbue Poll with a distinct pathos and leads us to believe that, for Dickens, at least implicitly, Poll's barbering, his shaving off of beards and head-hair, is redolent of death and destruction. Most important is the fact that many of the birds Poll sells are to be shot for sport by their buyers, such as the dashing young Bailey (NO:813).[3] Thus, the fact that Poll's shop bell is cracked and rings "most mournfully" (NO:311), harmonizes well with the lives of its doomed and captive occupants. Poll's shop, as viewed from the street, reveals "in every pane of glass. . . at least one tiny bird in a tiny bird-cage, twisting and hopping his little ballet of despair, and knocking his head against the roof. . . "(NO:311).

Thus, whereas Bailey, in his wisdom, aliveness and unpredictability eludes classification and stereotyping as a free bird, Poll is a symbol of limiting classification and also of death as a caged one. Poll's identification with his shop comes close to self-imprisonment. While the animal smells of his shop stand on the one side for animal fecundity (note NO:418), his "clammy cold right hand, from which even rabbits and birds could not remove the smell of shaving-soap" (NO:419) betokens his essential connection with sterility and death. The stereotyping of birds in their separate species-specific corners and the compartmentalization and multiplication of rabbits in hutches, is, in the long run, a sterile occupation, and it is this more than anything that suggests his eunochoid nature. Bailey's way of life is much the more creative, as we shall see.

## THE JOKE

The joke which takes place between them is here given in full. It is a joke without a punch-line, and moreover, is largely gestural rather than verbal. Mr. Bailey pays a visit to his friend Poll:

> On the little bell giving clamorous notice of a visitor's approach (for Mr. Bailey came in at the door with a lunge, to get as much sound out of the bell as possible), Poll Sweedlepipe desisted from the contemplation of a favourite owl, and gave his young friend hearty welcome.

'Why, you look smarter by day,' said Poll, 'than you do by candlelight. I never see such a tight young dasher.'

'Reether so, Polly, How's our fair friend Sairah?' (Mrs. Gamp).

'Oh, she's pretty well,' said Poll. 'She's at home.'

'There's the remains of a fine woman about Sairah, Poll,' observed Mr. Bailey, with genteel indifference.

'Oh!' thought Poll, 'he's old. He must be very old!'

'Too much crumb, you know,' said Mr. Bailey; 'too fat, Poll. But there's many worse at her time of life.'

'The very owl's a-opening his eyes!' thought Poll. 'I don't wonder at it, in a bird of his opinions.'

He happened to have been sharpening his razors, which were lying open in a row, while a huge strop dangled from the wall. Glancing at these preparations, Mr. Bailey stroked his chin, and a thought appeared to occur to him.

'Poll,' he said, 'I ain't as neat as I could wish about the gills. Being here, I may as well have a shave, and get trimmed close.

The barber stood aghast; but Mr. Bailey divested himself of his neckcloth, and sat down in the easy shaving chair with all the dignity and confidence in life. There was no resisting his manner. The evidence of sight and touch became as nothing. His chin was as smooth as a new-laid egg or a scraped Dutch cheese; but Poll Sweedlepipe wouldn't have ventured to deny, on affidavit, that he had the beard of a Jewish rabbi.

'Go **with** the grain, Poll, all round, please,' said Mr. Bailey, screwing up his face for the reception of the lather. 'You may do wot you like with the bits of whisker. I don't care for 'em.'

The meek little barber stood gazing at him with the brush and soapdish in his hand, stirring them round and round in a ludicrous uncertainty, as if he were disabled by some fascination from beginning. At last he made a dash at Mr. Bailey's cheek. Then he stopped again, as if the ghost of a beard had suddenly receded from his touch; but receiving mild encouragement from Mr. Bailey, in the form of an adjuration to 'Go in and win,' he lathered him bountifully. Mr. Bailey smiled through the suds in his satisfaction.

'Gently over the stones, Poll. Go a tip-toe over the pimples!'

Poll Sweedlepipe obeyed, and scraped the lather off again with particular care. Mr. Bailey squinted at every successive dab, as it was deposited on a cloth on his left shoulder, and seemed, with a microscopic eye, to detect some bristles in it; for he murmured more than once, 'Reether redder than I could wish, Poll.' The operation being concluded, Poll fell back and stared at him again, while Mr. Bailey, wiping his face on the jack-towel, remarked, 'that arter late hours nothing freshened up a man so much as a easy shave.' (NO:460-461)

## ANTHROPOLOGICAL ANALYSIS: THE JOKE STRUCTURE

According to Handelman and Kapferer (1972:484) a joke "emerges" from a negotiable "license to joke" extending from the individual at whom the joking is directed. In this sequence, the license might be considered to be Bailey's invitation to Poll to give him a shave, and his occupation of the "easy shaving chair." Both thereby agree to make fun of each other. But the license comes from a deep source. Poll at first stands aghast, not reacting instantaneously, but responding to the **way** in which Bailey places himself in the chair "with all the dignity and confidence in life." This momentarily transfixes and fascinates the barber. Bailey's love of life, as seen in his seeming precocity of experience (and which the joke is very much an expression of) has a power of its own which cannot be denied and becomes, not merely a license, but a command to which Poll must respond regardless of his rigidly stereotyped nature.

The joke also "emerges" from a very complicated social setting, a context of the novel wherein Bailey and Poll stand in a symbolic relation to each other, one as a sportsman who shoots birds, and the other as a barber who rears birds and is very much a bird himself; a context wherein Bailey is symbolic of the difficulty of classifying the slippery, the elusive, the vital, and Poll is symbolic of the sterility of pigeon-holing. This points out two aspects of the joke noted by Mary Douglas (1968) in her classic work on jokes. First, the joke is a "spontaneous joke", as opposed to a "standardized joke", in that its meaning is a reflection of the social relations of the participants (1968:365). Second, the joke is a reversal, whereby it is "potentially subversive of social order," causing a "victorious tilting of uncontrol against control...an image of the levelling of hierarchy, the triumph of intimacy over formality," and an instance where a dominant pattern is "disparaged" or "supplanted" by a previously hidden one (Douglas 1968:366, 369). Milner (1972) and Johnson (1975) have analyzed the reversals that occur in the semantics of many jokes. According to Johnson, "jokes consist of two clauses: One that defines the domain of play, or reversal, and the second which constitutes the play within which the operation of the reversal takes place" (1975:170). In reversal, an order AB in the bounding domain is rearranged to the new order BA in the joke, with the new order making use of material in the old (Johnson 1975:158).

The formal structure of the piece of fun under consideration is somewhat more complicated than a mere reversal. It involves an additional factor which negates the reversal and thus makes it harmless. For want of a better term I will call this total structure a "double reversal."

This form turns out not to be uncommon in the complicated course of everyday humor. I observed an example one day while sitting in a cafeteria. Two maintenance personnel were reconnoitering a prospective repair job and had with them a ladder and a paint brush. Before I realized what I was seeing, a joke took place and the men and props had disappeared. One of the men, smiling mischievously at his companion, took up the paintbrush and began to paint the ladder. A joke without words, this action entailed a sight-gag reversal. A ladder is usually the means to the end of painting, not the object of painting. A second reversal, however, was readily apparent. The paintbrush in use had no paint on it. This fact, the reverse of the one where a brush, when used in that way, usually has paint on it, negated any harm or result that might have come about by wasting paint on a ladder. The interaction between Poll and Bailey appears to have this kind of structure, but also much more meaning.

We have already established that Poll is closely identified with his shop and the birds which he raises and sells. He is a metonym of the feathered kingdom. Bailey, on the other hand, in his role as sportsman, is a destroyer of the members of that domain, its natural enemy. In one dimension of their relation, Poll and Bailey can relate to each other as humans and as birds. In another, they are in a state of opposition. This is a bounding context elucidated in symbolic terms. Thus, when Bailey invites Poll to give him a shave, he invites him to reverse this relationship. His facial hair becomes symbolic of the feathers of the bird and the bird now becomes the aggressive hunter who is challenged to "go in and win," to enjoy the sporting life. The participants temporarily and superficially exchange roles. But a negative fact obviates this invited attack and renders it harmelss: the face has no hair, the razor is actually removing no "feathers." A "double reversal" is the result, so that the relationship between the two remains essentially undamaged. Thus for Poll, Bailey more than ever becomes a figure of fun and a cherished companion.

Dickens' construction of the joke appears to be based on his own ethnographic observance of an apparent "law of sympathy" between birds and beards, as found in the barber shops of his time (NO:418). He may have had in mind an analogy between the feathers of birds and the hair of men. The removal of the feathers of a bird generally imply the death of the creature. By analogy, for Dickens, the removal of human hair might symbolize a sort of death or castration (as for Edmund Leach 1958). After all, the barber shop is pervaded with an atmosphere of sterility, despair and death, and Poll's shaving of Bailey is a reversal of the hunter-hunted role but made "only a joke" by the fact that Bailey really is not a bird in the sense that he has no "feathers."

## ANTHROPOLOGICAL ANALYSIS: THE SOCIAL STRUCTURE

Douglas (1968) has significantly pointed out that there is frequently some relation between a joke structure and the social structure in which it is performed. We can use this to help us understand the meaning of the Bailey-Sweedlepipe joke, within the context of their relationship and of the total social structure of the novel. As she says, ". . . all jokes are expressive of the social situations in which they occur" (1968:366). The joke shows that "an accepted pattern has no necessity. Its excitement lies in the suggestion that any particular ordering of experience may be arbitrary and subjective" (1968:365). Jokes brighten "the oppressiveness of social reality" and "express the creative possibilities of the situation" while "representing a temporary suspension of the social structure" (1968:372).

The first level of social structure to be considered is that between Poll and Bailey. Bailey invites Poll to challenge the implicit symbolic pattern that obtains between them, to make light of formal relations, note other potential possibilities in the situation, and experience a certain freedom. Bailey helps Poll to free himself of his classificatory and stereotyped view of life. Bailey might be a boy, but he is to be shaved and treated like a man anyway. Poll might be a "bird," and Bailey the slayer of birds, but this can be harmless and temporarily reversed in the play-world. We noted a certain inertia in Poll before the shaving: this suggests the boundary which must be crossed before the way things "are" can be made light of. The result is not a slaying of Bailey, of course. The revelation of freedom through "strange behavior" received by Poll at Bailey's invitation—the major event that takes place between them in the novel—has another result in their longer-term relationship: it forges a stronger social relation between them and an eventual companionable partnership where their similarities and differences can become operationally useful to them. Something changes in their relationship, we later find out, and Poll comes to have a new and more promising view of life. When Bailey returns to life after being presumed dead by Poll in a coach accident, the following scene takes place:

> 'Look here!' cried the little barber, laughing and crying in the same breath. 'When I steady him he comes allright. There! He's all right now. Nothing's the matter with him now, except that he's a little shook and rather giddy; is there, Bailey?'
> 'R-r-reether shook, Poll—reether so!' said Mr. Bailey....
> 'What a boy he is!' cried the tender-hearted Poll, actually sobbing over him. 'I never see sech a boy!' It's all his fun. He's full of it. He shall go into the business along with me. I am determined he shall. We'll make it Sweedlepipe and Bailey. He shall have the sporting branch (what a one he'll be for the matches!) and me the shavin!. I'll make over the birds to him as soon as ever he's well enough. He shall have the little bulfinch in the shop, and all. He's sech a boy!' (NO:813).

This may seem a limited liberation: Poll and Bailey continue in the same path in relation to the kingdom of birds. But the link that has been fashioned between them, largely through their joking, takes on added significance when viewed in terms of the novel as a whole. For a second level to be considered is the relationship between Poll and Bailey's joking relation, on the one hand, and the structure of the society, the "little culture" depicted by Charles Dickens, on the other.

This broader society has been brilliantly analyzed by the eminent critic J. Hillis Miller (1968). We do not have space to do more than state his evaluation of that society, without the necessary evidence for that evaluation which he provides:

> The arena of **Martin Chuzzlewit** is the present...in which society in the sense of an integrated community has been replaced by a framented collection of isolated self-seeking individuals...selfishness exists in the novel not only as the ethical bent of the characters, but also as the state of isolation in which they live. The novel is full of people who are wholly enclosed in themselves, wholly secret, wholly intent on reflexive ends which are altogether mysterious to those around them (1968:123).
>
> The self-enclosed inhabitants of the London of **Martin Chuzzlewit** live...in close proximity to other human activities of which they are totally ignorant. On the other side of the wall of one's own cell in the beehive there is another cell, and who can tell what is going on there (1968:132)?
>
> ...most of the characters are unwilling to consider...reciprocity, and instinctively try every means they can find to do without other people (1968:140).

To do this, the characters attempt to separate their private, inner, deceptive selves from the false selves which are the exposed surfaces presented to others. But

> The characters of **Martin Chuzzlewit** are doubly at the mercy of others: on the one hand, another person may at any time pierce the carefully constructed social shell, and, on the other, even if this does not happen, each person depends absolutely on the others, since it is only in their eyes that the public self exists at all (1968:143).

As a result

> There is no help for it. Each man must seek some kind of direct relationship to other people, a relationship which recognizes the fact of their consciousness, and makes it an integral part of the structure of his own inherence in the world (1968:144).

Miller notes that although this last is a basic insight the novel gives us, the characters are larely unsuccessful in convincingly achieving this aim in their own right. It is done by artificial means, ties of love and marriage seemingly imposed on the characters by the wealthy patriarch, old Martin, who asks them to join hands (Miller 1968:156-157). The link between Bailey and Poll arises out of their own interaction and thus appears to be an exception. In their own limited way they achieve a meaningful integration. They live in an atomistic social structure, wherein the condition is one of superficial, deceptive or almost nonexistent interpersonal relations. In constructing the joke situation, Bailey reverses this. Bailey is trying to fashion a stylistic definition of himself as an adult, whereas Poll's problem is the one of being the prisoner of classification. Through the joke Bailey manages to wrench him into the recognition of arbitrary, free, unclassifiable, playful behavior as a possibility and changes his life by revealing Life—with a capital L—to him. As Poll says when he thinks Bailey is lost: "And what a Life Young Bailey's was!" (NO:751). The joke helps them to achieve meaningful contact in a society where isolation is the rule. It is the temporary victory of anti-classification against classification, freedom against self-imprisonment. On one level, and for a moment, it reverses the symbolic relation between Bailey and Poll. On another level, and for a longer term, it reverses a world of isolated and sterile individualism into a world which, for the jokers, promises to be one of equal status and convivial productivity. The Sweedlepipe-Bailey joking relationship is, in a mild way, indicative of what ought to be in society.

NOTES

[1]The page numbers quoted for this work refer to the New Oxford Illustrated Edition (abbreviated as NO) which appeared in 1951.

[2]Dickens' character is based on sociological fact. As Mayhew noted eighteen years later, the barbers of Nineteenth Century London were also "assiduous rearers" of birds, especially of canaries (1967:61).

[3]Mayhew made reference to such birds being shot at *battues* or shooting-matches (1967:62).

REFERENCES

Dickens, Charles, 1951, The Life and Adventures of Martin Chuzzlewit. London: Oxford University Press. (The New Oxford Illustrated Dickens)

Douglas, Mary, 1968, The Social Control of Cognition: Some Factors in Joke Perception. Man n.s. 3(3):361-376.

Handelman, Don and Bruce Kapferer, 1972, Forms of Joking Activity: A Comparative Approach. American Anthropologist 74(3):484-517.

Johnson, Ragnar, 1975, The Semantic Structure of the Joke and Riddle: Theoretical Positioning. Semiotica 14(2):142-174.

Kennedy, Veronica M.S., 1972, Mrs. Gamp as the Great Mother: A Dickensian Use of the Archetype. The Victorian Newsletter 41:1-5.

Leach, Edmund, 1958, Magical Hair. Journal of the Royal Anthropological Institute 88: 147-164.

Levi-Strauss, Claude, 1967, The Savage Mind. London: Weidenfeld and Nicholson.

Mayhew, Henry, 1967, London Labour and the London Poor. Vol. II. London: Frank Cass and Company Ltd. (Reprint of 1861-62 Edition)

Miller, J. Hillis, 1968, Martin Chuzzlewit. In Dickens: Modern Judgements. A. E. Dyson, Ed. London: Macmillan. pp. 118-157.

Milner, G. B., 1972, Homo Ridens: Towards a Semiotic Theory of Humour and Laughter. Semiotica 5(1):1-30.

Pratt, Branwen Bailey, 1975, Dickens and Freedom: Young Bailey in Martin Chuzzlewit. Nineteenth Century Fiction 30(2):185-199.

# CHAPTER III

# The Play-World
# of Children

## GAMES AND VALUES IN ICELAND[1]

George W. Rich, California State University, Sacramento

Studies of socialization have more often than not sought to illuminate the connection between child-rearing patterns and cultural values without paying particular attention to child culture itself. The problem has been a pronounced one: children have been considered notoriously poor informants about their behavior (see Brukman 1973:56), and even more so about the processes by which they come to replicate a version of their culture. Hence, most observational emphasis has been placed on the actions of adults toward children, much to the detriment of a needed emphasis on the actions of children themselves. And as inconceivable as it may seem many socialization studies never so much as mention children playing.

During the course of ethnographic research in Iceland, focusing on the subjects of social organization and child-training patterns, I took the opportunity to direct my attention to children's games. I had employed a number of specific instruments (such as the Parental Attitude Research Instrument and a modified Role Profile Test) in addition to the time tested interview and observation techniques of anthropology, and had arrived at a point where I could generalize about the fit between predominant Icelandic values and child-training patterns. But stimulated by a number of important observations made by John Roberts, Brian Sutton-Smith and their associates, and provided with ideal conditions for observing children playing on a daily basis, I also undertook an extensive analysis of children's play routines. I observed and elicited descriptions of over 200 games and activities and measured children's play preference and involvement patterns, and in this respect shifted the locus of ethnographic observation from the sociocultural context in which children are reared, to the children themselves.

The purpose of this paper is to report my findings in brief with respect to the relationship between dominant Icelandic values, child-training patterns, and children's play patterns.[2] As a matter of course these findings should serve as one test of the Conflict-Enculturation Hypothesis. But particular attention will also be brought to bear on a specific and pervasive conflict as reflected in the game patterns.

## SOCIAL CHARACTER: A SUMMATION

The few sketches of Icelandic national character that have been made by scholars, both foreign and native, agree on all major points (see Thompson 1960, 1969; Griffiths 1969; Gislason 1970, 1973). Icelanders are an industrious, independent, and achievement-oriented people. For centuries Iceland remained the most isolated of the Scandinavian societies, becoming a repository of an ancient pre-Christian ethos—a pragmatic, achievement-oriented, individualistic world view made to fit life in a rugged environment (see Rosalie and Murray Wax 1955). There they codified their values in such native concepts as **mannvit**, **frid**, and **drengskapur**; and the behaviors considered expressive of these values would provide the basic meat for a renown national saga literature.

A glance at Icelandic achievements in the modern world attests to the continuity of these values in modern life. If we compare Iceland with 18 of the world's technologically most advanced societies, Iceland ranks 8th in overall per capital consumption; this amongst societies which far surpass Iceland in natural wealth (OECD 1973). Such an achievement has not occurred as a product of fateful and favorable circumstances, such as an abundance of easily exploitable resources, or a good proximity to the hub of the Industrial Revolution. Rather, in spite of relatively severe environmental limitations, six centuries of foreign domination, and the need to import virtually everything but fish, potatoes, and wool, the Icelanders have achieved what they have only with talent, perseverance, and a strong national will, translated along the way into personal motivation to achieve and get ahead.

When asked to characterize the ideal Icelandic boy and girl, Icelandic parents tended to emphasize three principal traits: **sociability, talent,** and **independence** (in that order). The characterizations were replete with such words as : honest, cooperative, reasonable, and understanding (all sociability traits); skillful, mentally alert, creative, noble-minded, and resourceful (traits of personal talent); and determined, self-disciplined, hard-working, independent, ambitious, self-reliant, and assertive (all expressions of independence-achievement values). Notably there were no appreciable differences ideally ascribed to boys and girls; and instrumental measures confirmed that these values are essential ingredients of the attitudes of parents toward children.

Research focusing on parental attitudes and actual child-training practices revealed that both ideals and practices have a conspicuous orientation. Not only is there a predominant emphasis on the value of achievement, but in almost every way the pattern of achievement training fits what other studies and experiments in achievement motivation have shown to be most conducive to internalizing the need for achievement (e.g. McClelland 1961; Rosen and D'Andrade 1959; Winterbottom 1958).

Socialization in independence, self-reliance, and responsibility is appropriately early. Comparisons with world samples (see Whiting and Child 1953) reveal, for instance, that the Icelanders begin to socialize their infants in independence and self-reliance at a very early age. Using such common self-reliance indices as weaning and toilet training, the average period of initial indulgence is a short 2-3 months and 6 months respectively. The Icelanders place greatest emphasis on the self-assertion and autonomy aspects of independence training, leading to what Day and Biemiller (1969) have characterized for the Icelanders as an early development of **autonomous morality**—a developmental prerequisite to independent decision-making, wherein the child is given the opportunity and is taught at an early age to assume the burden of making his own moral decisions.

Related to this is a moderate emphasis on responsibility training. Most children are assigned routine domestic chores by age 5-6, and by the age of 12-13 are expected to assume more or less full responsibility for the consequences of their actions.

Most studies of socialization for achievement have concluded that authoritarianism, restrictiveness, and interference contravene the values of achievement, self-reliance, and autonomy. And as though Icelanders have acquired their system from a guide to independence training, there is commensurately a **low** emphasis on parental authority and obedience. Icelandic parents are notably **unauthoritarian, unre-**

**strictive,** and generally **unconcerned** with obedience, as we conceive it. Children are given what many outsiders would consider unusual leeway in determining the course of their own actions. Doting, restrictive, or dominant parents are considered potentially detrimental to the development of sound character in children. One of the consequences, as revealed in data obtained through the **Role Profile Test,** is that authority and dominance are criteria which play a very small part in the children's own accounts of their interpersonal relations with relatives (Rich 1976:295-329; see also Day and Biemiller 1969).

Finally in this all too brief characterization, one pervasive value crosscuts the others. It is a strong emphasis on the value of sociability, on the value of affiliating with others, of establishing rewarding associations with people outside the primary group, of cooperating, and of establishing enduring friendships. It is as though in the course of their history the Icelanders have tacitly recognized the potentially pathological consequences of too strong an emphasis on self-assertion, autonomy, and independence, and have mediated these important values through fostering the need to cooperate and affiliate.

The value of sociability pervades the system, in the subtle persuasions towards other-directedness, in the early training in the use of polite rhetoric (expected by age 3), in developing a sensitivity to the needs of others, and in the conspicuous provision of wide opportunities for children to establish voluntary associations. For instance in the town of 11,000 people where the research was carried out, there are 37 children's associations and clubs, and a child of any social standing whatsoever belongs to at least a few. The emphasis on the value of sociability as a check on independence is also reflected in parental attitudes towards children's play.

Children are integrated into autonomous play groups at an early age. Mothers often usher their 3 or 4 year old youngsters out of the home in the hands of their older siblings or nurturant neighborhood children, not expecting to see much of them until the important midday meal. The children play unsupervised for hours on end, sometimes in nearby stairwells, sometimes directly in front of their houses, but most often in adjacent and nearby fields which are exclusively children's territory, rarely invaded by adults. Parents avoid assuming supervisory roles and rely on older children to relay distress calls. They place a high priority on the child's opportunity to play in autonomous groups, not only because it gives parents a few hours of quiet to themselves, but also because it is believed to be important for character development. In the most value-laden statements, it was expressed by some as the child's right to be left alone; to let him decide what he wants to do (autonomy-independence value). By others it was expressed as the child's opportunity to learn to get along with others (sociability value). At least one mother refused to assign routine domestic duties to her children, because it would interfere with their playtime while not in school; and another mother professed to ignore her children's failure to perform customary chores, "as long as they were doing something good, like playing with their friends."

## PLAY PREFERENCE AND INVOLVEMENT PATTERNS

As mentioned at the outset, the objective in examining children's play patterns was to shift the locus of observation from the socialization of the children to the children themselves, as they take a hand in their own socialization. A test of the Conflict-Enculturation Hypothesis was hence chosen as an appropriate format for exploring the probable relationship of the children's games back to Icelandic values and child-training practices.

In abbreviated form, the Conflict-Enculturation Hypothesis, developed by Roberts and Sutton-Smith (1962), postulates that the principal motivation for involvement in particular types of games is socialization anxiety. Attendant upon socialization is a certain amount of anxiety with regard to the performance of trained-for and culturally appropriate behaviors. Conflict engendered by the child-training practices of a culture leads to an interest in particular types of play activities which pattern the conflict. Either through role reversals sanctioned in the game, or through the performance of behaviors manifesting culturally-appropriate values, competence in the prescribed style of behavior is exercised, and anxiety is assuaged. From this perspective, games are salient cultural models which provide a context for buffered socialization, having the benefit of being **liminal** to the real world in which the exercise social competence may be inhibited, and where incompetence would have more dire consequences.

Based on broad correlationary analyses of the occurrence of types of games in association with various child-training patterns in different societies, Roberts and Sutton-Smith have asserted the following: that societies which emphasize achievement training in the socialization of children tend also to show a marked preference for games of physical skill; societies which emphasize obedience training produce children who gravitate toward games of strategy; and societies which emphasize responsibility training produce children with a marked interest in chance games. Again, theoretical continuity for the correlations lies in socialization anxiety theory. Achievement training emphasizes the development of individual skills, independence and self-assertion.

Children will develop anxiety with regard to exhibiting these attributes and will seek to assuage their anxiety in competitive activities in which the outcome is determined by individual skill and self-assertion. Anxiety engendered in obedience-training (which involves the early imposition of rules and restrictions) can be assuaged in games of strategy; and anxiety engendered in responsibility training can be assuaged in games of chance, since the individual may assume or deny responsibility for the outcome usually depending on whether he wins or loses, respectively.

## HYPOTHESES

Based on what had been learned about predominant Icelandic values and child-training patterns, the game data was approached to see if the emphases on various values and general orientation of child-rearing would show a similar consistency in the game data. If so, I could anticipate the following: 1) that the children would show a predominant interest in games of skill, reflecting the strong emphasis placed on independence and achievement training; 2) that with the moderate concern for responsibility training, games of chance would figure only moderately in the preference and involvement patterns of the children; 3) that with the negligible concern for obedience, and with the laxity of training in this area, games of strategy would be unimportant. 4) Finally, due to the absence of significantly different ideals, attitudes and training practices for males and females, the play patterns would not be markedly different for boys and girls.

## PROCEDURES

In addition to carrying out broad and systematic observations of children playing, I initiated two major surveys to obtain quantifiable data: a Play-Preference Survey and Play-Involvement Survey. In both cases approximately 75% of the town's children between 8-12 years of age were sampled. In the first case, the children were asked to list games and activities they played, being sure to list their favorite activity first. And in the second, the children were asked to check from a large inventory only the activities they actually became involved in.

Content and structural analyses were performed for each activity, and each was classified as either a **pastime,** a form of **simulation** play, or a **game**; and the games were classified as either principally games of **skill, chance,** or **strategy** utilizing criteria employed by Roberts and Sutton-Smith (1962). Other features of the games were analyzed—such as the structure of relationships in teams, and built-in handicap systems—but these features were not employed in testing the hypotheses. The results of the surveys are organized in the following tables to display the distribution of **play preferences** by type, sex, and age (Tables I, II, and III); rates of **involvement** in play types by age and sex (Table IV); and occurrence of sexually-exclusive forms of play by type (Table V).

I
Total Play-Game Preferences
Favorite "Game" by Type

|        | Strategy | Chance   | Skill    | Simulation | Pastime  |
|--------|----------|----------|----------|------------|----------|
| Total ·| 0        | 7        | 283      | 30         | 66       |
| P=     |          | < .001   | < .001   | < .001     | < .05    |

II
Play-Game Preferences
Favorite Play Type by Sex

|         | Strategy | Chance | Skill  | Simulation | Pastime |
|---------|----------|--------|--------|------------|---------|
| Male    | 0        | 4      | 158    | 5          | 18      |
| Female  | 0        | 3      | 125    | 25         | 48      |
| P=      |          | .70    | < .001 | < .001     | < .001  |

III
Play-Game Preferences
Favorite Play Type by Age

|     | Strategy | Chance | Skill | Simulation | Pastime |
|-----|----------|--------|-------|------------|---------|
| 8   | 0        | 4      | 39    | 6          | 6       |
| 9   | 0        | 2      | 68    | 14         | 9       |
| 10  | 0        | 0      | 59    | 4          | 25      |
| 11  | 0        | 1      | 66    | 6          | 19      |
| 12  | 0        | 0      | 51    | 0          | 7       |
| P=  |          | .02    | .70   | .02        | .02     |

119

IV
Average Rate of Participation in
All Play-Games by Type and Sex

|  | Skill | Chance | Strategy | Simulation | Pastime |
|---|---|---|---|---|---|
| Male | 44.18 | 51.15 | 78.25 | 37.69 | 52.56 |
| Female | 47.57 | 47.10 | 64.40 | 39.14 | 53.85 |
| P= | .70 | .70 | < .05 | .99 | .99 |

V
Sex-Linked Games
and Play Forms

|  | Skill | Chance | Strategy | Simulation | Pastime | Total |
|---|---|---|---|---|---|---|
| Male | 17 | 0 | 1 | 7 | 7 | 32 |
| Female | 28 | 5 | 0 | 7 | 7 | 47 |

Figures represent the number of games under each type from the total corpus in which involvement by sex is different at < .10 level of significance.

A summary of the results shows that some patterns emerge confirming the hypotheses. Not a single one of the 386 children surveyed listed a game of strategy as a "favorite" game (despite the fact that chess is a national board game amongst Icelandic adults). A significantly low number of children designated games of chance; and an inordinantly large number of children designated games of physical skill (Table I). In the latter case there was a significant difference by sex (Table II). A significantly larger percentage of the boys' favorite games were games of skill; but this is attributable to the fact that a significantly larger number of girls chose amusing pastimes and forms of simulation play as favorite activities. For the girls, the vast majority of favorite activities were nevertheless games of skill.

The distribution of preferences on a developmental scale reveals significant differences by age, in all cases except games of physical skill (Table III). These games are the dominant favorites for children of all ages in the sample. Chance games, however, are significantly more important to the younger children (8-9 years olds), as are, for the most part, the forms of simulation play. The preference for simple pastimes, however, increases significantly for 10-11 year old females.

The play-involvement data complements in every way the general pattern revealed in the play-preference survey. The most important observation generated from this data is with regard to the developmental transformation of the play repertoire. The ages of 12 and 13 are important transition stages, for at this age there is a significant rejection of chance games, simulation play, creative pastimes, and lower-order skill games, and a significantly intensified interest in the highly structured and team games. This corroborates the ethnographic observation that the sheer size of the play repertoire constricts at this time. This constriction and focus on the more mature games of skill reflects an interest in severing the identity with younger children through eliminating activities characteristic of them. Notably, this corresponds to a social phenomenon in which children of this age are subjected to subtle pressure to mature, to assert their independence, and to demonstrate their ability to achieve as **Fermingardagurinn**, the major rite of passage out of childhood, approaches.

One final pattern of interest ought to be noted. The transformation of the play repertoire with maturation is different for boys and girls. Both the play preference and involvement data, as well as examinations of the play repertoire on an individual basis, confirm the casual observation that the girls not only have larger play repertoires than the boys, but also incorporate a wider range of play forms and maintain early-learned play forms for a longer period of time. Boys, on the other hand, constrict their repertoires earlier, bringing them to focus almost exclusively on skill games.

As a lesson in the utility of the study of play to ethnographers, this observation forced a re-examination of the data and led to some purposeful inquiry. Could it be that there were subtle differences in the socialization pressures affecting boys and girls that were not accounted for either in expressed parental attitudes or early child-training practices? The suddenly increased role of pastimes and simulation play in the overall pattern at the ages of 10-11 (just prior to the elimination of young children's play forms) proved, on re-examination of the data, to be due almost solely to the girls' reincorporation of simulation play forms (primarily playing mommy, playing doctor, playing store), in which the girls are involved in simulations of real-life domestic roles, intensifying their identification with the consistently available female models, or perhaps modeling and intensifying a transition conflict more exclusively female in nature. For at the same time, the play repertoires of girls included more games played in common with boys, than vice versa, and the largest class of exclusively **girls' games** was composed of rigorous physical skill games (Table V).

One test of a scientific theory is to see if the proposition will empirically generate data not considered in its formulation in the first place. The case summarized here confirms the Conflit-Enculturation Hypothesis in this respect. There is indeed a correlation of the type proposed in the hypothesis, between the play activities of Icelandic children and the conspicuous orientation of the value systems and child-training patterns. Icelandic children show by far the greatest interest in games of physical skill, competitive activities in which the outcome is determined by the exercise of individual skills and in which the individual, pitted against others, is required to assert himself. This corresponds with the strong emphasis on achievement training and the constituent values of self-assertion and independence. Games of chance rate a very distant second amongst the three principal types, commensurate with the moderate (but still relatively light) emphasis on responsibility training, and reflecting the probability that little or no anxiety with regard to responsibility is generated in the early socialization process. And the notable derth of strategy games in the play repertoire corresponds, as suggested in the hypothesis, with the negligible concern for obedience training.

The fourth hypothesis is only partially confirmed. The play repertoires of boys and girls are not markedly different. For both, games of physical skill vastly dominate the overall repertoire and the preference and involvement patterns. This confirms the ethnographic observation that there are few important differences either in parental ideals or training practices for boys and girls; that both are equivalently affected by the pervasive emphasis on achievement-independence values. However, developmental inconsistencies, especially in the revival of simple pastimes and simulation play by 10-11 year old girls, warrant further research.

SOCIABILITY AND CONFLICT

One of the elements of play yet to be explored is the relative sociability of game forms. Game sociability has been used before as a criterion for game analysis. Van den Berghe (1975:246-48), for instance, distinguishes play forms which reflect the need for affiliation from those which are solitary (such as solitaire and gambling). In that most games are to some degree sociable they function in developing an awareness of others.[3] But games which involve large numbers of participants are of higher sociability than games (such as chess) which require few participants. High sociability games place special requirements on the individual. The individual must remain cognizant of the roles of a greater number of "others," and must continually monitor the latter's behavior in constructing his own. This task is often facilitated by the formation of teams and the assignment of roles to specific individuals.

In Iceland, like most western industrial societies, the maintenance of the socio-economic order hinges to a large extent on instilling in children the positive value of achievement. Successful socialization in the achievement motive in turn rests on children learning to assert their independence and on learning to derive intrinsic pleasure from accomplishing tasks by themselves (Rosen and D'Andrade 1959). This does not mean that the value of cooperation is eschewed. Quite to the contrary, achievement-oriented societies generally place an emphasis as well on getting along with others and on cooperating to accomplish tasks (McClelland 1961:192). Hence, one might say that in such societies there is a built in conflict of primary dimensions. Children are generally trained quite rigorously in the values of independence, achievement, and self-assertion; but as though there is an implicit awareness of the social dangers of rearing children who are too independent or too autonomous, there is a counter emphasis on sociability and other-directedness. The ideally competent individual in such a society must, then, perform something of a "balancing act" between developing his self-worth through asserting himself and getting ahead as an autonomous individual, and doing so while maintaining an awareness of the needs of other individuals and the groups he associates in.

As noted already, the child-rearing patterns in modern Iceland are most distinguished by the emphasis placed on the virtues of independence and achievement; but there are also subtle though pervasive pressures for sociability. Indeed the most common admonition toward misbehaving children is to cooperate and get along. This dualistic orientation, though probably characteristic of achievement-oriented societies in general, engenders a conflict which has pervaded Icelandic social life throughout the ages. Consistently at the core of the Icelandic saga sociodramas, for instance, is the conflict over whether the individual should assert himself or submit to the demands and needs of the group (see Rich 1976:220-54). The same is reflected in Icelandic children's games. We have seen from the cursory analysis of play preference and involvement patterns that the conspicuous emphasis on achievement motivation, the commensurately low emphasis on obedience, and moderate concern for responsibility in early child training are reflected in the children's game preoccupations. The children gravitate largely toward games of physical skill, reflecting some anxiety with respect to individualism, self-assertion, and achievement. But a large number of the children's games, and the vast majority of their favorite ones, are high sociability games which foster affiliation and cooperation.[4] At an early age, the children are initiated into games which not only require self-assertion and the exercise of individual skills, but ones which also place ego-centric and socio-centric values in conflict. The social situation is modeled in which the individual players must assert themselves as individuals and simultaneously monitor and incorporate the roles and needs of others in a cooperative enterprise. These functions may be common to all multi-player games, but they are especially crucial, and are hence intensified, in a society where the inordinate emphasis on independence and individualism might be socially pathological unless mediated by a counter-emphasis on sociability.

In view of the potentially broad interpretations of these results, but the limited scope within which the findings have been discussed, it might suffice as a means of concluding to bring back into focus and re-iterate three principal points. First, a limited contribution comes from using the abstract play data to test the Conflict-Enculturation Hypothesis. Though the hypothesis, originally derived from a cross-cultural study, has been tested through a number of successful subsystem replications (e.g., Sutton-Smith, Roberts, and Kozelka 1963; Sutton-Smith and Roberts 1967), few attempts have been undertaken to test it cross-culturally (see Georges 1969). As one such test, the foregoing analysis generally validates the hypothesis; or stated differently, the hypothesis lends theoretical continuity to the correlations established between the predominant values in Icelandic culture, the conspicuous orientation of child-training patterns, and play preference and involvement patterns.

Secondly, while the Conflict-Enculturation Hypothesis focuses primarily upon the principal types of actions which determine the outcome of a game (i.e., strategy, skill, chance), the present study goes beyond these variables to consider the sociability factor in games. This expansion was precipitated by two ethnographic observations: the emphasis on potentially contradictory values, achievement and sociability, and the extent to which Icelandic parents foster and encourage high sociability play together with the role of high-sociability games in the play repertoire. In bringing these observations to bear on a pervasive conflict of values throughout Icelandic history and culture, an additional dimension of socialization anxiety theory was added to the Conflict-Enculturation Hypothesis, and the games were seen as modeling conflicts in another way as well.

Finally, the data analyzed above were obtained not out of an exclusive interest in Icelandic children's play, but in the context of a broader ethnographic study. The observation was instrumental to broader ethnological objectives, and was undertaken as a convenient means of shifting the locus of attention from behavior toward children to the behavior of the children themselves. In this way the play research proved not only to be a useful corroborative research tool, but a valuable source of insight as well. For instance, the emergence of anomalous types of developmental play patterns for boys and girls, not originally hypothesized, amplified the need for further ethnographic research in a specific area, exemplifying the extent to which an analysis of children's play patterns may serve as a sensitive index of culture.

NOTES

[1] The research on which this paper is based was carried out in northern Iceland, August, 1973-August, 1974, supported by grants from the Wenner-Gren Foundation for Anthropological Research, the National Science Foundation, the American-Scandinavian Foundation, and the United Nations International Institute of Education (Fulbright-Hays).

[2] There are many ways in which the observations to follow should be qualified, but space restrictions prohibit this here. The characterizations of Icelandic values and child training practices are out of necessity brief. For detailed discussion of these see Rich (1976).

[3] The sociability factor and the concept of "game" itself have become muddled in the popular metaphor in which "game" becomes synonymous with ritual or structured interaction. Popular sociology (e.g., Berne, *Games People Play* [1964] and Goffman, *Strategic Interaction* [1969]) tends to equate everything from a dinner party to a seduction encounter with "game." Since games have rules and internal structure, all interactions which have rules and structure are thereby games and are sociable events. The simple distinction being made here with respect to the sociability elements in games rests on the varying expressions of the need to affiliate.

[4] Of 135 activities classified as games, 42 (31 percent) are central person games in which players develop cooperative strategies in their adversary relationship to *han* (he); and 23 (17 percent) are spontaneous team games. These types, and especially the latter, figure much higher amongst the games designated by the children as "favorite" activities.

REFERENCES

Berne, Eric, 1964, Games People Play: The Psychology of Human Relations. New York: Grove Press.

Brukman, Jan, 1973, Language and Socialization: child culture and the ethnographer's task, in Learning and Culture. *In* Proceedings of the 1972 Annual Spring Meeting of the American Ethnological Society. Seattle: University of Washington Press. Pp. 43-58.

Day, Lilia and Andrew Biemiller, 1969, Autonomy and Conformity in Icelandic School Children. Mimeographed. Sir Sandford Fleming College. Peterborough, Ontario, Canada.

Georges, Robert A., 1969, The Relevance of Models for Analyses of Traditional Play Activities. Southern Folklore Quarterly 33:1-23.

Gislason, Gylfi, 1970, Iceland (1918-1968): a Lecture Delivered 14 November, 1968. University College, London. Scandinavian Studies Jubilee Lecture. Colchester: Benham and Co., Ltd.
1973, The Problem of Being an Icelander: Past, Present, and Future. Reykjavik: Almenna Bokafeligid.

Goffman, Erving, 1969, Strategic Interaction. Philadelphia: University of Pennsylvania Press.

Griffiths, John C., 1969, Modern Iceland. New York: Praeger.

McClelland, David, 1961, The Achieving Society. Princeton: D. van Nostrand.

OECD, 1973, Organization for Economic Co-Operation and Development, Economic Survey: Iceland. Paris: OECD.

Rich, George W., 1976, Core Values, Organizational Preferences, and Children's Games in Akureyri, Iceland. Doctoral Dissertation, University of California, Davis, California.

Roberts, John M. and Brian Sutton-Smith, 1962, Child Training and Game Involvement. Ethnology 2:166-85.

Rosen, Bernard C. and Roy D'Andrade, 1959, The Psychological Origins of Achievement Motivation. Sociometry 22(3):185-218.

Sutton-Smith, B., Roberts, J. M., and R. M. Kozelka, 1963, Game Involvement in Adults. Journal of Social Psychology 6:15-30.

Sutton-Smith, B. and J. M. Roberts, 1967, Studies of an Elementary Game of Strategy. Genetic Psychology Monograph 75:3-42.

Thompson, Laura, 1960, Core Values and Diplomacy: a Case Study of Iceland. Human Organization 19:82-85.
1969, The Secret of Culture: Nine Community Studies. New York: Random House.

Van den Berghe, Pierre, 1975, Man in Society: a Biosocial View. New York: Elsevier.

Wax, Rosalie and Murray Wax, 1955, The Vikings and the Rise of Capitalism. The American Journal of Sociology 61:1-10.

Whiting, John W. M. and Irvin L. Child, 1953, Child Training and Personality: a Cross-Cultural Study. New Haven: Yale University Press.

Winterbottom, Marian R., 1958, The Relation of Need for Achievement to Learning Experiences in Independence and Mastery. In Motives in Fantasy, Action, and Society. J. W. Atkinson, Ed. New York: D. van Nostrand. Pp. 453-78.

## PLAY AND PERSONALITY IN DENMARK

Robert T. Anderson and Edna M. Mitchell, Mills College, Oakland

PROBLEM AND METHOD

National character is a statement about how the people of one nation tend to differ in measurable ways from the people of another. It is a statement about how a Dane, for example, is likely to differ from a

Swede or a Norwegian. Further, national character is a statement about how the complex process of socialization that shapes and molds infants and young children also differs from one nation to another. It is clear that nations which differ in basic personality structure, differ as well in how they raise their children. We see, for example, that national differences in personality are related to national differences in socialization in the work of Herbert Hendin (1965) in Scandinavia. He was able to measure significant differences in basic personalities of Danes, Norwegians and Swedes. He then demonstrated that such differences appear to reflect differences in family life, particularly in the patterning of dependency between children and parents.

National character research has focused upon ways in which personality may reflect techniques of socialization and the extent to which one nation may differ from another. Attention to these areas of concern has been at the expense of research upon a key assumption, namely, that child-rearing practices are significantly uniform throughout the population. This persistent failure to explore the extent to which nations are internally consistent in the process that shapes personality constitutes a major weakness in basic personality studies. Geoffrey Gorer, for example, argued that the adult Russian personality grew out of child-care practices that included the swaddling of infants. Unfortunately, he did not explore the extent to which children were socialized identically by all Russians (Gorer and Rickman 1949). Since it is clear that Russia was permeated with cultural differences related to socio-economic class, regionalism and the variables of urban and rural residence, we cannot simply assume the existence of nation-wide uniformity in how parents raised children. In so far as Gorer did not adequately investigate this matter, the value of his findings is diminished, as Anthony F. C. Wallace (1970:149-152), among others, has pointed out. Ruth Benedict has been similarly challenged for not investigating the extent to which practices assumed to be uniform in Japan do in fact cut across socio-cultural divisions that otherwise split the nation into more or less discrete sub-groupings (Benedict 1946; Bennett and Nagai 1953).

This largely unexplored problem in national character research is particularly appropriate for anthropological investigation, since it may be defined as a problem in diffusion. To what extent are child-rearing practices shared uniformly throughout a nation? Who communicates with whom to maintain a statewide process of imitation in early-childhood practices, particularly as a process of diffusion that overcomes the barriers of class and urban-rural divisions? Or, is the very notion of national character a mirage and the sharing of patterns of socialization a false assumption?

In a preliminary effort to seek answers to these questions, we explore a selected aspect of socialization — patterns of play; in a single case study — Denmark. We take as given that play and peer groups function to shape personality.[1] We focus upon a time in history when Denmark was fragmented by class and urban-rural divisions, the turn of the century (approximately 1885 to 1915). Data was derived from a questionnaire sent to older people by the Ethnological Surveys Department of the Danish National Museum. The surveys were first undertaken in 1941 when a questionnaire on harvesting implements was sent to at least one respondent in every parish in the nation. In 1969, Nina Fabricius inaugurated the thirty-third survey with a series of 138 questions on play and toys. Printed in a set of four booklets and mailed with instructions and follow-up correspondence, it produced 713 responses now on file in the museum.[2]

Denmark around 1900 was a nation of diverse standards of living. At an apex of affluence were families of the aristocracy and middle class that resided on estates or in large homes. Their mode of living contrasted with that of the urban poor, who were inadequately educated, poorly paid and badly housed. In the countryside, land-holding farmers lived very differently from impoverished cottagers, small-holders and fishing people. Although the population was becoming culturally more uniform, these extremes along urban-rural and poor-rich axes remained worlds apart in styles of living. To incorporate these dimensions into this study, questionnaire responses were categorized into four groups: (1) urban-affluent, (2) urban-poor, (3) rural-affluent, and (4) rural-poor. Contrary to our initial expectations, the data did not permit us to quantify our findings.[3] Similarities and differences are none-the-less clearcut. Differences are most striking with regard to toys.

## TOYS AND PLAY

Poor children, rural or urban, possessed almost no purchased toys. For example, the son of a poor civil servant in Copenhagen (born 1888) could not remember any toys being bought in his childhood until probing revealed that he owned a pair of purchased ice skates. So far as he could recall, his sister had been given only crocheting and knitting needles. A woman born to a Copenhagen working-class family (1856) also reports that she and her five siblings possessed no purchased toys, although she later mentions a porcelain head bought for her doll. Another woman from the same milieu (1881) remembers a time when an uncle, about to sail to America, asked her what kind of a toy she would like as a going-away gift. A jump-rope was her response, and when he gave one to her it became her first store-bought toy. Later an aunt gave her a doll with a wax face and eyes that closed. Somehow she also acquired a number of pins with colored glass heads (**nipsenale**), juvenile collectors' items much prized by children in those days.

In contrast to the poor, the children of wealthy families might own many expensive toys. The collection of the National Museum includes a variety of doll houses, rocking horses, magic lanterns and mechanical gadgets that once delighted middle-class and aristocratic children. Turning from museum artifacts to survey protocols, we find descriptions of what particular individuals owned. The son of a professor of medicine, born in 1897, describes the following purchased toys, some of which he shared with a brother: a rocking horse with hair, saddle and bridle, a hobby horse, tin soldiers, a wooden fortress with drawbridge and tower, a box of building blocks, a doll theater, games (such as dominoes), balls, a trundling hoop, a top, roller skates when they first appeared on the market, a diabolo, glass pea-shooters, and stilts. Still other items, such as a sled, were probably bought. In the summer, he had a small row-boat to play with at the family summer estate.

Stella Hansen Anderson, born in 1900 as the daughter of a successful businessman in Copenhagen (and incidentally, the mother of one of the authors of this paper), when interviewed with the National Museum questionnaire was able to recall the quantity and quality of purchased toys that contrasted dramatically with the sparse possessions of poor children. Although a doll, doll carriage, and set of miniature cups and saucers of porcelain, constituted her most precious possessions, she also had been given pins with colored glass heads, a trundle hoop, a spinning top, a diabolo, several balls, a sled and a pair of ice skates. In addition, her father kept a sailboat and an iceboat for recreation on Lake Furasoen, where they maintained a vacation home.

We appear to document an enormous difference when the play of privileged-class children is compared with that of the poor. We will now argue that differences in the possession of purchased toys implied few or no real differences in play habits.

First, it must be noted that many of the toys purchased by the well-to-do occupied only a very small place in the activities of children who owned them. Mechanical toys, rather common in the collection of the museum, provided amusement only briefly and occasionally. A windup clown, for example, soon lost its novelty. Educational toys, much touted after their success in the Crystal Palace Exhibition in London in 1851, introduced children to simple principles of optics, mechanics, magnetism or chemistry, primarily by permitting the observation of some principle in action. A popular toy in many variations was an optical device, the primitive ancestor of modern movies, which passed drawings rapidly before the eye to give an illusion of motion. Since the number of drawings was limited, such a toy tended to be amusing rather than challenging, good for some moments on a rainy day, but not for frequent use.[4]

Second and more important, toys could be made at home. All of the much-used possessions of the children of affluence were available to poor children in home-made forms. Any father could manufacture a pair of stilts for his son. Boys made their own kites. Trundle hoops were improvised from barrel rings. A few pieces of wood easily produced an ice sled, and at a time when few children owned ice skates, all possessed wooden shoes that slid splendidly, especially when metal plates were attached with knobbed nails. A plank across a tree stump or an over-turned barrel became a seesaw. It took only a length of rope to make a jump-rope, while rope plus a piece of wood for a seat produced a swing. Balls were seldom bought since, in addition to needle work and other home crafts, women and girls made balls by wrapping bottle corks in woollen yarn and sewing on stout covers of bright colors. Dolls of cloth, customarily made by women, were normally dressed in sewn, knitted or crocheted garments and, less commonly, attached to a doll house or room made and furnished by some father or uncle.

Third and perhaps most important, much play took place without the use of toys or equipment at all. Children were expected to improvise materials and exercise fantasy. No significant equipment was needed for hopscotch, hiding, chasing, guessing and singing games. Children from every milieu were accustomed to use whatever was at hand as props for playing. The leaves of fall, swept into piles on four sides, made a kind of room familiar to many, although rooms, houses and stores were improvised in other ways as well. Rich or poor, children played store, selling sand, pebbles, berries and leaves for money made of paper. Rich as well as poor brought chestnuts home in the fall to polish and fit with toothpicks for the creation of farms and zoos. The doctor's son, who owned many toys by contemporary standards, recalled a favorite game. He and his brother were permitted at times to turn the dinner table over and to hang the legs with blankets to form a tent. So housed, they sat on pillows and played "Arabs," clothed in turbans made of towels and cloaks improvised from an adult bathrobe and a raincape. Imagining their horses to be tethered just outside, they dined on the end-slices of rye bread washed down with water from old soda-water bottles. Except for turning over the table, which suggests unusually lenient parents, children in a poor family might have done the same.

## MECHANISMS OF UNIFORMITY

When the use of purchased play materials is examined in the context of materials and facilities as a whole, differences melt into practices shared by all. Yet modern agencies of diffusion did not then exist or were still relatively undeveloped. At that time, national uniformities in play did not derive from official policy, state agencies or a network of nursery schools and day-care centers. Commerce played a very limited role, although a few inexpensive toys spread widely (wooden tops, pins with colored glass heads, colored pictures for trading and pasting in albums, tin soldiers, expensive but nearly ubiquitous pocket knives for boys and doll heads for girls). The mass media did not yet include radio and television. Newspapers and magazines, however, reached people in every geographical area and socio-economic level. These published media became the sources of extensive play with paper, including cut-out paper dolls and paper theaters. Children also cut out ordinary illustrations in a collecting fad that put empty cigar boxes to use as treasure chests.

The mechanisms of diffusion of the 1970s were largely absent at the turn of the century. Other sources of uniformity were present, however. One such source may be characterized as ecological. Children tended to be uniform because the environment of play created by adults was uniform across class and urban-rural boundaries.

First, the use of time was consistent for children throughout the nation; little time was available for play. Denmark was unusual for a nation of peasants in that enough schooling to eliminate illiteracy was an established reality. Not only did the poor as well as the rich send their children to school, they did so with the feeling that basic education was useful and important. Homework exercised a heavy claim on after-school hours. So also did chores in all homes. In a pre-industrial economy, children provided a necessary source of help in hauling water and fuel into homes, in multiple daily trips to the store (in town), in feeding and watering animals (on farms), and in carrying slop pails. Even in well-to-do families, children might be expected to help in the endless housecleaning tasks. Despite a fulltime servant and a "non-working" mother, Stella Hansen Anderson was expected to keep the parlor dusted and to help mind her younger brother. In all classes, childhood was regarded as a short prelude to adult responsibilities in which it was more important to become educated and to develop good work habits than it was to play. In the use of time, we conclude, early forms of universal education and industrial development established uniformities that affected children of all classes and parts of the nation.

Second, space use was also subject to equalizing influences. In warm seasons, country children, rich or poor, encountered an abundance of space in which they could play out of doors. They had access to fields, forests and yards. They were not provided with playgrounds other than sparcely equipped school yards on school days, so games that involved teams frequently took place on roads. Traffic, in that era before the automobile, was light and less dangerous than in our time.

Urban children, rich and poor, had some access to parks or wooded and open areas even in Copenhagen, although parts of large cities differed in this regard. Much urban play was confined to neighborhoods in which streets, sidewalks (then still rather new) and apartment-house courtyards provided the only daily opportunities. In working-class neighborhoods, courtyards typically were cramped, dark places where play was barely tolerated by adults. The children of such places were disadvantaged as compared with children in better neighborhoods. Urban playgrounds were primarily limited to facilities for small children, with swings and seesaws the most common equipment. On the whole, summer space was better for rural children than for urban, for rich children than for poor. All, however, played predominantly in areas not designed or set apart specifically for play.

Space in winter was a different matter. Out-of-doors play in a land of ice and snow tended to offer equal opportunities to all. Children built snowmen, characteristically with lumps of coal as buttons, a carrot for a nose, and an old hat as a headpiece. Sledding was popular, though limited everywhere by the absence of high hills and mountains. Often children hitched rides by attaching ropes to passing horse carriages. Ice play included only a limited amount of skating, but much sliding and sledding by boys in standing position who pushed themselves with staves between their legs.

Indoors play in winter was confining for all. Even the well-to-do were reluctant to heat more rooms than they felt was necessary. The small wealthy-elite equipped nursery rooms for young children. All other children played in the kitchen (poorer families), living room (the most common) or dining room (if it existed), where the floor or table provided a play surface. Winter hours indoors were prime times for playing with toys for those who had them, but all classes entertained themselves with play that required simple materials available to all. The turn of the century was a time when paper play was highly developed, based upon techniques of folding, cutting and pasting rather than drawing or coloring. The use of space, we find, was shaped by adults in an environment that imposed the rigors of a northern climate and limited energy resources.

Ecological factors set the basic parameters of play as restrictions on the use of time and space. The nature of play within these parameters was shaped by diffusion among children. Diffusion among children constitutes a process of imitation that has been observed by others. Folklorists are familiar with it as the basis for historical continuity in the culture of children. Direct transmission from child to child has preserved some kinds of play over centuries of time. In England, Iona and Peter Opie report that "[b]oys continue to crack jokes that Swift collected from his friends in Queen Anne's time; they play tricks which lads used to play on each other in the heyday of Beau Brummel; they ask riddles which were posed when Henry VIII was a boy" (1959:2). Such findings by folklorists raise few questions about the mechanism of diffusion, however, since it is assumed that younger children learn from the older in a single play environment. We are concerned, however, with transmission that crosses class and rural-urban barriers. We are also concerned with the totality of play rather than of aspects only. How could uniformity of this sort and on this scale take place? The attitudes of adults towards play appear to provide the answer.

The questionnaire devised by Fabricius included one question that proved particularly relevant to this issue. Respondents were asked, "What was the general feeling of adults concerning play? Was play, for example, considered a waste of time, or perhaps healthy and beneficial for the young?"[5] In our examination of responses to this question we were at first puzzled by the ambiguous nature of the responses. In part, ambiguity undoubtedly resulted from the fact that former children are attempting to discuss how their parents felt. More significantly, however, ambiguity appears to reflect the fact that it was not a question considered by the people at that time. Lack of agreement or clarity in responses to this question, and the frequent answer of "I don't know," derive, we conclude, not so much from differences of opinion as from indifference. Adults gave little thought to the value of play or the nature of play, so long as it did not become destructive or intrusive into their own activities. Children were left to fend largely for themselves in their free time, to appropriate space and materials as best they could. Even in wealthy families, where a serving girl might be hired to care for preschool children, the responsibility was thought of primarily as custodial. Adults frequently made toys for their children, but parents did not regularly spend time playing with them or directing their play.

It is this attitude of unconcern, we feel, that created a situation in which play could become uniform even though adult styles of living were highly diverse. Children, unlike their parents, were not segregated on the urban-rural or wealthy-poor axes, despite some partial barriers.

As concerns class divisions, residential patterns did keep certain children apart in their play, a tendency strengthened in the upper classes by the feeling that "well-bred" children ought not to play with those of the slums. Yet National Museum survey protocols consistently document ways in which rich and poor children did in fact play together. The richer the family, the more likely it was to espouse segregation, but also the more likely to follow other customs which brought children together. For one, wealthy families were more likely to employ live-in and other domestic and estate servants whose children played with the children of employers as a matter of course. In addition, the children of the very rich played with nearby rich and middle-class children, who played in turn with lower-middle-class and "nice" working-class children in adjoining areas, who played with working-class children of a poorer sort, and so on. Even though it was uncommon for the children of the very rich to play with the children of the very poor, children at the extremes were culturally in contact through intermediate children.

The division between town and country was equally permeable to children. Every year, and increasingly by 1900, country families moved to urban centers to find work, thus bringing village children into urban play environments. Conversely, middle-class and upper-class children spent summer vacations in rural localities, often with country kin. Distances were short and movement was constant.

In all, patterns of play were free to diffuse the length and breadth of Denmark because children were in contact across barriers that divided their parents and because they shared a similar environment as concerns the use of time and space. Above all, an adult attitude of indifference made this potentiality for diffusion a reality.

The process of nation-wide diffusion among children is so simple that its importance can be overlooked. Adult culture traits were not equally free to diffuse. Differences in wealth, occupation and place of residence correlated with differences in styles of clothes, houses, furnishings, food, ideas and values. The leisure of children did not differ greatly by class or occupation, whereas adults differed strikingly in the amount of free time they had. If play was the work of children, as Rousseau expressed it, the work of adults was necessarily as different as farmer, worker, estate-owner and industrialist. If the social interaction of children was essentially simple, direct and unsegregated, the interaction of adults was shaped by differing modes and rules of etiquette. Finally and most importantly, whereas no one seemed greatly concerned that children played essentially in the same manner in different social strata, traditional European attitudes of cultural differentiation still inhibited diffusion among adults. That is, the upper class still endeavored in many ways to remain different from lower-class people, and townspeople still felt it embarrassing to be similar to country folk (Anderson 1975:29-33, 75).

## CONCLUSIONS

Based upon responses from individuals in every part of Denmark who were children at the turn of the century, we find that patterns of play tended to be uniform throughout the nation. Despite cultural differences that sharply distinguished Danes as rich versus poor and as country versus urban, these key features of the process of socialization were uniform. We conclude, therefore, that a basis for the maintenance of a Danish basic personality type was present at that time.

In uncovering the process of diffusion that lay behind national character in this case study, we find an answer to our initial question which rapidly transforms itself into still further questions. Two above all are insistent. First, was Denmark around 1900 unusual as concerns diffusion among children? Do parents in other nations supervise and control the play of children more than was the case in turn-of-the-century Denmark? Are the social barriers of adults applied more rigorously to children in other nations? Does this case study even reflect the situation as it was in Denmark itself at an earlier time? In short, to what extent is Denmark around 1900 representative of how patterns of play diffuse in other societies?

Second, our findings concerning play tell us nothing about the diffusion of family practices. Were families throughout Denmark similar in habits of child care? Did parents relate to children in comparable ways everywhere throughout the nation? We offer no answers, but this much is clear: To the extent that the diffusion of family practices took place, it had to have been a thoroughly different process from that which resulted in uniformities in patterns of play, because the active agents of diffusion would have been adults rather than children.

Our findings, then, are offered with an awareness of their limitations. They suggest one conclusion that is unambiguous, however. They provide a basis for knowing that a complex nation of differentiated sub-cultures could be sufficiently uniform in the socialization patterns of play so that an aristocrat, a peasant, a merchant and a worker, although each grew up to be rather different in psychological characteristics, nevertheless could share basic personality traits that identified them equally as Danes.

NOTES

[1]In experimentation with monkeys, Harry and Margaret Harlow (1962) found that infants deprived of maternal contact, but permitted to play daily with their peers, grew to be nearly normal adults, in contrast to infants deprived of both mothers and peers. One must, of course, exercise caution in extrapolating from animal studies to conclusions about human beings.

[2]For a descriptioin of the surveys see Hojrup (1966). The director of the Third Division of the National Museum, the Danish Folk Museum (Dansk Folkemuseum), is Holger Rasmussen. The curator directly in charge of survey files is Ole Hojrup, assisted by Bodil Madsen. Their staff includes Charlotte Bogh, who is presently developing distribution maps of toys and games, and Inger Tolstrup. Ib Varnild is the curator of toys and games. We are pleased to acknowledge our debt to these members of the museum staff as well as to Hanna Mathiassen and, above all, George Nellemann.

[3]These surveys greatly refine older techniques for eliciting memory culture. In survey No. 33, however, the findings remain incomplete in three critical ways: (1) respondents almost never reported the ages at which they engaged in specified forms of play; (2) they almost never reported the frequency of specified play forms, although in many cases some forms were designated as "very popular" or "much done;" (3) they rarely answered all of the questions asked, thus leaving uncertain the completeness of their responses.

[4]In a Danish experiment, children were given a choice of playing in either a room with mechanical toys or in one with simple building blocks. For the first two days, that with mechanical toys was by far the most popular. Thereafter, children preferred the room with simple toys (Hegeler 1955).

[5]*Hvordan var de voksnes indstilling i almindelighed til leg? Blev leg for eksempel regnet for tidsspilde — eller for noget, der var sundt og godt for born og unge?*

REFERENCES

Anderson, Robert T., 1975, Denmark: Success of a Developing Nation. Cambridge, Mass: Schenkman.

Benedict, Ruth, 1946, The Chrysanthemum and the Sword, Patterns of Japanese Culture. Boston: Houghton Mifflin.

Bennett, J. W. and Michio Nagai, 1953, Echoes: Reactions to American Anthropology — Japanese Critique of the Methodology of Benedict's 'Chrysanthemum and the Sword.' American Anthropologist 55:404-411.

Gorer, Geoffrey and J. Rickman, 1949, The People of Great Russia. London: Cresset Press.

Harlow, Harry F. and Margaret K. Harlow, 1962, Social Deprivation in Monkeys. Scientific American 207(5):136-146.

Hegeler, Sten, 1955, Hvordan finder jeg det rigtigt legetoj til mit barn? Copenhagen: Stig Vendelkars Forlag.

Hendin, Herbert, 1965, Suicide and Scandinavia, A Psychoanalytic Study of Culture and Character. Garden City, N.Y.: Anchor Press/Doubleday.

Hojrup, Ole, 1966, The Work of the National Museum's Ethnological Surveys Department. *In* Dansk Folkemuseum & Frilandsmuseet: History and Activities. Holger Rasmussen, Ed. Copenhagen: Nationalmuseet.

Opie, Iona and Peter Opie, 1959, The Lore and Language of Schoolchildren.. Oxford: Clarendon Press.

Wallace, Anthony F. C., 1970, Culture and Personality. 2nd ed. New York: Random House.

## THE USES OF ORDER AND DISORDER IN PLAY: AN ANALYSIS OF VIETNAMESE REFUGEE CHILDREN'S PLAY

Christine Emilie Robinson, Stanford University

Adults often assume that children freely join play groups and will be able to play as long as they know the game rules. However, some play forms demand a cultural sophistication which many children do not have. By sophistication I mean more than knowing the rules; some games require knowing the rules so well you can ignore or distort them. The rules referred to are not merely game rules; they are social rules which shape non-play behavior and influence children's behavior in play. These games are the spontaneous, seemingly structureless activities in which children chase, wrestle and taunt each other, enjoying freedom from everyday social restraints.

These data are based on observations of the play of nine to twelve year old Vietnamese refugee children in four San Francisco area schools.[1] Simple observation shows that Vietnamese children are developing American social skills in play. However, on closer observation it becomes clear that their participation in play is limited by their unfamiliarity with American culture. A major difference between Vietnamese children's play and the play of their American peers lies in their play preferences. Vietnamese children tend to choose highly structured games for the security of the structure, even though their American peers often choose games with structures they can destroy.

The school experience of Vietnamese refugee children varies greatly. The four schools I chose for observation have student populations ranging from predominantly White to predominantly Black. School programs for limited-English speaking students range from all day English as a Second Language programs, to limited or non-existent special language programs.

Despite the differences in school environments, I found two patterns in the play of Vietnamese children. First, Vietnamese boys have very different patterns of play involvement than Vietnamese girls. All Vietnamese boys play actively, while few girls participate in play or games. Secondly, Vietnamese children play rule-governed games almost exclusively. They rarely participate in the spontaneous, free-flowing play created by their peers.

These patterns reflect two common notions about play. First, boys and girls in most cultures have different play patterns (Sutton-Smith and Roberts 1962), and secondly, the play of nine to twelve year olds is often described as rule-governed (Piaget 1962). The play preferences of Vietnamese children reflects these characteristics perfectly, but the play preferences of their peers conform less closely.

## SEX DIFFERENCES IN PLAY INVOLVEMENT

Part of the difference between the Vietnamese boys' and girls' participation rests in the nature of traditional boys and girls games. Certain games that are labelled "boys' games" and "girls' games" have existed for generations. Boys' games are traditionally aggressive and competitive, while girls' games are passive and accommodating (Sutton-Smith, Rosenberg and Morgan 1963). When asked what they played in Vietnam, most boys said soccer, while girls said jump-rope and badminton (Robinson 1976). Play experience in Vietnam parallels the experience of American boys and young girls, but American girls over nine years of age are often not satisfied with passive traditional girls' play.

By the age of nine, many American girls are discontent with their role on the playground. Their traditional games do not offer them the challenges they used to offer. After several years of jump-rope and hopscotch, most girls have reached the game's skill ceiling. Meanwhile, girls have not developed the skills needed for extended competitive games and seem envious of boys' deep involvement in play (Lever 1976). For these reasons, girls often list "bugging the boys" as a favorite pastime.

Most playground activities geared to children over nine years of age are competitive and aggressive. Team sports take on new importance to fourth graders. Boys' games build progressively toward competitive team sports, but girls learn to sublimate aggression and competition in their early play. Girls learn cooperation in order to play together, not to cooperate for a desired goal, such as winning a game. Boys' team sports, in contrast, require cooperation for success. Boys are able to combine cooperation, competition and aggression in their games, but these behaviors are at odds in girls' play. Girls rarely sustain games which require cooperation, competition and aggression. Thus, they frequently turn to spontaneous play to release aggression (Robinson n.d.).

Vietnamese girls seem reluctant to participate in even slightly aggres-

sive play. They often stand or sit near the games, participating vicari-
ously. For example:

> Van[2] (fifth grade) was with a group of boys and girls standing on either side
> of a chain-link fence. They threw a frisbee from one side to the other. Chil-
> dren near the fence tried to intercept the frisbee as it went over the fence.
> Van leaned against the fence, near those who were leaping for the frisbee.
> She smiled, laughed and watched the game eagerly, but she did not partici-
> pate. She was holding a brown shopping bag in one hand and never put it
> down to try to catch the frisbee. (Field notes 2/18/77. Black school 10:30-
> 10:45 a.m.).

In contrast, all of the Vietnamese boys play actively. They frequently
play four-square, tag football and a modified basketball game. They
play aggressively and competitively. For example:

> Dinh and Thiet (fourth grade) were playing six-square (four-square with two
> additional players). The ball came low into the inside corner of Dinh's
> square. He lunged at the ball, fell forward onto his knees and left elbow but
> recovered the ball and kept it in play. Another ball came to him before he
> could get up, and he threw himself on his back to recover it. He got up,
> dusted off his hands and responded to the exclamations of the on-lookers
> with a look of "what else was I supposed to do? I *had* to get the ball." (ESL
> school 2/18/77, 1:45-2:00 p.m.).

The difference between Vietnamese boys' and girls' play reflects both
general sex differences in play and the specific play patterns of Vietnamese children. Vietnamese boys were prepared for competitive group
play by playing soccer and other team sports in Vietnam, but girls' play
experiences in Vietnam did not prepare them for the play of older
American girls. They were familiar with structured, cooperative, non-
competitive games which have been abandoned by their American
peers. They seem unwilling to join in the brief, spontaneous chasing and
taunting that marks much of the play of their peers.

Language limitations seem to be felt more strongly by Vietnamese
girls because girls' play is generally more verbal than boys' play. As
Millar points out, "Girls are, generally speaking, linguistically more
skillful from an early age than boys in our society, and when they are
aggressive, tend to use their tongues rather than their fists" (1968:196).
Differences in verbal style are particularly evident in interactions at the
predominantly Black school. When asked whom she plays with after
school, Van said, "My sister. I don't have many friends. I don't like the
Black kids very well; they are too mean. They say mean things to me.
They use bad words" (home visit 3/4/77).

One conclusion from this study is that Vietnamese girls rely less on play for social interactions than do boys. Vietnamese girls interact with other girls on the playground, but their interactions are usually limited to talking to one or two girls, whereas boys play with large groups of boys. The girls' limited participation in play may have significance for their adaptation to American culture because they cut off an important channel of social learning. They do not learn game rules which can be transferred to social rules. Avoidance of games with rules may have repercussions on Vietnamese girls' confidence to later play with the rules.

## PREFERENCE FOR RULE GOVERNED GAMES

All Vietnamese boys play during recess, but they limit their play participation to rule governed games. When Vietnamese girls play, they also play rule governed games. Free-flowing, spontaneous play exists on all of the playgrounds, but the Vietnamese children choose rule governed games instead. Since they are free to choose their play activity, there must be a reason why they prefer rule governed games to spontaneous play. It seems that the security of rule governed games is attractive to Vietnamese children. Their limited knowledge of more subtle rules of play in the United States makes the freedom of spontaneous play somewhat frightening.

The structure of each activity determines whether it is a game or play. Games are relatively predictable. They are governed by a set of predetermined rules; participation is geared to a known goal (making baskets, scoring points, gaining territory, etc.). Quite often games are competitive. Play, on the other hand, does not have clearly defined rules or roles for participants. No one wins in play, and players are free to come and go without destroying the shape of the activity.

According to Piaget, children are cognitively unable to play rule governed games until after they are seven years old. They remain interested in rule governed games into adulthood because these games are the "ludic activity of the socialized being" (1962:142). He goes on to say:

> In a general way it can be said that the more the child adapts himself to the natural and social world the less he indulges in symbolic distortions and transpositions because instead of assimilating the external world to the ego he progressively subordinates the ego to reality (1962:145).

The play of Vietnamese refugee children fits Piaget's model perfectly. The younger children (kindergarten and first graders) often play alone, creating the fantasies of solitary play, while the older children play rule governed games exclusively. This does not explain why the older Vietnamese children's peers often play non-rule governed games. I suggest that they have learned the game rules and now enjoy turning the rules over and playing with deeper social rules and structures.

Vietnamese children choose play forms with well defined boundaries and well defined roles. They rely on the game's structure to clarify and define their position in relation to the other players. It is not clear if they are retreating from the confusion of learning a new culture into the safety of rules, or if they are leaning toward a structure they can work within. According to Caillois, all game players try to eliminate confusion; "The confused and intricate laws of ordinary life are replaced in this fixed space and for this given time by precise, arbitrary, unexceptionable rules that must be accepted as such and that govern the correct playing of the game" (1961:7).

The role Vietnamese children take in decision making and conflict resolution also points to their desire for well defined boundaries. In most cases, Vietnamese children avoid threatening and poorly defined play interactions. They usually stand back while decisions are made and conflicts settled. For example:

> Pham (sixth grade) was playing four-square with a large blonde boy, an Asian boy and a Chicano boy. The blonde boy (best described as a bully) controlled the game. He was standing in the first square bouncing the ball. Suddenly, he jammed the ball into Pham's square. Since Pham had no warning, he could not reach the ball in time, and he ran obediently onto the field to retrieve it. Meanwhile, the Asian boy stood up to the bully, saying that he hit the ball out. Their argument continued after Pham returned with the ball. Pham's only contribution to the discussion was to bounce the ball on a spot outside the square where he thought the ball landed (White school 2/7/77, 10:30-10:45 a.m.).

Pham's reaction to the conflict was to let the other boy argue with the bully, although Pham was the injured party. His only involvement in the argument was to non-verbally emphasize the rules.

Vietnamese children often state rules when disputes arise, but they do not participate actively in arguments or discussions. They seem much more concerned with following the rules than in negotiating for better positions. Sutton-Smith noticed a similar insistence on rules among first grade children. He says:

> The rules give the children a way of functioning as a group...As the players become more experienced in the ways of groups their attitude toward such rules can become more flexible. The very rigidity of the rules is a guarantor for the players against the chaos of their own and others' idiosyncratic behavior (1971:89).

The Vietnamese children are like the young children described by Sutton-Smith; they too are uncertain about their role in group play. Therefore, they want well defined roles in their play interactions.

The children who are fairly sure of their status on the playground and understand the social rules, create novel play situations by transcending and over-turning social rules. In contrast, children unfamiliar with American culture find rule governed games novel because they learn new social rules. Berlyne (1960:21) writes that we are most responsive to an intermediate degree of novelty. We are indifferent to situations that are either too remote or too familiar. Different criteria for novelty influence the play patterns of Vietnamese children and their American peers. A novel situation for an immigrant child may seem boring to an American child because it is too familiar, while a novel situation for an American child may be too foreign for an immigrant child.

Novel play forms for many children do not have pre-established rules and well defined boundaries and roles. These play forms will be referred to as spontaneous play. This play appears chaotic, but it has an underlying structure and unstated boundaries. Spontaneous play does not rely on rules to mark the distinction between play and non-play behavior. Instead, players create a "play frame" or a boundary between play and non-play behavior. A play frame is created through signalling an unstated message, "this is play" (Bateson 1972:187). The players must understand the messages and the unstated boundaries in which they play because there are no rules to rely on. The lack of rules and preestablished play patterns gives children freedom to do whatever they want and assume any role they please. This freedom can be frightening if the play frame is not carefully maintained and clearly understood.

Children's spontaneous play goes beyond preparing for future roles and understanding social relations. It actually allows children to "play with play." Children turn over the social order and expected behaviors and create disorder and chaos for the pure enjoyment of experiencing the unknown and otherwise unknowable (Sutton-Smith in press, Robinson n.d.).

Spontaneous play often involves what Clifford Geertz (1972) calls "deep play." People engage in deep play when the stakes are so high it is irrational to be involved in the activity. Children's play seems to involve fairly low stakes, except when spontaneous play turns upon the social structure and cultural norms. This would be the deepest of play if the social structure were static. The intensity and depth of spontaneous play is evident when a child's play frame breaks, and he or she asks, "is this play?" At this point, the child no longer enjoys the disorder in the play world and flees to the security of the rule governed structured world.

Previous discussions of spontaneous play have not recognized the importance of a shared cultural base. New social structures and interactions intrigue those who are so secure in their culture they can think about changing it. If children do not fully understand the social structure and the rules spontaneous play turns against, play boundaries, infra-structures, and signalling, will not be strong enough to hold children in spontaneous play. Vietnamese children avoid spontaneous play with American peers because they do not understand the rules well enought to break them. They are still trying to establish boundaries and understand social relations in their everyday world. They engage in play forms that strengthen social relations and clarify social rules rather that participating in play that breaks down the social structure they are trying to build.

Children do not participate whole-heartedly in spontaneous play unless they are sure of the social rules they violate. Vietnamese children will gain this security by first mastering rule governed games. I do not mean they must become good athletes; rather, they must understand the rules along with what lies beneath the rules.

A parallel development of rule manipulation occurs in children's riddling. Children go through three stages in learning to riddle. They begin with learning the structure and linguistic rules and end with transcending and distorting the rules. First, children learn the linguistic code, in this case, the question/answer sequence. They enjoy asking riddles such as, "what two letters do Indians live in? T.P." Once the code is learned, they play with and distort the linguistic sequence by demanding answers that do not follow logically from the question, for example, "What is black and white and read all over? A bloody zebra." Children eventually subordinate the linguistic code to their interpersonal relations and substitute victimization as the proper response to the question. They ask a question such as, "Do you want a Hawaiian punch?" and follow it by punching the child in the face (McDowell 1974).

CONCLUSION

The development of riddling skills is analoguous to the development of play skills. Rules of proper speech or play behavior are learned in the first stage. At this time, children enjoy mastering rules they will use in daily life. Learning rules loses its novelty once children are proficient in them. Childen then begin testing the sensation of rule distortion. Players are not bound by the rules because they are playing, either physically or linguistically. Eventually, the riddles or games transcend the limits of their codes. Communication in both cases goes beyond verbalization or patterned interaction into what Bateson calls "metacommunication" (1972:191).

Vietnamese children are essentially in the first stage, learning the linguistic and social codes. Vietnamese girls are at a disadvantage because they are avoiding both spontaneous play and rule governed games. They are like the child who never tells a riddle. They stand back and observe the social interactions of play, but they do not learn what it is like to participate in the play. The girls learn the social rules, just as the non-riddler learns the question/answer sequence, but they do not learn how to play with the codes. In contrast, Vietnamese boys are learning social rules through play and may eventually know them well enough to play with them. These data suggest that Vietnamese boys will gain a deeper understanding of American culture than will Vietnamese girls because of their participation in play.

Vietnamese boys are learning American cultural rules through the informal channel of play. They will learn to play with the rules and adapt to changes in American society, if they go beyond rule governed games. Vietnamese girls in contrast, are learning social rules through the more formal channel of school and adults. They may be less prepared for change than Vietnamese boys because school and adults do not give children an opportunity to play with the rules they have learned.

The difference between Vietnamese and American children's play patterns points to another level of play beyond those recognized by Piaget. Children do not stop progressing in play once they have learned its rules. Rule governed games are an important aspect of play, but they are not the ultimate play form. They might be the ultimate form in a static, unchanging society, but today children must become flexible and adaptive to change. Spontaneous play offers them this opportunity.

NOTES

[1]Field work was conducted from October, 1976 through March, 1977. Twenty two Vietnamese children were enrolled in the four schools; twelve of them were in the 4-6th grades.

[2.]Names have been changed. Schools will be referred to by their ethnic make-up, except one school will be called ESL school because the Vietnamese children only play with other limited English speaking children.

REFERENCES

Avedon, Elliot M., 1971, The Structural Element of Games. In The Study of Games. Elliot M. Avedon and Brian Sutton-Smith, Eds. New York: John Wiley and Sons. pp. 419-426.

Bateson, Gregory, 1972, A Theory of Play and Fantasy. In Steps to an Ecology of Mind. San Francisco: Chandler. pp. 177-193.

Berlyne, D. E., 1960, Conflict, Arousal and Curiosity. New York: McGraw Hill.

Caillois, Roger, 1961, Man Play and Games. New York: Free Press of Glencoe.

Denzin, Norman K., 1975, Play, Games and Interaction: The Contexts of Childhood Socialization. Sociological Quarterly 16: 458-478.

Geertz, Clifford, 1972, Deep Play: Notes on the Balinese Cockfight. Daedalus, 1-37.

Lever, Janet, 1976, Sex Differences in the Games Children Play. Social Problems 23: 478-487.

McDowell, John, 1974, Interrogative Routines in Mexican-American Children's Folklore. Working Papers in Sociolinguistics 20.

Millar, Susanna, 1968, The Psychology of Play. London: Penguin.

Piaget, Jean, 1962, Play Dreams and Imitation in Childhood. New York: W. W. Norton.

Robinson, Christine, 1976, Survey of Social Conditions of Vietnamese Refugee Families in San Francisco. For Center for Southeast Asian Refugee Resettlement. unpublished manuscript.
    n.d. Sex-Typed Behavior in Children's Spontaneous Play. unpublished manuscript.

Sutton-Smith, Brian, 1971, Play, Games and Controls. In Social Control and Social Change. John P. Scott and Sarah F. Scott, Eds. Chicago: University of Chicago Press. pp. 73-102.
    in press. Games of Order and Disorder. In The Dialectics of Play. Schorndorf: Verlag Karl Hofmann.

_____, and J. M. Roberts, 1962, Child Training and Game Involvement. Ethnology 1:166-185.

_____, R. B. Rosenberg and E. P. Morgan, 1963, The Development of Sex Differences in Play Choice During Preadolescence. Child Development 34:119-126.

## THE EFFECT OF PRESCHOOL PLAY ACTIVITIES ON CHILDREN'S ANTISOCIAL BEHAVIOR

Patrick H. Doyle, University of Houston, Clear Lake City

INTRODUCTION

The majority of preschool programs rely on play activities to engender the desired behavior in children. As the most frequently cited goal of parents sending their children to preschool is for them to learn to "get along," it is of major importance to delineate the relationship between play activities and antisocial behavior. In the absence of such knowledge it is very possible that the provision of certain activities is unwittingly encouraging antagonism among children. Thus the purpose of this study was to investigate the effect of play activities on antisocial behavior. In particular, attention was given to the development of higher order categories of preschool play in order to provide more understanding of the effects of play on antisocial behavior.

# METHOD

The location of the research was the Wayne State University Nursery School (Detroit, Michigan). Comprised of a one-story building, adjoining patio and playground, the preschool provided a typical curriculum including such play activities as sand, art, puzzles and roleplay. The data were collected in the form of videotape chronicles of each child as he or she went through a preschool session. As there were 20 children, 20 videotape chronicles were obtained with a mean of approximately two and one half hours in length. (As is customary in preschools the children attended half-day session.)

Analysis of the 20 videotape chronicles yielded 6,003 social interactions. Identification of the social interactions was accomplished according to the following operational definition: Uninterrupted reciprocative behavior, verbal or non-verbal in which the focal child is half or more involved with a substantially constant social milieu. (An inter-rater reliability check provided an agreement of 88 percent.)

Each social interaction was further classified according to the play activity in which it occurred. Initially 66 play activities were identified from the videotapes, however, these were collapsed into just 14 relatively broad categories which, generally being more abstract, provided a basis for greater understanding of the effects of play on behavior.

The following are the 14 broad play categories, their usual or standing patterns of behavior, and the original play activities collapsed to form them:

1. Individual art props—this category has as its standing behavior pattern the individual's employment in some sort of drawing or construction. This would include cutting, painting, sewing, etc. The play activities comprising the category are: art, art easel, playdough, sewing, fingerpaint and puppet construction.

2. Science props—this one engenders various fine motor manipulations in setting and resetting the equipment. In general the children discover relationships around them by actively probing the environment. The component activities are: balance scale, magnifying glass, battery and bell, magnets, inspecting rock collection, microscope and clock face.

3. Large blocks—this is characterized by stacking the blocks so as to form an enclosure, climbing on them, etc. (Large blocks was one of the initial 66 play activities and was maintained as a distinct play activity.)

4. Small interchangeable blocks—the child interlocks, stacks, or arranges pieces which form a structure or pattern. The designation interchangeable is supposed to emphasize the usefulness one person's small blocks, or otherwise shaped components, have to the others in the acti-

vity. Because one child's "Lincoln logs" can serve equally well in another's project, there ought to be more tendency toward encroachment than in puzzles for example. In the latter activity a piece from one puzzle is of no value in assembling another. The corresponding activities are small blocks, tinker toys, felt-magnetic boards, and wheels and spindle.

5. Puzzles—the standing pattern of behavior is the manipulation and placement of the parts of the puzzle. Besides jigsaw puzzles, sequence story cards were added to this category.

6. Large model props—this category and the next are similar except in the size of the props. Basically the children model adults in playing with life-sized props which are usually adult prerogatives. Playing in the kitchen sink, wearing high heels or a policeman's cap are examples. The activities encompassed are camera, clothing, kitchen and dolls-dollbed.

7. Small model props—like the preceding designation this one concerns imitating adults, except on a smaller scale, as in playing with a dollhouse or race cars on a table. The constituent activities are dollhouse, roadway table set, stand up figures and small vehicles.

8. Roleplay—this is the enacting of an identity or role other than the child's own such as policeman, spiderman, or batman. Roleplay like large blocks was one of the original 66 activities; in this case, however, the designation has been broadened to include puppet play since the children assume the puppet's identity in directing its movements.

9. Waterplay—it is characterized by children filling and pouring from containers into other glasses, buckets, etc. There is also considerable interest and pleasure in the dramatic effects of pouring the water into a container from a few feet above it. Waterplay was one of the original activity designations.

10. Audio-visual displays—the child is usually passively concentrating on props providing either an aural or visual presentation. The corresponding activities are: bulletin board, gerbil cage, displays, individual reading, record listening and tape recorder.

11. Sand—generally the participant is concerned with the molding of different shapes in the sand. This is accomplished with digging tools and kitchen molds. Sand was another one of the original 66 activities.

12. Musical instruments—the child is playing the xylophone, piano, etc. Instrumental music and piano were combined to form this category.

13. Large muscle multiple niche—this involves the child in either jumping, climbing, dancing, pushing someone in a vehicle, swinging, or another muscularly robust activity. The degree of motor behavior is not

sufficient, however, for an activity to fit in this category; the activity must also contain a prop which provides for more than one concurrent participant. For example, the teeter-totter actually requires two people to operate it effectively; likewise, scaling a climber can concurrently involve two and even more at once. The activities determined to entail large muscle behavior as well as provide for more than one performer (i.e. possess multiple niches) are the following: climber, dance-march, go-kart, obstacle course, teeter-totter, climber houses (both indoor and outdoor), climber swings (both indoor and outdoor), pedal motorcycle (two seater), half moon rocker for four children, teeter-totter assembly, ball playing, wooden buggy and long jump-rope. (Long jump-rope is included because the physical length of the rope determines the number of children who can play with it simultaneously. If it is long, then three children are accommodated, one on each end twirling and one in the middle jumping. **Short** jump-ropes, on the other hand, have to be used individually with the jumper holding each end.)

14. Large muscle single niche—such play involves much the same pattern of behavior relative to the use of the large muscles as the preceding category, but has provisions for only one person to use the prop at a time. As indicated above, children cannot sufficiently extend a short jump-rope to permit two to hold the rope and a third to jump, so it must be used individually and is therefore a single niche activity. In addition to short jump-rope, the activities in this category are pedal delivery truck, rocking horse, slide, sweep with broom, tricycling, shoveling-play and ride-on trucks.

Having identified the social interactions by play activity the next step was to determine if the social interactions were more apt to be marred by antisocial behavior in some activities than others. Thus whenever a social interaction occurred, it was coded for the existence of antisocial behavior. The exact frequency was not distinguished, only whether one or more antisocial behaviors occurred.

The following is the antisocial code: malicious, teasing, ridiculing, name calling, quarreling, attacking, pushing, fighting, rejecting, forcibly taking another's place or prop, disrupting another's progress, squealing in protest of another's actions, resisting another's efforts, threatening, or rebuking. (Inter-rater reliability was 94 percent.)

RESULTS

Figure 1 indicates the differences in rates of antisocial behavior across activities. The indicated play activity rate were accomplished in the following fashion. First, for each child and by activity, the number of social interactions involving one or more antisocial behaviors was divided by the total number of social interactions. This obtained the percentage of each child's social interactions in each activity which included antisocial interchanges. Second, these percentages were averaged by activity to obtain a mean antisocial behavior rate for each play activity.

According to Figure 1 the highest rate is that of small model props in which eight children participated. In this type of play, the children averaged one or more antisocial behaviors in more than .440 (44.0 percent) of their social interactions. The lowest rate of antisocial behavior was found in puzzles in which seven children participated. The mean of .040 indicates on the average only one social interaction in twenty-five included antisocial behavior during puzzle play.

The range between the high (small model props) and low (puzzles) play activities is substantial being .400. In relative terms, small model props attained a mean antisocial rate per child more than 10 times that of puzzles.

In order to test the hypothesis that these differences are attributable to the play activity, the logical competing hypothesis was formulated. According to the alternative view, in as much as the children varied in their selection of play activities, the different antisocial rates may be attributable to biased proportions of high and low antisocial-acting children across the play activities. In other words, differential rates in play activities may stem from the particular children participating in a specific activity rather than the nature of the play. To check this possibility the following null hypothesis was developed: children who entered both lower and higher rate play activities will not have higher antisocial behavior rates in the latter.

The data do not bear out the null hypothesis as shown in Table 1. The table presents the results of Wilcoxon matched-pairs signed-ranks tests for all the combinations possible between the upper and lower four ranked activities. Since these tests only compare the scores of matched-pairs, i.e. the same child in two differernt activities, according to the null hypothesis there should be few significances.

## FIGURE 1

### Mean Rate of the Children's Social Interactions in Each Activity Which Contain One or More Antisocial Behaviors

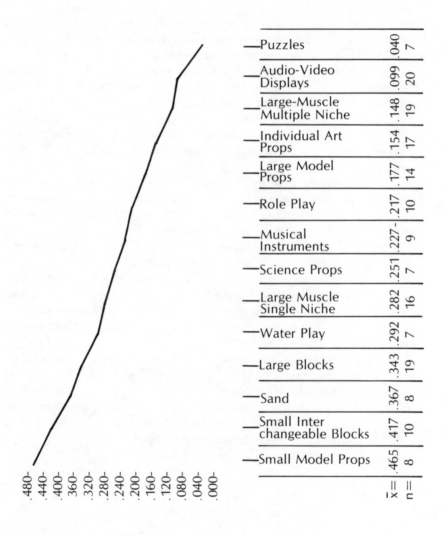

Table 1

Significance Levels of Tests
of Null Hypothesis Comparing Upper and Lower
Four Ranked Activities

| | Play Activity | Lower | Four | |
|---|---|---|---|---|
| | | Individual Art Props | Large Muscle Multiple Niche | Audio-Visual Displays | Puzzles |
| **Upper** | Small Model Props | .0398* (5) | NS (6) | .0398* (5) | |
| | Small Interchangeable Blocks | NS (7) | NS (6) | | |
| **Four** | Sand | NS (9) | .0232* (6) | .0232* (6) | |
| | Large Blocks | .0196* (13) | .0054** (13) | .0060** (12) | .0398* (5) |

Notes:

Figure in parentheses is number of untied pairs in Wilcoxon calculation.

Empty cell indicates insufficient number (fewer than four) of untied pairs for significance test.

*Indicates .05 level of significance for one tail test.

**Indicates .01 level of significance for one tail test.

Though there are 16 combinations possible, insufficient sample size reduced the total to 12. However, in fully eight of the 12 tests the null hypothesis was rejected at the .05 or better level of significance. Thus these data seem to lend support to the alternative hypothesis that involvement in antisocial behavior is to an important degree a function of the play activity.

Table 2 is a summary of the findings in terms of the clustering of the play activities into general designations such as high or low with respect to engendering antisocial behavior. These designations are determined by the discontinuities in the rates which are ranked in descending order. This table aids in making the results more comprehensible by organizing the results into only five categories rather than 14 individual antisocial rates. In addition, it provides an ordinal value for each activity to compare to the findings of other studies.

## DISCUSSION

To further assess the validity of these findings it is important to make comparisons with previous studies. Hence, Updegraf and Herbst (1933) report that between clay and small blocks the latter resulted in more uncooperative behavior such as "successful and unsuccessful attempts to take other's material." This seems to agree with the Doyle findings in which small blocks ranked second while individual art props including clay was eleventh.

Table 3 graphically depicts the degree of agreement between Doyle's antisocial behavior rankings and those of Green's quarrels (defined as "antagonism...expressed verbally, by argument or calling names, by physical force, such as kicking, pulling or biting, or spatially by pulling out the tongue and making faces" [1933:339]).

Only the activities in the two studies which are common to both were selected for comparison. Lines connect the activities which correspond to each other in the two studies. More than one line may connect activity classifications because of one being more inclusive than the other. Thus small interchangeable blocks and puzzles both connect with fine manipulation. Whether activities were the same was determined by consulting the primary source for the description of the activity. The general designations of the tendency to engender antisocial behavior from Table 2 are parenthetically indicated for the Doyle activities. In the activities from the other study the parenthetical designations are those which would be predicted from the Doyle study.

## TABLE 2

### Tendency for an Activity to Engender Antisocial Behavior During Social Interaction

| Activity | Rate | Designation |
|---|---|---|
| Small Model Props | .4648 | Very High |
| Small Interchangeable Blocks | .4168 | Very High |
| Sand | .3673 | High |
| Large Blocks | .3430 | High |
| Water Play | .2915 | Moderate |
| Large Muscle Single Niche | .2823 | Moderate |
| Science Props | .2513 | Moderate |
| Musical Instruments | .2269 | Moderate |
| Role Play | .2167 | Moderate |
| Large Model Props | .1766 | Low |
| Individual Art Props | .1538 | Low |
| Large Muscle Multiple Niche | .1478 | Low |
| Audio-Visual Displays | .0992 | Low |
| Puzzles | .0400 | Very Low |

It is immediately apparent from the table that one activity pairing is grossly discrepant across the two sets of findings. This is small interchangeable blocks and the fine manipulation activity whose connecting line intersects almost all the others in the table. Otherwise a high degree of correspondence between the two studies exists; the only predicted tendency out of order involves the same pair.

This discrepancy is readily explainable. Fine manipulation is a more general activity category than used here for the same play, so it contains not only small interchangeable blocks but individual art props and puzzles as well. Though lumped together by Green these types of play are substantially different with respect to engendering antisocial behavior. For example, on the surface puzzles appear very similar to small interchangeable blocks; both require the participant to sit at a table and finely manipulate small props to accomplish an interlocking structure. However, several crucial physical factors distinguish puzzles from play such as Lincoln logs and tinker toys.

TABLE 3
Comparison of Findings of Doyle and Green

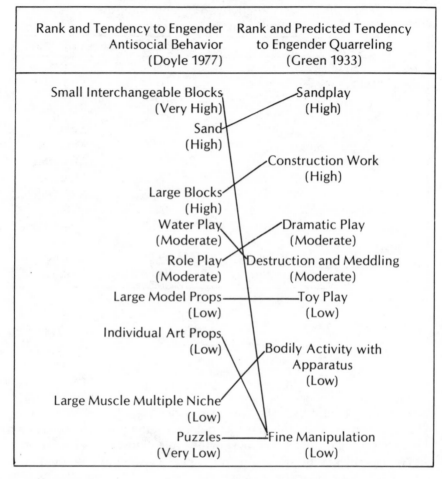

| Rank and Tendency to Engender Antisocial Behavior (Doyle 1977) | Rank and Predicted Tendency to Engender Quarreling (Green 1933) |
|---|---|
| Small Interchangeable Blocks (Very High) | Sandplay (High) |
| Sand (High) | |
| | Construction Work (High) |
| Large Blocks (High) | |
| Water Play (Moderate) | Dramatic Play (Moderate) |
| Role Play (Moderate) | Destruction and Meddling (Moderate) |
| Large Model Props (Low) | Toy Play (Low) |
| Individual Art Props (Low) | |
| | Bodily Activity with Apparatus (Low) |
| Large Muscle Multiple Niche (Low) | |
| Puzzles (Very Low) | Fine Manipulation (Low) |

First, in puzzles the pieces involved are **not interchangeable**. Those from one puzzle are usually not serviceable in another. Psychologically this physical feature appears to make considerable difference with respect to engendering antisocial behavior. In playing with interchangeable blocks dispossessing someone else of his pieces can be a path, while giving up your own is a barrier, to a goal. In fact, the longest duration conflict observed in the 1800 minutes of children's pre-school days occurred in Lincoln logs and involved contesting for a prop which one child wanted and another was already using in his project. In contrast, one child's puzzle pieces are of no value to the assembling of someone else's puzzle: if anything, the inclusion of pieces from another puzzle are apt to confuse the child's efforts and therefore ownership of them is actually a barrier to the goal of the activity. In these terms it can be seen why, though both are fine manipulation activities, one could be very high in antisocial behavior and the other very low.

Another physical feature which distinguishes small interchangeable blocks and puzzles is the precariousness of the projects. Whereas puzzles lay flat on the table top, block structures are built to a considerable extent perpendicular to it. Puzzles are expanded horizontally, and block structures vertically so to speak. This places the latter's center of gravity in a precarious position; a passerby only needs to lightly bump the structure to dislodge parts or topple the entire effort. Therefore, inspecting and handling a block structure by other children is likely to trigger a confrontation. So on account of the physical precariousness of blocks, other children showing interest in the structure are likely to be seen as threats to the original child's building goals. This is not the case in puzzles.

The horizontal, as opposed to vertical, expansion of puzzles also results in the project being less visible. Children must be quite close to the puzzle itself to appreciate it, consequently there is less of a tendency for other to be attracted to it. The situation is similar to a sign in a store window which having fallen down ceases to be seen except by the individuals in close proximity to the window. This suggests a puzzle is somewhat less likely to foster competition for props, simply because less children notice it than blocks.

In summary, the physical dimensions of noninterchangeability of prop pieces and the vertical versus horizontal expansion involved in fitting the pieces together appear to manifestly distinguish puzzles and small interchangeable blocks; though otherwise quite similar, these features make them diametric opposites in antisocial behavior levels. Thus, in terms of antisocial behavior, small interchangeable blocks is not comparable to puzzles and both should not be included in fine manipulative activities. If we delete the small interchangeable blocks and fine manipulation pairing then the agreement between the two studies is quite high indeed; the ordinal values agree perfectly.

The next comparison is with the Parten (1932) study which did not systematically delineate the different activities' antisocial densities, although it does describe the behavior which was usual in each one. The only one in which there was mention of antisocial behavior was sand. Behavior there was described as including "smashing other's mold," "seizing his vessel" and "disputing boundary lines." This would tend to indicate that sand was the highest in antisocial behavior among the

Parten activities and this would have been predicted from the Doyle data. Of the activities common to the two studies sand was apparently highest in both Doyle and Parten.

Based on the interchangeability principle sand would have been predicted to be high in antisociality at any rate. Like Lincoln logs, sand is building material which is equally useable by all the participants in their respective projects. Hence, someone else's sand could be a path to the goal of completing a project; if sand grains are conceptualized as very fine pieces of building material sand play could even be classified under small interchangeable blocks.

There is substantial agreement between Doyle and the other studies which together span a total of four decades. This is particularly so in terms of agreements in tendencies such as high or low as opposed to specific ranks. Consequently it should be concluded that antisocial behavior is activity related.

The capability of the play activity to materially affect antisocial behavior has obvious implications. It first forces a reevaluation of the tendency to attribute the behavior to the child; a high rate of antisocial behavior may to a large extent be the result of participating in activities in which other individuals are likely to be barriers rather than paths. Thus, the tendency referred to earlier for children attending preschool to increase their antisocial aggression could be due to inadvertent activity programming. Consequently it might be possible to reverse or at least modify this trend by simply adjusting activities.

Moreover, rather than waiting until problems arise it would seem incumbent on programmers to evaluate their preschool curricula in terms of the presence of activities which are likely to induce not only antisocial but any undesirable behavior. However, to adequately accomplish this would require delineating the underlying dimensions which would mean further research. So it would appear that the present knowledge should be applied in the preschool while additional research furnishes increasingly effective alternatives.

## REFERENCES

Green, L., 1933, Friendship and Quarrels Among Preschool Children. Child Development 4:327-352.

Parten, M., 1932, Social Participation Among Pre-school Children. Journal of Abnormal and Social Psychology 27:243-269.

Updegraf, R., and E. Herkst, 1933, An Experimental Study of the Social Behavior Stimulated in Young Children by Certain Play Materials. Journal of Genetic Psychology 42:373.

## THE DEVELOPMENT OF ENVIRONMENTAL COMPETENCE IN GIRLS AND BOYS[1]

Susan Saegert and Roger Hart, City University of New York

While carrying out research on the development of children's use, knowledge and experience of the landscape, one of the authors dis-·covered surprising differences in the activities, and in particular the manipulation of the environment, by boys and girls (Hart in press). Commonly, learning is studied in the more obvious location, where education occurs—in schools. It was a premise of Hart's research, how-ever, that in the child's learning about the physical world (local geo-graphy in particular) and, in fact in all aspects of behavior, the out-of-school environment is an equally important ground for learning. In play, games and work around the home, girls and boys are given very different opportunities to experience and learn. Having made these ob-servations it became clear through discussion that in many other aspects of children's activities and intellectual performance there were similar dramatic differences between the sexes. In this paper we review some of the differences in the environmental experiences of boys and girls and relate these to a much studied intellectual domain, that of spatial ability. We believe both of these are significantly affected by the different attitudes, rules and expectancies governing the lives of the two sexes.

### THE SPATIAL ACTIVITY OF BOYS AND GIRLS

The aspect of behavior which first led Hart to look more closely at the different behaviors of boys and girls, in what was primarily a develop-mental study, were clear differences in the parentally defined spatial range restrictions of children over six years of age. This alone is an in-teresting observation for there is no biological basis for such different treatments. In reviewing the evidence on differences in physical strength, Tanner concludes that only at adolescence do boys become "more adapted for the tasks of hunting, fighting, and manipulating all sorts of heavy objects" (1970:95). Even then it is not clear how much this greater adaptation is the result of different childhood experiences. Findings from studies on the activity level of boys and girls are not very consistent. It is true that seldom have girls been found to have a higher activity level but, more important, the summary of evidence suggests no sex differences during the first year of life (Maccoby and Jacklin 1974). This leads us to the central concern of this paper: to what extent do parents' attitudes about boys and girls lead them to make different environmental experiences available and to encourage or restrict certain activities.

Until recently, studies of child development commonly failed to look at sex differences at all. One of the reasons for this has been the influence of the most prevalent psychoanalytic theory of sex role learning—"identification". According to this theory, advanced by Freud and developed by many others, children only begin to identify with one parent or the other after they have noticed the difference between sexes and identified themselves as belonging to one group or the other. Following this group of theories, such identification could not occur until the "phallic stage"—about three years of age. Because of this, and because sex role learning was considered to be a process which can occur only with the full awareness of the child, it would have been considered meaningless to study sex differences before the child had identified with one of the parents. In recent years, however, numerous alternative theories of sex role learning have been introduced. Also, many behavioral scientists have come to realize that boys and girls may be differentially treated by adults in many ways according to their sex, even though the children themselves may be unaware of sex differences, their own sex category, and the appropriate sex role they are expected to adopt. A study by Moss (1967) suggests that this differential treatment of boys and girls in the first year of life is unlikely to be a simple matter of studying which behaviors occur spontaneously and which are the result of different parental treatments; it is more likely to be a complex interactive process. She found that at the third week of life boys were more irritable than girls and hence, their mothers spent more time responding to them. The mothers also stressed boys muscles more and stimulated/aroused them more.

Lewis (1972) has attempted to examine some of the various ways in which girls and boys are responded to differently from a young age. He stated that parents are more likely to talk to girls throughout infancy. However, behaviors such as touching, holding, kissing and rocking vary with the age of the infant. From birth he found that boys were more likely to receive such handling, but after six months the pattern was reversed. At two years, he found boys more willing to venture further away from the mother. Lewis concluded that during the first two years of life, socialization takes place to wean boys away from maintaining physical contact with others to a much greater extent than for girls.

Studies of child-rearing, both by psychologists and anthropologists, commonly use "restrictedness" versus "autonomy-granting" as one index of socialization practice. Surprisingly, in their excellent comprehensive review of the literature on sex differences, Maccoby and Jacklin concluded that "the bulk of evidence is that there is little or no difference in the socialization of boys and girls when it comes to independence-granting" (1974:319). They even report a tendency in the preschool years towards a greater restriction of boys but note that the findings between studies are not consistent (Hatfield **et al.** 1967, Radin 1973, Sears **et al.** 1957, Baumrind 1971). Further evidence from these studies suggests that both mothers and fathers are more likely to follow up these restrictions with punishment for boys than they are for girls (Hatfield **et al.** 1967, Baumrind 1971). Few of the studies reviewed by Maccoby and Jacklin included investigation of parental restrictions and punishments regarding spatial range, and then only as one question among many given to parents. Also, most of the studies relied on parental interviews, and of those few which observed behavior, it was only for brief periods in the home or in a nursery school. We are familiar with five studies which they did not cite, concerning the spatial ranges of older children, and each has suggested significantly more liberal definitions of spatial range for boys than for girls. Each study differs somewhat in the manner in which the data were collected. In 1972, as part of a larger study on the environmental behavior of all children aged four to twelve in a New England town, Hart asked each child to describe "the area you are allowed to play in outside your house by yourself, without asking special permission from your parents". The children found it easy to describe this area using environmental details and, because of his familiarity with the environment, Hart was able to draw the boundary lines on a large-scale aerial photograph. Follow-up interviews with the parents of six families representing sixteen children, confirmed the accuracy of these descriptions. Additionally, the children were asked to describe those places they were allowed to go to with "special permission" from their mother or father. This data also reveals significant sex differences, but because there were numerous qualifications given by the children depending on whether other children were with the child, the day of the week, and the time of the day, the evidence is less satisfactory. From a comparison of the means in Table 1, it seems there is little difference in range according to sex amongst the youngest children. It was not possible to make statistical comparisons for each age group as the sample was too small for some ages, but in comparing the five to eight year olds with the nine to twelve year olds, the older group does seem to exhibit greater differences.

Table 1
Averages of Areas Girls and Boys May Play Within
**Without** Having to Ask Special Permission

|  | Girls | Boys |
|---|---|---|
| Grades 1-3 | $\bar{X} = 1.38$ (N = 12) | $\bar{X} = 1.90$ (N = 23) |
| Grades 4-7 | $\bar{X} = 2.97$ (N = 19) | $\bar{X} = 4.77$ (N = 15) |

This finding is congruent with that in a similar study by Tindal (1971). In her study of "home range", second and fourth grade girls and boys in suburban and urban environments of similar economic backgrounds were asked to draw on an aerial photograph the places he or she walks or cycles to, and the paths taken. Measurement was then made of the total "non-redundant path length" (i.e., no paths, whether walked or cycled, were included more than once in the summation). No investigation was made of parental restrictions but as can be seen from Table 2, not only are boys ranges significantly larger than the girls, but the home range of fourth grade (ten year old) boys over girls is proportionately larger than that of second grade (eight year old) boys over girls.

Table 2
Mean Home Range of Black Elementary School Children
(Mean given in feet, standard deviation in parentheses*)

| Sub-Group | No. of children | Mean Home Range |
|---|---|---|
| Urban 2nd grade girls | 12 | 2833 (1157) |
| Urban 2nd grade boys | 13 | 4128 (1342) |
| Urban 4th grade girls | 13 | 3518 (1009) |
| Urban 4th grade boys | 12 | 5816 (2923) |
| All Urban | 50 | 4074 |
| Suburban 2nd grade girls | 12 | 3962 (1781) |
| Suburban 2nd grade boys | 13 | 5209 (1378) |
| Suburban 4th grade girls | 13 | 3905 (1293) |
| Suburban 4th grade boys | 12 | 6207 (3134) |
| All Suburban | 50 | 4810 |

*Extracted from Tindal (1971:31)

In the study of child-training in rural Puerto Rico, Landy (1957:136) had similar findings. On a scale to measure restrictiveness of physical mobility based on ratings of interviews with mothers, the median for boys was 2.5 and for girls 3.0 (where 4.0 was "extreme restriction"). Landy also investigated frequency of checking upon the children by their mothers and found a median of 3.0 for boys and 3.5 for girls (where 4.0 is high). No data are provided on the development of this difference, but it is noted that after six to seven years of age when utilitarian roles are found for the children, while girls become less "clingy" and become more of a "companion" to the mother, they are not given as greater freedom of physical mobility as are the boys. This begins to suggest one of the dynamic factors in these differences. The mother, usually responsible for the caretaking of children, brings girls more quickly into line with the woman's role in the home than the mother or father does for boys. Hart found in New England that while boys and girls are expected to run errands and do some chores, domestic chores (particularly staying around the house and looking after young children) are commonly the duty of the daughters, not the sons.

Two other studies of the spatial range of children are known to us, both of them with Bantu-speaking societies in Kenya (Munroe and Munroe 1971, Nerlove **et al.** 1971). The purpose of the studies was to explore the relationship between environmental experience and spatial ability. These studies employed a more direct measure of spatial range than either the child-reported parental restrictions of Hart's study, the child-reported actual "home ranges" of Tindal's study, or Landy's parent interview. In the first study, fifteen boys and fifteen girls between the ages of three and seven were sorted in pairs on the basis of age matching. Each of these sample members were then observed a total of twenty times in their natural setting around the village and their location recorded. Analysis of children's distances away from their respective homes, revealed a significant tendency for males to be farther away from home than their age-matched female counterparts. However, these scores included observations of the children when they had been instructed by an older person to carry out some assigned task away from the home, such as fetching water. Just as Hart had found it necessary in his study to distinguish between "free range" and "range with special permission", so Munroe and Munroe found that observations involving directed activities should be separated for study. They therefore went over their data again and extracted only those observations made of children during their "free" or "undirected" time. They found in thirteen of the fifteen pairings that the male was rated as more distant from home on the average than the female ($p < .01$, sign test). In addition, the proportion of free time was analyzed. This was found to be greater in boys in only nine of thirteen cases; an insignificant difference until they looked more closely at the ages and found that in eight cases out of the nine oldest pairs, boys were as free as, or freer than, the girls. In the second study, using the same techniques with another Bantu-speaking group, "free range" of children proved to be non-significant in differences between boys and girls, but because the activities of this society were very different the analysis was modified. It was concluded that although herding was a directed activity, it left the child relatively free to meander to different places over varying routes and hence, was effectively the same as "free range".

In summarizing the state of our knowledge on sex differences in spatial behavior, it seems there is need for further study. There is sufficient evidence to question Maccoby and Jacklin's belief that no sex differences exist in independence granting. Maccoby and Jacklin were lead to their conclusion by the fact that most of the studies reviewed were of four to five year old children; this is easily the most studied group in child psychology, largely because it is the most accessible population for study! The studies by Hart, Tintal, and Munro and Munroe, suggest a gradual increase in the boy-girl differences with age. Even a postscript comment by Maccoby and Jacklin points in this direction. In reporting the work of Newson and Newson on child-rearing in Nottingham, England, they note that although in their extensive research on four year olds, no sex difference had been found in the range of movement inside and outside the home, personal communication with the authors had revealed that in the longitudinal study the girls, now seven years old, were being treated differently from the boys (Maccoby and Jacklin 1974). They were receiving more "chaperonage", such as being met after school, than the boys. Their whereabouts must be know more than with the boys and they were more often in the company of an adult. The suggestion by Maccoby and Jacklin is that the parents have a greater fear of molestation of the girls and that this is an anticipation of further chaperonage in adolescence. The informal observations by Hart on this question in the New England village, were that while this may have been in the minds of some parents, the greater restraint of girls was related to a whole complex of attitudes to boys, versus girls. The most striking feature of Hart's interviews with the children about parental range restrictions and the one which led him to first notice the many sex differences in his data, was the ambiguous response he received from the boys as opposed to the girls. Boys would describe one boundary and then give the name of another place beyond the boundary. On further questioning, it would commonly be revealed that the rules, usually made by both parents, were in fact administered by the mother only, and that she often turned a "blind-eye" when her boy breaks the boundary: "well, she knows that I go, but I'm not supposed to". Such comments as this were most frequently made by the older boys in the village. Again from casual observations it was noted that if the boy should get into trouble outside the formally agreed upon range, such as falling into the river, he must be ready to be punished. Implicit in this special treatment given to boys by their mother, seems to be the attitude that "boys will be boys", meaning that we must expect them to explore more, engage in more rough play, be more physically active and even get into trouble more, but that they must expect punishment equal to, or even greater than, that given to girls. Such are their attitudes toward the making of a man.

## THE CONSTRUCTIVE ACTIVITIES OF GIRLS AND BOYS

In his developmental study of children's relationship to the physical environment, Hart found another marked difference between the behavior of most boys and girls. Boys modify the landscape more frequently and more effectively. For example, in creating settings for their play, boys build physical structures much more frequently than do girls. Girls also have houses, forts and so on, but they physically manipulate the environment less. More frequently they modify the spaces in their imagination, so that bushes become walls, lateral branches of trees make excellent shelves, and rocks are used as seats. Such imaginative creation of spaces also occurs with boys, but commonly after about seven years of age, boys build forts and other structures with walls, windows, seats and even roofs. When girls do build such places, rarely do they create walls even though considerable effort may go towards the detailed elaboration of the interior with drapes, bottles, pots, pans, etc. None of the structures built entirely by girls had fixed walls or roofs. Also, boys made many more models in the dirt, manipulated streams with dams and channels, made and managed gardens, built sled runs and jumps, and in general made their mark on the landscape more than girls. On the few occasions observed by Hart where girls did create models in the dirt, alone or with other girls, they built models of houses and rooms and decorated the interiors and the pathways, while boys built cities, highways, airports and racetracks. When girls were found in these latter activities, it was in play with boys. On one occasion, while interviewing all of the children in the school about their "favorite places", Hart was pleasantly surprised to find a fourth grade girl describing a "giant city" that had been built at the back of her house. In pursuing this interesting discussion, however, his pleasure was quickly subdued as the girl explained that it was built by an older boy and that she could not possibly have built anything like this by herself because she was a girl and "only boys know how to build things". She described how, because of this, she and her younger sister only helped make the roads and cleaned things up. Why should an extremely confident and competent girl, rated at the top of her grade in school, speak in this way? We believe the answer lies largely in the multiple reminders girls and boys receive from adults and from peers as to what are and are not suitable activities for them. But first we shall review a well known alternative description and exploration of the play constructions of boys and girls.

As part of a long-range developmental study of children, Erik Erikson, a psychologist, devised a simple technique to assist him in the preparation of a dynamic biography of 75 boys and girls, then aged twelve years (Erikson 1951). Each child would enter a room with him and find a square table and two shelves with toys—blocks, people, cars and animals. Erikson told them that because he would like to know what kind of moving pictures children would make if they had the chance, he would like them to construct an "exciting" scene out of an imaginary moving picture. On completion of the scene, the children told him what they had created. Although it was not the purpose of the study, Erikson, like Hart, received a definite impression of differences in the constructions of girls from those of boys. After the presence or absence of certain configurations, such as enclosures, bridges, streets, etc., had been rated in each of these scenes, he summarized the masculine and feminine variables in constructions. Typically characteristic of boys creations were "elaborate buildings", "complicated structures", the "channelization of traffic through tunnels and street crossings", and the "erection of high structures" (1951:111). In comparison, girls constructions typically included "simple walls which merely enclose interiors, with an emphasis by ornamentation on the vestibular access to the interior", "interiors without walls", and "intrusion into such an interior of a dangerous or mischievous animal or male creature" (1951:111). In summary, then, the similarities with Hart's observations are quite striking: "Boys more often than girls erect buildings, cover them with roofs, provide them with ornaments and other objects which stick out: towers, guns, etc." (1951:102). But unlike Hart, Erikson finds explanation entirely in the psychodynamics associated with the different sex organs, and sex impulses of boys and girls:

> Without prejudging discussion, one basic fact can be stated now, namely the analogy between the sex differences in play configurations and the primary physiological sex-differences, that is in the male the emphasis on

the external, the erectable, the intrusive, and the mobile—in the female, on the internal, on the vestibular, on the static, on what is contained and endangered in the interior (Tanner and Inhelder 1955:112).

While we have no basis to entirely dispute Erikson's ideas as to why boys tend to build more elaborate structures and girls commonly create interior spaces, we doubt that symbolism is the only or even the prime reason. Social direction regarding the suitability of activities for one sex or the other is so pervasive that construction skills, practices and interests are bound to differ in a free play situation, regardless of questions of sexual awareness and the sex urges of boys and girls. Girls are being prepared to work within these interior spaces and in their play reflect this role, while boys are being prepared for their adult roles as creators and builders. Specifically with housing, Erikson should have noticed that girls are encouraged from early on to decorate and to play out social events in interiors—notably in dolls' houses, while boys are encouraged to build them. This discussion cannot be supported by hard evidence though for many persons, reflection on their own early childhood should offer support for these comments. It is important that we begin to try to understand some of the powerful effects of socialization. Erikson's data has been too easily picked up uncritically by too many persons. Gesell and Ilg (1942) also found from observations of children that boys are better at block-building activity. But the information we have reveals that blocks are more commonly provided to boys than girls. It is, therefore, not surprising. If we wish to truly evaluate the constructive ability of girls as well as boys, we would either have to establish equivalent skills in the girls' world and evaluate boys and girls ability with these, or preferably offer a training program in which girls used blocks as much as boys, before being evaluated. To our knowledge, neither of these research approaches have been utilized. What, for example, would be the result of a study of constructive ability in which the test involved cutting out and sewing clothes for a doll?

The evidence that there are different preferences for toys by boys and by girls, even during the first year of life, is substantial (Bronson 1971, Goldberg and Lewis 1969, Jacklin **et al.** 1973, Kaminski 1973), but it is not clear which attributes of the toys influence their selection. However, in reviewing the evidence from experimental studies with children under two years of age, Maccoby and Jacklin are able to conclude that the manipulability of a toy is not related to sex differences in preference. But certainly after two years of age boys and girls develop very different interests and attitudes. Parents commonly speak as though such differences are inherited rather than learned from themselves and from others. In a study of pre-school socialization, Pitcher found that:

165

Parents commented often on the boys' preoccupation with bulldozers, trucks, cement mixers. The boy, as the parents reported, was interested not only in objects but in making them work (1974:81).

The very clear preferences revealed by older children are likely to have been learned due to the selective provision of toys by parents, and from other children. Unfortunately though, there has been little investigation of the selectivity of parents purchases of toys for children and to what extent these purchases are based on preferences established by the children or vice versa (Maccoby and Jacklin 1974). Maccoby and Jacklin seem surprised that blocks are thought of as "boyish" and suggests that societies may begin to label as "masculine" those toys that differentially attract boys, even if there is no relationship to a masculine role, as with firemans' hats or toy trucks (Maccoby and Jacklin 1974:278). This surprises us, for building is clearly thought of as a male activity in this society, as are the associated skills of design, engineering, mathematics and the skilled construction trades; blocks are most "boyish" as the first tool in the development of these "manly" trades. This selective use of toys is found in the schools as well as in homes. In an "area usage" test for the sex-typing of four year olds, boys spent more time in that part of a large nursery school play-room where blocks, wheel toys and carpenter tools were found, in comparison to girls whose time was spent rather in the dress-up clothes, cooking equipment and doll house areas (Sears 1963). Some of these investigators have suggested that these different uses of toys (they might better be called tools) influence the development of children's interests, attitudes and intelligence, but direct evidence on this is lacking. Pitcher (1974) also found in the "free drawings" and "tell me a story" exercises, a greter interest in "persons" from girls and in "things" from boys. In the drawings, over 50% of the girls said they had drawn persons, only 15% of the boys did so. The boys drew in just as great a proportion—cars, park benches, trains and trees.

In summarizing the various findings in the environmental behavior of children, girls are constrained both in their movements and in the nature of their manipulation of the environment. It seems that girls are practicing and being prepared for roles in the home and boys for roles outside.

## SEX DIFFERENCES IN SPATIAL ABILITY

The different amounts of self-directed spatial exploration and opportunities for free manipulation of the environment that seem to characterize girls and boys, especially as they get older, quite probably has serious consequences for the development of certain cognitive abilities. Very strong evidence exists indicating that boys, by adolescence, have begun to demonstrate greater ability to visualize spatial configurations and to solve problems requiring visual-spatial skills.

All commonly used tests of intelligence and ability for children and adults contain a spatial subtest such as the Block Design Subtest of the Wechsler Intelligence Scale for Children, the Spatial Subtest of the PMA, and the various spatial subtests of the Differential Aptitudes Test. Factor analytic studies of mental abilities have for a long time indicated the existence of a visual-spatial dimension of mental abilities (e.g., Thurstone 1944, Michael **et al.** 1957, Werdelin 1961). The spatial subtest of the Thurstone Primary Mental Abilities (PMA) Test includes the following tasks: (1) a standard American flag is presented with a set from which the subject must choose the same figure rotated out of four alternatives also containing mirror reversals; (2) the subject is presented with a drawing of a system of gears, and asked to describe the resultant motion in other parts of the system when a specified motion occurs in one part; (3) the subject must judge from a two-dimensional picture of a pile of blocks the number of surfaces that would be visible from a different perspective than his own. Other spatial abilities tests have concerned copying geometric figures, maze performance, perception of distance and spatial relationships, and aiming at a target.

Generally males excel in these various tests of spatial ability as has been amply documented in reviews for the past twenty years (e.g., Anastasi 1958, Fruchter 1954, Maccoby and Jacklin 1974, Sandstrom 1953, Tyler 1965, Werdelin 1961). Interestingly, sex differences are rarely found until about the age of eight. Prior to this time girls are just as likely to excel as boys; males do not establish a clear superiority in spatial abilities until adolescence (Maccoby and Jacklin 1974). Though most of these spatial tests are not considered as measures of analytic ability, these differences in spatial ability seem also to be related to differences in mathematical ability, thus giving them increased significance for the child's cognitive growth (e.g., Werdelin 1961, Mellone 1944, Guilford **et al.**, 1951).

The questions of the existence of male superiority on another type of spatial test, that of field independence, has become something of a **cause celebre** among researchers as the whole issue of sex differences has become increasingly political. This set of tests, designed by Witkin and his colleagues (1962), purports to measure analytic ability. Although the test consists of several subtests (the Rod and Frame Test [RFT], the Embedded Figures Test [EFT], the Body Adjustment Test and Block Design, sex differences in favor of the male tend to occur only on the visual measure of the RFT, EFT, and Block Design. In her review article, Sherman (1967) cites numerous studies in which these measures of field independence are shown to correlate highly with non-analytic spatial abilities. In a similar vein, Maccoby and Jacklin (1974) point out that other tests that could be though of as a measure of analytic ability do not find males performing better. In fact, one such test, anagram solution, which clearly involves breaking sets and restructuring, reveals female superiority. As with the other measures of spatial ability, sex differences do not become established until adolescence.

There are a number of reasons why the field independence questions have been so hotly debated and why it is of special relevance to our concern with the environmental experience of girls and boys. Witkin **et al.**, (1962) used the concept of articulation to distinguish the operation necessary for field independence. This means the ability to differentiate figures from ground; the process involved is like that involved in **any kind of problem solving** (although it could be seen as a perceptual task) in that an organization must be projected onto the field by the person in order to perform well. Witkin and his colleagues advanced the hypothesis that encouragement of autonomy and support for independent endeavor, together with a secure environment, provides the developmental background for a field independent person. In their original work with an all-male sample, Witkin and his colleagues found a relationship between maternal attitudes and behavior supportive of autonomy, and field independence in the child. Thus, it seems that this issue has assumed importance because field independence has been presented as a general cognitive skill representing what is thought of in colloquial terms as the ability "to think for one's self" and prototypic of all types of problem solving. Secondly, the character trait it is taken to represent, and the socialization seen as relevant, are central to our concepts of stereotypic male and female traits. Such attributes as competence and independence are more often used to describe males than females; further, these are seen as traits that characterize the ideal mentally healthy adult (Broverman **et al.** 1970). When questions of changes in the roles and ideal conceptions of women and men are raised, those negatively disposed to such changes used evidence of normative differences in abilities to justify the naturalness and rightness of current sex roles and stereotype (e.g., Garai and Scheinfeld 1968, Hutt 1972).

Clearly the ability to visualize and analyze spatial relationships is of value generally and is perhaps critical for certain occupations like engineering and architecture. Its relationship to other skills, such as mathematical reasoning and general problem-solving, makes its even more desirable as an attribute. How this ability develops seems to be a complex process.

The evidence concerning the heritability of spatial abilities supports a genetic explanation to some degree. Correlational studies reveal stronger relationships between the spatial ability scores of fathers and daughters, and mothers and sons. Further, there is little correlation between fathers' and sons' scores, whereas a weak correlation exists for mothers and daughters (Stafford 1961, Corah 1965, Hartlage 1970, Bock and Kolakowski 1973). This all suggests that high spatial ability is determined by a recessive gene carried on the X chromosome. That is, the mother's trait will determine that of the son; further, boys, having only one X chromosome, will be more likely to display the high ability trait because of the absence of a second X chromosome bearing a dominant, lower ability gene. Bock and Kolakowski (1973) argue that spatial ability has two components, one genetically sex-linked and the other not. Their predictions, based on this hypothesis, are well supported by their data. These authors estimate that approximately 50% of all men and 25% of all women would show this trait. As Maccoby and Jacklin (1974) note in their review, this percentage of women still far excedes that of women in engineering and architecture.

An additional physiological argument has been presented for the hormonal determination of spatial abilities (Broverman **et al.** 1968). In a comment on this article, Singer and Montgomery (1969) present the theoretical contradictions involved in this argument as well as much incompatible evidence. Kagan and Kogan (1970) and Maccoby and Jacklin (1974) further criticize Broverman and his colleagues' position and present recent non-supportive evidence.

Despite the evidence for the heritability of spatial skills, data on the training of such skills also suggests that it is in part learned. Van Voorhis (1941) and Brinkmann (1966) found that special instruction in spatial visualization significantly improved children's performance in mathematics. Kato (1965) and Goldstein and Chance (1965) found that subjects performed better on spatial tasks after direct training. Unfortunately, no analyses of sex differences were performed in any but the Goldstein and Chance study. These investigators found that the original superiority of males on the EFT was erased by training of both males and females. Females gained proportionally more from the training experience, thus equalizing the scores of the two sexes, even though males also improved.

These training studies all involved classroom exercise-type interventions rather than experience in the child's daily environment. When we turn our attention to the kinds of spatial experiences a child has in his or her daily life, the issue of sex role socialization begins to merge with that of the learning of spatial abilities. If we designed a more thorough environmental enrichment program, girls would be encouraged to explore and manipulate their environments freely. This might easily conflict with parents' ideas of feminine behavior. In Hart's study, we have seen that the boys in a New England village are much more free to roam and to explore their environment that are the girls, and that the quantity and quality of their building endeavors differs greatly for the two sexes. Perhaps related to this, early analysis of their ability to spatially represent the physical environment in model-map form indicates superior performance from the boys. Each of these trends are more apparent in late childhood and adolescence than for younger children.

ENVIRONMENTAL EXPERIENCE AND INTELLECTUAL PERFORMANCE

To our knowledge, no studies exist specifically relating the environmental experience of Western children to the development of their spatial abilities. A number of studies in other cultures do, however, address this issue. In the two studies of African tribes reported above (Nerlove **et al.** 1971, Munroe and Munroe 1971) in which the male children in both tribes ranged further from home in their daily activities, the males also performed better on several tests of spatial ability. Within sexes, those girls and boys who had larger free activity ranges also performed better on the spatial tests. These studies are only correlational in nature but certainly suggest the possibility that the greater restriction of girls activities in their environments is related to their lower spatial ability. Not until girls, previously demonstrating poor spatial ability and constricted activity ranges, are allowed and encouraged to use a greater range, then again tested, can the question really begin to be answered.

A cross-cultural comparison of American Eskimo and African Temne subjects on field independence provides some relevant evidence (Berry 1966, MacArthur 1967). Overall, the permissive, autonomy-encouraging Eskimos demonstrate more field independence than do the traditional, more authoritarian Temne tribe. But more interesting for our purpose, no sex differences were found among Eskimos while the usual male advantage occurred in the Temne sample. A possible explanation could be offered in terms of genetic selection. Since Eskimos must deal with an exremely monotonous environment, the ability to make fine discriminations may have been evolutionarily selected. However, Eskimo children are treated very much the same, regardless of sex. Exploration and autonomy are encouraged in both; girls and boys alike go on extensive hunting trips with their fathers. In the camps or villages, sex differences in adult role performance are relatively slight. These circumstances suggest the possibility that the lack of sex differences in measures of field independence may be attributable to the egalatarian and autonomy-supporting orientation Eskimos have toward the socialization of girls and boys.

One other study of field independence exists relating social role to performance on this test (Preale **et al.** 1970). The field independence of (a) middle eastern, (b) western and (c) kibbutz-reared Israelis was compared. Group (c) tested more field independent than (b) who were more so than (a); the ordering of proportion of leaders and high status individuals from each group was the same. The authors of that article proposed that field independence and attendant skills cause the privileged position of the kibbutz-reared population. An alternative explanation could be that the kibbutz and its inhabitants are extremely highly valued by the people of Israel and that this adds to their prestige. Perhaps this position of confidence contributes to this groups' ability to project their definition of problems and goals onto the environment with some assurance that the projection will fit.

Maccoby and Jacklin's discussion of personality mediators of cognitive abilities suggests that for girls, aggressiveness, a sense of personal potency and activity level are positively related to cognitive abilities. Overall, boys do not show these relationships. Boys who identify with their mothers, and girls who identify with their fathers, tend to have greater spatial abilities. In both sexes, impulsivity is negatively related to such performances. They summarize their conclusions as follows:

> . . . the studies of personality correlates of intellectual performance have continued to suggest that intellectual development in girls is fostered by their being assertive and active, and having a sense that they can control, by their own actions, the events that affect their lives. These factors appear to be less important in the intellectual development of boys—perhaps because they are already sufficiently assertive and have a sufficient sense of personal control over agents, so that other issues (e.g., how well they can control aggressive impulses) become more important in how successfully they can exploit their intellectual potential (1974:133).

Because the quality of the lives of girls and boys is often drastically different in so many ways, any simple relationship between freedom to explore and manipulate the environment and spatial abilities runs the risk of greatly oversimplifying what is probably the true situation. There does seem to be a genetic base for the development of spatial abilities. However, this base seems not to be developed into adult skills even in the girls and women who would possess it. Further, evidence suggests that specific training in spatial tasks and visual-spatial skills can do much to improve these abilities in all children, tending to eradicate any initially existing sex differences. In addition to specific training, the beneficial effects of support for environmental manipulation and exploration are also indicated by cross-cultural studies. Even more generally, the development of a sense of autonomy and assertiveness seems to facilitate this and other intellectual abilities, especially for girls for whom the cultural norms often involve at least the appearance of dependency and restraint.

Perhaps our interest in this paper could best be summarized as a concern with the development of environmental competence in both girls and boys. By this we mean the knowledge, skill and confidence to use the environment to carry out one's own goals and to enrich one's experience. This issue, more general than activity range, construction or spatial abilities, makes salient the special disabilities girls seem to suffer in many areas of competence. First of all, a number of different kinds of studies find that girls and women do not consider it appropriate or rewarding to be competent. Komorovsky (1946) and Wallin (1950) report that college women feel it necessary to "play dumb" in male company. Horner (1970) offers support for this point with her findings that a motive she calls "fear of success" is common among women, especially bright, productive, nearly-successful women. Two studies of children indicate that this apparent lack of pleasure in intellectual achievement begins early. Crandell (1969) found that brighter boys expected to do better on a new task; I.Q. correlated negatively with girls' predictions of success. Similarly, Sears (1963) reported a positive correlation between boys' I.Q.'s; for girls, there was no correlation. Recently, kindergarten boys who tested high on creativity and intelligence were found to be more open, expressive, playful, curious and, to some extent, more self-confident. In contrast, highly creative and intelligent girls appeared less open, less expressive, less self-confident and less effective in peer relations (Singer and Rummu 1973).

One problem faced in attempting to develop environmental competence in girls has to do with a sense that the activities and skills involved are for boys only. Generally, children have been found to spend more time, on, prefer, and perform better, on tasks and in play labeled as appropriate for their own sex (Liebert **et al.** 1971, Montemayor 1974, Stein **et al.** 1971). In assessing the relative abilities of females and males, this problem makes any inference of the presence or absence of an internalized trait extremely difficult. For example, Carey (1958) found that a simple discussion of attitudes toward problem-solving erased an initial male advantage. After the pretest, a one hour discussion was conducted with both male and female subjects (college sample) concerning attitudes toward problem-solving and achievement; then the post-test was administered. A control group also took the pre- and post-tests with no intervening discussion. Women solved significantly more problems correctly after the discussion; men in the experimental group and all control group subjects showed no such improvement. We also noted how in Hart's observations, girls in the village were not encouraged to see environmental competence as appropriate to their sex. Hart's observations of the very different opportunities given to girls versus boys to freely manipulate the environment, must surely affect their cognitive representations of the environment and their spatial abilities. The difference In the experience of the two sexes is analogous to (and usually includes) the difference between the knowledge about an environment gained when one is a passenger in a vehicle and when one is the driver.

We have seen that girls tend to be restrained by parents, teachers and peers in their environmental exploration and manipulation because such activities are considered masculine. Thus, not only is a possible area of competence and adventure denied them, but the attendant restrictions could be expected to undermine their self-confidence in these areas. Both lack of experience and lack of confidence would in turn tend to diminish girls' spatial abilities and perhaps generalize to other types of problem solving. Certainly, the stereotypes and their related restrictions do not support the development of skill in using the environment for attaining goals. The difference in the experience of the two sexes is analogous to (and often includes) the difference between being a passenger in a car and driving it. The driver is allowed decision-making, experimentation and self-directed learning of the environment, while the passenger can only suggest and observe.

NOTES

[1] Also to be published in Burnett (in press).

REFERENCES

Anastasi, A., 1958, Differential Psychology: Individual and Group Differences in Behavior. New York: Macmillan.

Baumrind, D., 1971, Current Patterns of Parental Authority. Developmental Psychology Monograph 4.

Berry, J. W., 1966, Temne and Eskimo Perceptual Skills. International Journal of Psychology 1:207-209.

Bock, D. R. and D. Kolakowski, 1973, Further Evidence of Sex-Linked Major-Gene Influence on Human Spatial Visualizing Ability. American Journal of Genetics 25:1-14.

Brinkmann, E. H., 1966, Programmed Instruction as a Technique for Improving Spatial Visualization. Journal of Applied Psychology 50:179-184.

Bronson, W. C., 1971, Exploratory Behavior of 15-Month Old Infants in a Novel Situation. Paper at the meeting of the Society for Research in Child Development, Minneapolis.

Broverman, D., Klaiber, E. L., Kobayoski, Y. and W. Vogel, 1968, Roles of Activation and Inhibition in Sex Differences in Cognitive Abilities. Psychological Review 75:23-50.

Broverman, I. K., Broverman, D., Clarkson, F. E., Rosenkrantz, D. S. and S. R. Vogel, 1970, Sex-Role Stereotypes and Clinical Judgements of Mental Health. Journal of Consulting and Clinical Psychology 34:1-7.

Burnett, P. (Ed.), In Press, Women in Society: New Perspectives. Chicago: Maaroufa Press.

Carey, Gloria, 1958, Sex Differences in Problem Solving as a Function of Attitude Differences. Journal of Abnormal and Social Psychology 56:256-260.

Corah, N. L., 1965, Differentiation in Children and their Parents. Journal of Personality 33:300-308.

Crandell, V. C., 1969, Sex Differences in Expectancy of Intellectual and Academic Reinforcement. In Achievement-Related Motives in Children. C. P. Smith, Ed. New York: Russell Sage Foundation.

Erickson, E. H., 1951, Sex Differences in the Play Configurations of Pre-Adolescents. American Journal Orthopsychiatry 21:667-692.

Fruchter, B., 1954, Measurement of Spatial Abilities: History and Background. Educational and Psychological Measurement 14:387-395.

Garai, J. E. and A. Scheinfeld, 1968, Sex Differences in Mental and Behavioral Traits. Genetic Psychology Monographs 77:169-299.

Gesell, Arnold and Frances L. Ilg, 1942, Infant and Child in the Culture of Today. New York: Harper & Row.

Goldbert, S. and R. Lewis, 1969, Play Behavior in the Year-Old Infant: Early Sex Differences. Child Development 40:21-31.

Goldstein, A. G. and J. E. Chance, 1965, Effects of Practice on Sex-Related Differences in Performance on Embedded Figures. Psychonomic Science 3:361-362.

Guilford, J. P., Green, R. F. and P. R. Christiansen, 1951, A Factor Analytic Study of Reasoning Abilities. II. Administration of Tests and Analysis of Results. Report No. 3, University of Southern California, Psychology Laboratory.

Hart, R., In press, Children's Experience of Place. New York: Irvington Publishers.

Hartlage, L. C., 1970, Sex-Linked Inheritance of Spatial Ability. Perceptual and Motor Skills 30:610.

Hatfield, J. S., Ferguson, L. R. and R. Alpert, 1967, Mother-Child Interaction and the Effects of Message Structure on Persuasion. Journal of Personality and Social Psychology 38:365-414.

Horner, M. S., 1970, Femininity and Successful Achievement: Basic Inconsistency. In Feminine Personality and Conflict. J. M. Bardwick, E. Douran, M. S. Horner and D. Gutman, Eds. Belmont, California: Brooks Cole Publishing Company. pp. 45-74.

Hutt, C., 1972, Males and Females. Middlesex, England: Penguin Books.

Jacklin, C. N., Maccoby, E. E. and A. E. Dick, 1973, Barrier Behavior and Toy Preference: Sex Differences (and Their Absence) in the Year-Old Child. Child Development 44:196-200.

Kagan, J. and N. Kogan, 1970, Individuality and Cognitive Performance. In Carmichael's Handbook of Child Psychology I. P. Mussen, Ed. New York: J. Wiley. pp. 1273-1365.

Kaminski, L. R., 1973, Looming Effects on Stranger Anxiety and Toy Preferences in One-Year Old Infants. Master's thesis, Stanford University, Stanford, California.

Katon, N., 1965, A Fundamental Study of Rod-Frame Test. Japanese Psychological Research 7:61-68.

Komorousky, M., 1946, Cultural Contradictions and Sex Roles. American Journal of Sociology 52:184-189.

Landy, David, 1965, Tropical Childhood. New York: Harper & Row.

Lewis, M., 1972, State as an Infant Environmental Interaction: An Analysis of Mother-Infant Behavior as a Function of Sex. Merrill-Palmer Quarterly 18:95-121.

Liebert, R., McCall, R. and M. Hanratty, 1971, Effects of Sex-Typed Information on Children's Toy Preferences. Journal of Genetic Psychology 119:733-736.

MacArthur, R., 1967, Sex Differences in Field Dependence for the Eskimo: Replication of Berry's Findings. International Journal of Psychology 2:139-140.

Maccoby, E. E. and C. N. Jacklin, 1974, The Psychology of Sex Differences. Stanford, California: Stanford University Press.

Mellone, M. A., 1944, A Factorial Study of Picture Tests for Young Children. British Journal of Psychology 35:9-16.

Michael, W. G., Guilford, J. P., Fruchter, B. and W. S. Zimmerman, 1957, The Description of Spatial-Visualization Abilities. Educational and Psychological Measurement 17:185-199.

Montemayor, R., 1974, Children's Performance in a Game and Their Attraction to it as a Function of Sex-Typed Labels. Child Development 45:152-156.

Moss, H. A., 1967, Sex, Age and State as Determinants of Mother-Infant Interaction. Merrill-Palmer Quarterly 13:19-36.

Munroe, R. L. and R. H. Munroe, 1971, Effect of Environmental Experience on Spatial Ability in an East African Society. Journal of Social Psychology 83:15-22.

Nerlove, S. B., Munroe, R. H. and R. L. Munroe, 1971, Effect of Environmental Experience on Spatial Ability: A Replication. Journal of Social Psychology 84:3-10.

Pitcher, E. G., 1974, Male and Female, In And Jill Came Tumbling After: Sexism in American Education. J. Stacey, S. Berand and J. Daniels, Eds. New York: Dell.

Preale, I., Amir, Y. and S. Sharon (Singer), 1970, Perceptual Articulation and Task Effectiveness in Several Israel Subcultures. Journal of Personality and Social Psychology 15:190-195.

Radin, N. A., 1973, A Comparison of Maternal Behavior with Four-Year-Old Boys and Girls in Lower Class Families. Unpublished manuscript.

Sandstrom, E. L., 1953, Sex Differences in Localization and Orientation. Acta Psychologia 9:82-96.

Sears, P. S., 1963, The Effect of Classroom Conditions on the Strength of Achievement Motive and Work Output on Elementary School Children. Cooperative Research Project No. OE873, Stanford University.

Sears, R. R., Maccoby, E. E. and H. Levin, 1957, Patterns of Child Rearing. Evanston, Illinois: Row, Peterson.

Sherman, J., 1967, Problems of Sex Differences in Space Perception and Aspects of Intellectual Functioning. Psychological Review 74:290-299.

Singer, D. L. and J. Rummu, 1973, Ideational Creativity and Behavior Style in Kindergarten Age Children. Developmental Psychology 8:154-161.

Singer, G., and R. B. Montomery, 1969, Comment on Roles of Activation and Inhibition in Sex Differences in Cognitive Abilities. Psychological Review 76:325-327.

Stafford, R. E., 1961, Sex Differences in Spatial Visualization as Evidence of Sex Linked Inheritance. Perceptual and Motor Skills 13:428.

Stein, A., Pohly, S. and E. Mueller, 1971, The Influence of Masculine, Feminine and Neutral Tasks on Children's Achievement Behavior, Expectancies of Success and Attainment Values. Child Development 42:195-207.

Tanner, J. M. and Barbel Inhelder (Eds.), 1955, Discussions on Child Development, VIII. Proceedings of the Third Meeting of the "WHO" Study Group on the Psychobiological Development of the Child, Geneva. London: Tavistock Publications.

Thrustone, L. L., 1944, A Factorial Study of Perception. Chicago, Illinois: University of Chicago Press.

Tindal, M., 1971, Home-Range of Black Elementary School Children. Place Perception Research Reports, No. 5, Clarke University.

Tyler, L. E., 1965, The Psychology of Human Differences. New York: Appleton-Century-Crofts.

Van Voorhis, W. P., 1941, The Improvement of Space Perception Ability by Training. Doctoral dissertation, Pennsylvania State University, University Park, Pennsylvania.

Wallin, P., 1950, Cultural Contradiction and Sex Roles: A Repeat Study. American Sociological Review 15:288-295.

Werdelin, L., 1961, Geometrical Ability and the Space Factors in Boys and Girls. Lund, Sweden: University of Lund.

Witkin, H. A., Dyk, R. B., Paterson, H. F., Goodenough, D. R. and S. A. Karp, 1962, Psychological Differentiation. New York: J. Wiley.

## FUNCTIONS OF SCHOOL ATHLETICS: BOUNDARY MAINTENANCE AND SYSTEM INTEGRATION

Andrew W. Miracle, Jr., Texas Christian University

Increasingly, American schools are becoming more heterogeneous, with a student population drawn from various social classes and ethnic groups. The natural patterning of these diverse elements of the community tends toward voluntary segregation. As boundary maintenance devices, school athletics tend to separate participants by certain social criteria including sex, social class and racial or ethnic identification.

Several examples could be cited. Recently, Wyatt (1976), in a study of a desegregated southern high school, has shown that pick-up basketball contributes to the cohesion evident in the separate clique systems of blacks and whites and that it also helps maintain the separation between the two groups. Colfer (1976) has stated that high school basketball also can function to foster sex differentiation within school and community structures.

However, school athletics need not always serves as boundary maintenance devices. In fact, they may serve as a socialization mechanism which tends to promote systems of interaction and reciprocity, appropriate and necessary for the incorporation of socially, racially, ethnically and linguistically heterogeneous groups in the school population. In such situations, school athletics might be said to serve an integrative function by increasing the effective level of cross-cultural, cross-class interaction and communication, thus promoting equilibrium within the school system.

For example, Precourt (1976) has shown how basketball can cross-cut social groupings, community structures and social identity relationships. In his study of a small Appalachian community and its school, Precourt concluded that basketball "bridges the gap between various community contexts and identity groupings" (1976:4).

There are many common examples of diverse groups playing the same sport, even playing it together. Tindall (1973b:17), however, has cautioned us not to be mislead by the apparent use of the same label for what may represent essentially different systems. Utes and Anglo-Mormons both play a game they each call basketball, but this shared label disguises the fact that the games are different. Wyatt (1976) found the same phenomenon among black and white students in a single high school. In such cases, playing basketball might reinforce group identities and prejudices, since the rules of the game one observes effectively marks one's social identity and excludes one from the other group. Basketball, in such situations, might serve to maintain existing social boundaries.

My own research has examined school athletics in a broad spectrum of environments. Some examples and findings from these studies may shed light on the general questions under consideration.

## THE NATURE OF SCHOOL ATHLETICS

For the purposes of this paper, school athletics will be defined as structured play recognized as an official school activity.[1] Such activities are usually sponsored or supervised by a teacher or coach who is charged with certain responsibilities regarding the student participants. Following this definition, school athletics would included physical education classes, intramural programs and extramural or interscholastic sports. Thus, participation is sometimes voluntary (e.g., interscholastic sports) and sometimes mandatory (e.g., physical education classes).

During the period 1972-1976, I collected data in a single southern school district with a total population of 125,000 and a school population of 25,000. The school district includes major segments of lower class blacks and whites with rural backgrounds and middle class whites with rural and urban backgrounds. The residential clustering of these major segments is accompanied by distinct life styles and membership in different associations, with little interaction among the various segments. It is not surprising that a voluntary separation of students in the schools parallels that of the general population in the community. Apparently, patterns of behavior and association are established in the family environment and taught within the school setting. These basic patterns of natural groupings and interaction change in only a few specific instances. The system of organized school athletics is one arena where such variations can be observed.

One further characteristic of this school district needs to be discussed: the degree and extend to which people are involved with athletics. In this regard, I consider the district to be "typical" of most school districts I am familiar with throughout the southern United States. On the whole the population is neither maniacal nor **laissez faire** in its atitudes about school athletics. The district has produced several college athletes with a regional or national reputation but few professional athletes, and none of great renown.

Following the definition of school athletics stated above, two basic categories of school athletics can be identified: those which pertain to the time and space grids of physical education classes and those which are generally identifiable as after-school sports. In the district I studied, the patterning of these athletic activities is distinct for each level of schooling, i.e., elementary (kindergarten—grade 4), middle (grades 5-8), and high school (grades 9-12).

In elementary schools, physical education classes are occasionally taught by certified specialists. More often classroom teachers direct these activities; at such times they might be appropriately labeled a recess, rather than a physical education class. Certified physical education teachers sometimes offer highly structured activities designed to build specific skills or meet perceived psychomotor, cognitive or emotive needs of students. Most often, regardless of the skill of the teacher, the scheduled period of athletic activity is one in which the teacher selects the specific activity and then provides minimal assistance and supervision. The teacher-originated activities often proceed without adult interference until the scheduled period is over. Participation in these activities is frequently segregated along sex lines at the direction of the teacher. For example, baseball and football are played almost exclusively by boys; some games, such as kickball, may be played by mixed groups of boys and girls. Athletic activities in elementary schools, with few exceptions, are age-graded. There are no after-school sports.

Middle schools have full-time certified physical education teachers and better and more extensive facilities and equipment for athletic activities. Compared with elementary schools, middle school athletics are more structured, with a greater emphasis on complex-rule games. Middle schools also offer a variety of after-school sports programs. While there is a strict segregation of the sexes in activities related to physical education classes, a few girls have opted to play with boys in the after-school sports programs rather than participate in the all-girls leagues.

All high schools have several certified physical education teachers and professional coaches to direct their athletic programs. While some physical education classes are highly structured and well-planned by the specialized teachers, many high school physical education classes resemble elementary school recesses—the activity for the day is designated by the teacher, but student participation generally proceeds without interferences from the teacher. Physical education classes are not mandatory for all high school students, as they are for elementary and middle school students, though two years of physical education credits are required for graduation. Student attitudes toward physical education change after entering high school and for the first time in their student careers many students express a dislike of physical education. There is a great increase, however, regarding after-school sports in both the variety of the programs offered and the percentage of students participating.

## PATTERNS OF SOCIAL CLASS AND ETHNIC GROUP BEHAVIOR IN AMERICA

As was noted, the general patterns of segregation observed in the community were frequently replicated by voluntary separation along race and class line in the schools. Certain exception to this general pattern, however, need to be noted.

I observed integrated classes of first and second graders after a couple of months of socialization in the school environment. No race bias was apparent during athletic activities, although it was observed during normal classroom activities. Two students bound by kin ties or neighborhood ties might be inseparable in class and on the playground; this was true for whites and blacks. However, whether under teacher supervision or engaging in play outside the direct supervision of a teacher, no exclusion or segregation on the basis of race was detected.

In middle schools, racial bias was widely evident. However, sometimes in nonstructured situations, blacks and whites would play together with little or no regard for race (e.g., during free play at the lunch hour). This was frequently the case in team games (directed or nondirected) where talent was more appreciated as a criterion for participation than was race. In fact, in situations such as these, black and white students who previously may have begun a classroom fight or confrontation in which racial epithets were hurled, might play together, complimenting one another on a good play and rejoicing in a common victory. Obviously there was little carry-over from the playground to the classroom.

In high schools, in both class and play, there is almost complete segregation of blacks and whites—some of it structured by the system (e.g., railing or tracking of students and the courses they take) and some of it voluntary. In physical education classes voluntary interracial interaction was minimal, but sometimes it was promoted by the structured activities of a teacher. Usually, however, these structures were manipulated by students in such a fashion that one by-product was continued segregation. For example, it is common practice for the teacher to select team captains and then for the captains to choose team members through alternate selection. In less structured situations, the teacher simply announces for the students to form themselves into teams, without specifying the process. The frequent result of either method is teams composed largely of one race or the other.

Several factors contribute to this selection process, but one that is sometimes overlooked is that for many games there may be subcultural variations of the rules and structures (including prestige systems) associated with the games themselves (see Tindall 1973a, 1973b; Wyatt 1976). Often games have a white variant and a black variant. I noted such variants for volleyball and basketball. A major problem arises when black and white students try to play with each other or against each other in such situations. It is not recognized that they are playing different games which follow different rules and emphasize different talents. Not only are the games enjoyed more when everyone is playing by the same rules (i.e., when blacks play blacks and whites play whites), but there are fewer disputes. This latter result is appreciated by teachers who thus find it much easier to allow the segregated activities to continue than to restructure the physical education classes.

There were a few notable exceptions to this general description of physical education classes. In one high school, where the head basketball coach was black, everyone was instructed to play physical education basketball using what Wyatt (1976) has identified as "black" rules. In the classes I observed in this school, even in all-white games, black rules were used. In nondirected games of basketball and volleyball there was some racial segregation in the classes, however, the natural group-ings for these games appeared to be based primarily on ability (size and skill), with race (and even sex) being secondary.

In several schools the activities of the physical education program were highly structured, removing or inhibiting the students' control over participation, and thus the composition of teams. I observed this most often among young, enthusiastic teachers, and more often among middle school teachers than high school teachers.

## TEAM SPORTS: THE CASE OF FOOTBALL

Team sports such as football[2] tend to increase the variety and fre-quency of interaction among the diverse ethnic and social class elements in both school and community. A well-functioning team is an institution which does not recognize race or class differences within its limited parameters. Orientation toward specific goal achievement fosters a restructuring of attitudes and interaction patterns which emphasize abilities, not race or friendship groupings.

The achievement of a new value code appropriate to the efficient functioning of this talent-based, task-oriented team system, can be pro-moted by ritualized behavior. Rites of intensification validate both the values inherent in the goal (i.e., a successful football program) and the worth of expending the necessary energies to achieve the goal. Rites of passage are essential for unifying and channeling individual energies. Having endured common rites of passage, football players, both black and white, may surrender some personal identity, including blackness and whiteness, in exchange for team membership.

Sports which emphasize individual achievement, such as track, tennis, swimming or golf, do not promote the kind of interethnic and cross-class interaction associated with true team sports. The individually-oriented sports are similar to voluntary associations and tend to be characterized by homogeneity of class and ethnic identifica-tion and participation.

The effects of school athletics are not limited to the primary partici-pants. This is especially true for important team sports such as football. Football makes possible the existence of several tangential systems within the school which offer channels for meaningful activity to athletes and nonathletes. These other associations (e.g., the cheer-leaders, the pep club and the band) also may cut across race and class boundaries, thus increasing the range of interactive patterns. Because it touches so many systems, a sport such as football provides a school with a cohesiveness that might otherwise be difficult to obtain. The entire school is focused on football during the season, especially through such rites of intensification as homecoming and the pep rallies preceding the weekly games (see Burnett 1969). Such events may provide interracial and cross-class interaction that would not occur otherwise.

Football helps connect the school with various political and economic systems in the community. This is best demonstrated by the Athletic Association or Booster Club, which provides for community in-put and participation in the life of the school. In addition, football helps united the community, and the ritual of football gives expression to certain values and moral principles esteemed by the community.

Many high schools serve a heterogeneous community in which there is normally little interaction between blacks and whites or across class boundaries. The natural patterning of these diverse elements of the community tends toward voluntary segregation. Football is one of the few systems that can unite and focus the energies of these disparate elements in both school and community.

When it offers fair representation to various class and cultural segments, football has the potential to serve as a channel for cross-cultural and cross-class communication and interaction. In such a situation, high school football not only may integrate players of different race and social class backgrounds, but also it may integrate diverse elements of both school and community.[3]

CONCLUSIONS

It is a requisite of a social system that its members learn and conform to the relevant behavioral expectation embodied in the culture of the system (Nixon 1976:10). Since play forms are determined by the culture, they conform, or are congruent with, the norms and expectations of the society (or one of its component groups in complex societies). Or, as Tindall has stated, we may "presume that every aspect of sport is permeated by a non-obvious structure of social relations which is totally compatible with the behavior existing in the larger society" (1973a:20).

The conclusions drawn from the observations presented in this paper support such a perspective. Apparently one of the things that school children may learn is to segregate themselves along racial lines. Due to the residential clustering and distinct interactional patters in the community, few children have had much experience with children of a different race, ethnic background or social class before entering school. While first and second graders were not observed practicing frequent or habitual racial segregation, fifth graders were. Students learn to conform in school to norms which are characteristic of the general community.

The arena of play, however, is a special locus. Within this arena, it appears that individuals may be freed of certain traditional relationship obligations or normal expectations of behavior, that prevail in other spheres. Blanchard (1976) has noted that on the basketball court, the Ramah Navajo does not feel constrained to defer to traditional authority figures, such as mother's brother. Similarly, some black/white interaction was noted above, especially within the domains of interscholastic football, even though such interaction was not the norm for the community.

The interaction of blacks and whites that does occur in the athletic arena is learned behavior. It is important to note, however, that such integrative behaviors tend to be limited to the time and space grids of the athletic domain. Very little black/white interaction was observed in other social situations, even among veteran players.

It is suggested that orientation toward specific goal achievement (i.e., winning games) fosters a restructuring of attitudes and interaction rates. Specific abilities become the primary social criteria, while race is deemphasized. However, this talent-based social structuring is functional only within the boundaries of the task-oriented universe; more traditional patterns of organization continue to pertain in other spheres.

While participation in school athletics may offer students opportunities for interracial and cross-class interaction, interscholastic sports may serve to integrate various groups at the community level. School sports help to unite community members at various stages in the life cycle. In a sense, athletics is more than a coin of communication (see Cheek and Burch 1976:215). For many, it is a common experiential bond, a set of behaviors and related sentiments in which they have, or will have, participated at one level or another, in one or more roles, at various points along the life cycle.

In conclusion, American schools increasingly are becoming more heterogeneous, with a student population drawn from various social class and ethnic groups. The natural patterning of these diverse elements of the community tends toward voluntary segregation. Organized athletics is one of the few systems that may serve to unite and focus the energies of these disparate elements in both school and community. Some of the activities of a school athletic program may serve particular social class or ethnic elements. Others provide for the interaction of the diverse elements represented in the school and community and thus contribute toward the maintenance of equilibrium within school and community.

NOTES

[1]By school athletics, I refer only to organized athletics at the elementary, middle and high school levels. The activities of post-secondary institutions, that is, collegiate athletics, will not be considered here.

[2]For a more complete discussion of high school football, see Miracle (1976).

[3]A recent article in a popular magazine provided a graphic, but clear, example of this. The article describes the role of football in a rural Texas town. The School Superintendent relates the following: "When a black player and a white player got in a fight, [coach] led them into his office, took out a pocketknife, and made a small cut in each player's arm. As they stood in silence and watched the blood drip, they got the message: they were alike on the inside. Neither the school or the town has had any racial strife since. 'The harmony on the football field is one big factor in the harmony in this whole town,' (the Superintendent) says" (Winningham 1976:118).

REFERENCES

Blanchard, Kendall A., 1976, Basketball and Cultural Transmission: The Continuities and Discontinuities of American Indigena. Paper presented at the 75th meeting of the American Anthropological Association, Washington.

Burnett, Jacquetta Hill, 1969, Ceremony, Rites and Economy in the Student System of an American High School. Human Organization 28:1-10.

Cheek, Neil H. and William R. Burch, Jr., 1976, The Social Organization of Leisure in Human Society. New York: Harper and Row.

Colfer, Carol J. Pierce, 1976, Baskets, Baskets, Baskets, Boys. . . Paper presented at the 75th meeting of the American Anthropological Association, Washington.

Miracle, Andrew W., Jr., 1976, The Integrative Aspects of High School Football. Paper presented at the 11th Annual Meeting of the Southern Anthropological Society, Atlanta.

Nixon, Howard L., II, 1976, Sports and Social Organization. Indianapolis: Bobbs-Merrill.

Precourt, Walter E., 1976, Basketball, Social Structure and Cultural Transmission in an Appalachian Community. Paper presented at the 75th Annual meeting of the American Anthropological Association, Washington.

Tindall, B. Allan, 1972, Organizing Physical Education for Change: An Anthropological Perspective. In Sport in the Sociocultural Process. M. Hart, Ed. Dubuque: W. C. Brown. pp. 356-362.

1973a, The Hidden Curriculum in Sport. Paper presented at the Symposium on Sport, Games and Culture: Northeastern Anthropological Association meeting, Burlington, Vermont.

1973b, Exploration of a 'Troublesome Agenda' Based on the Non-Sharing of 'Property-like' Information. Paper presented at the American Anthropological Association meetings, New Orleans.

Winningham, Geoff, 1976, Friday Night Heroes. Texas Monthly Dec.:114-121.

Wyatt, Donald L., 1976, Pick-up Basketball: A Case Study of Clique Behavior Variation. Paper presented at the 75th Annual meeting of the American Anthropological Association, Washington.

# CHAPTER IV

# The Dichotomy of
# Work and Play

## INTRODUCTION

Perceptions of play are intimately related to one's culture. In the West, our understanding of play has been most significantly influenced by shared attitudes about what play is **not**. Play is not **work,** play is not **real**, play is not **serious**, play is not **productive**, and so forth. These attitudes, which are related to that complex of beliefs which has come to be known as the Protestant Ethic, have made it very difficult for Westerners to see that work can be playful while play can be experienced as work. Anthropologists, of course, have often found that the separation of work and play, which is characteristic of industrialized societies, is frequently absent in non-industrialized cultures, where the more important contrasts may be that between sacred and profane work (Turner 1974) and also between ritual and play (Handelman 1977a).

It is the contention of the authors in this chapter[1] that the giveness of the work-play dichotomy in Western societies must also be questioned. A number of studies point to the importance of this idea. For example, Turner (1973, 1974) has recently argued that in complex societies, play can be viewed as a type of **metalanguage** "for discussing,

185

criticizing, and defending the ideologies and outlooks that sustain the world of work" (1973:viii). In **Black Clubs in Bermuda** (1973), Manning documents in detail the complex relationships which exist between recreational clubs (e.g., sports associations, bars, etc.) and politics, "shows" and cultural identities, and games and the development of financial and business skills in Bermudian society. In contrast to Manning's discussion of work **at** play, Handelman (1974, 1975, 1977b; also Handelman and Kapferer, 1972) has presented an extensive ethnographic analysis of play **at** work. In particular he illustrates how jokes, pranks and games, which developed in a sheltered workshop in Jerusalem, allowed players/workers to express "critical sentiments without being held accountable, yet have the seriousness of their messages communicated" (1974:67). Finally, Csikzentmihalyi (1975) has recently used his notion of "flowing" to investigate the experience of play **in** games (e.g., chess) and **in** work (e.g., surgery). All of these investigations attest to the importance of pursuing **integrated**, as opposed to segregated, studies of play and work.

The specific papers in this chapter are intentionally problematic, but not with respect to the author's argument or presentation of material. Instead the "data" is itself problematic, and it is hoped that this material will illustrate the importance of formulating studies of play and work. In Mergen's study we see an example of shipyard workers whose job is not necessarily the unsatisfying, boring, and alienating activity that is often depicted. In the context of the shipyard, horse-play, defiance of restrictions, games, and friendship networks are all examples of play **at** work, and in our stereotyped Western conceptions of the work-place, these activities seem "out-of-place." In Schwartzman's discussion, the activities of a group of community mental health service providers are described. One pattern which developed in this context was labelled by participants as "dancing" and it appears to meet at least some of our traditional definitions of play. However, it began to seem more and more bizarre or "crazy" to participants and it brought them full circle to a point where they began to experience the behavior which they were supposed to **treat,** illustrating the tenuous nature of the frames—play, therapy, and madness. Dancing is an example of play **in** work.

Discussions of work **at** play and work **in** play are offered by Boyd, Theberge and Bowman. In Boyd's article we see how Native Americans **work** on constructing both individual and group identities during the play event of the Powwow, while Theberge clearly illustrates the problems faced by an athlete struggling to earn a living in the world of professional golf. Bowman describes examples of the spontaneous play behavior of adults and he illustrates how the "interactional work" of individuals enables them to achieve a sense of play. Bowman also suggests that we must call into question static conceptions of both play and reality which make it impossible (or is it just that it makes us uncomfortable?) to recognize that adults, as well as children, play.

Most importantly the authors wish to demonstrate the importance of theoretical and conceptual play. If we are flexible in our research orientations then we can accept the ambiguities and the frustrations inherent in the realization that both "play" and "reality" are **problematic achievements**. We will never understand play if we see **it** as "our problem" and do not simultaneously question the assumed givenness of reality (or work, or seriousness). In other words, an anthropology of play necessarily entails an anthropology of work.

—Helen B. Schwartzman

NOTES

[1]This chapter had its origins in a symposium, entitled "The Anthropology of Work and Play," organized by Helen Schwartzman at the Third Annual TAASP conference in San Diego, April, 1977. Mergen, Schwartzman, Boyd and Bowman participated in this symposium.

REFERENCES

Csikszentmihalyi, M., 1975, Beyond Boredom and Anxiety. San Francisco: Jossey-Bass.

Handelman, D., 1974, A Note on Play. American Anthropologist 76:66-68.

1975, Expressive Interaction and Social Structure: Play and an Emergent Game Form in an Israeli Social Setting. In Organization of Behavior in Face-to-Face Interaction. A. Kendon, R. Harris, M. Ritchie Key, Eds. The Hague: Mouton. pp. 389-414.

1977a, Play and Ritual: Complementary Frames of Meta-Communication. In It's a Funny Thing, Humour. H. J. Chapman and H. Foot, Eds. London: Pergamon. pp. 185-192.

1977b, Work and Play Among the Aged. Assen/Amsterdam: Van Gorcum.

Handelman, D. and B. Kapferer, 1972, Forms of Joking Activity: A Comparative Approach. American Anthropologist 74:484-517.

Manning, F., 1973, Black Clubs in Bermuda. Ithaca, NY: Cornell University Press.

Turner, V., 1973, "Foreword" to Black Clubs in Bermuda. F. Manning. Ithaca, NY: Cornell University Press.

1974, Liminal to Liminoid, in Play, Flow and Ritual: An Essay in Comparative Symbology. Rice University Studies 60:53-92.

## WORK AND PLAY IN AN OCCUPATIONAL SUBCULTURE: AMERICAN SHIPYARD WORKERS, 1917-1977

Bernard Mergen, George Washington University

Traditional distinctions between work and play have, until recently, forced a false dichotomy upon anthropologists and historians who have attempted to study the behavior of men and women on the job. The two disciplines have also tended to contrast pre-industrial with industrial societies; emphasizing the compartmentalization of work and leisure in the latter (Schwartzman 1976; Thompson 1963). Historians, especially, have approached the subject of work in Western cultures as if it were a foregone conclusion that technology has transformed every craft into a single, monotonous task. Relying heavily on the writings of dissidents and reformers, historians have usually assumed that the continuous demands for shorter hours, longer vacations and earlier retirement mean that workers find their jobs totally unsatisfying. While the desire to escape the drudgery of work remains a powerful incentive for reducing hours spent at boring tasks, there is ample evidence that most workers still find their jobs a mixture of "disgruntlement and small pleasures," and that it is the latter which provides the incentive beyond pay for their continued labor (Stearns 1975: 353).

This paper examines one group of American workers—shipyard workers—to show some of the mechanisms they have used over the past sixty years to provide some small pleasures in their work. My data comes from a variety of sources—union records, government reports, newspapers, autobiographies, novels, interviews and photographs—all of which obviously require careful and critical analysis. These sources document three distinct periods—1917-1919, 1943-1945 and 1975-77. The problems raised by the diversity of my sources of information, my interest in changes over two full working generations, and the need to describe and compare the work and play of shipyard workers, constitute the three major theoretical concerns of this paper. To develop methods for utilizing sources as different as a novel and a government report, we need to know as much as possible about the context in which the novel or the report was written, about the person or persons who wrote them, and about the purposes of their publication.

Similarly, making cross-time as well as cross-cultural comparisons requires a detailed knowledge of the work environment within the context of the surrounding culture (Miller 1969). The shifting connotations of the terms "work" and "play" force us to review the meanings which an activity may have for the individual engaging in it. For examle, attendance at a union meeting has one meaning for a rank-and-file member and another for a politically ambitious local officer. The third concern of this paper, the description and explanation of the work and play of shipyard workers, follows from this concern with cross-time and cross-cultural comparisons, because it offers a possibility of testing the hypothesis advanced by British sociologists that shipyard workers are able, because of the layout of the yards and the nature of their work, to develop a system of values which places an emphasis on play, defiance of restriction, leisure-taking, and camaraderie (Brown **et al.** 1973).

The work of Richard Brown and his associates in England has no equivalent in the United States. After securing information from almost 300 Tyneside shipyard workers about their leisure activities, club memberships, level of participation in trade union affairs, and political orientation, Brown's researchers observed men in the yard. Brown's conclusions provide a useful starting place for the analysis of the work routine of a distinct occupational group. English shipyard workers, according to Brown, belong to workingmen's clubs, spend much of their nonwork time there and in pubs, and do most of their socializing with other shipyard employees. At work they place great value on "being one of the lads," working at a pace which is acceptable to the majority of their work group, and maintaining a "witty, caustic and self-mocking style" in their conversations (Brown **et al.** 1973:98, 107).

Basically, this description fits American shipyard workers, if one substitutes civic and fraternal organizations for the British workingman's clubs. That the occupational or work-place culture of shipyard workers in the United States should resemble the British example in many ways is not surprising, since a significant number of American shipyard workers emigrated from England and Scotland in the 1920's (Mergen 1968). Nevertheless, the history of the shipbuilding industry in Britain and America is different, which accounts for some of the differences between the cultural systems described by Brown and the systems depicted here. Shipbuilding in the United States in the twentieth century has been an industry which boomed during war time and dwindled to insignificance in peace time. Moreover, most of the major shipyards are controlled by the giant steel companies, whose labor policies were inimical to union organization. In England, trade unions were strong in shipyards from the 1890's (Clegg **et al.** 1964). Technological changes also affected workers in varying ways. Welders, for example, replaced blacksmiths and riveters in American shipyards in the 1920's, but failed to achieve recognition as a separate craft within the labor movement because the standards for judging craft-work did not change until much later (Mergen 1972). The common assumption that cultural change is more rapid in the United States is unwarranted until we know more about specific groups and their perception of change (Goodenough 1963).

My earliest data on the work culture of American shipyard workers come from the records of the Emergency Fleet Corporation (EFC), a government agency which built and managed American shipyards

Plate 1

General view of Hog Island shipyard, Philadelphia, Pennsylvania, 1918. Financed and built by the Emergency Fleet Corporation, a government agency, and managed by American International Shipbuilding Corporation, this yard was designed to have fifty shipways. The typical linear plan allowed employees ample opportunity to control the pace of work as they moved from job to job.

Source: United States Shipping Board, Audiovisual Division, National Archives and Records Service. 32-CV-23-1C-39.

Plate 2

"Noontime at canteen—Reading the Hog Island News." This typical publicity photograph shows part of the 30,000 man work force in the shipyard. In addition to a newspaper and dining facilities, the company provided a YMCA, baseball and football fields, and a hotel.

Source: United States Shipping Board, Audiovisual Division, National Archives and Records Service. 32-CV-23-1A-410.

191

Plate 3

Cranes in the Bethlehem-Fairfield shipyard, Baltimore, Maryland, 1943. Photograph by
Arthur Siegel for the Office of War Information. The layout of shipyards changed little in
twenty-five years, although the cranes became larger. The opportunities for play
increased, as new groups of workers, notably women and Negroes, came into the shipyards. Initiation and socialization were always strenuous and sometimes harsh.

Source: FSA/OWI Files, Prints and Photograph Division, Library of Congress. USW3-
26460-E.

Plate 4

Lunchtime in Bethlehem-Fairfield shipyard, Baltimore. Workers pose by graffiti covered ship plates. Imaginative graffiti, mealtime sociability, and eccentric clothing were part of the play rituals in wartime shipyards.

Source: United States Maritime Administration, Record Group 357, 63 A-4136, 13/28: 41-47, Box 19, #1247, Federal Records Center, Suitland, Maryland.

during World War I. It was a subsidiary of the United States Shipping Board (USSB) which was created in 1917, to develop the merchant marine (United States Shipping Board 1917-1919). The USSB and the EFC made significant, if unintended, contributions to the occupational culture of shipbuilding by creating an Industrial Service Section under the father of personnel management, Meyer Bloomfield, and by cooperating in the establishment of the Shipbuilding Labor Adjustment Board (SLAB) which sanctioned union organization and collective bargaining. Bloomfield's ideas on the recruiting, training and welfare of workers resulted in a massive housing, recreation and public relations campaign designed to create good working conditions and high morale. Whatever culture existed in the prewar yards was unquestionably swallowed up in 1917-1918, when employment leaped from 80,000 in 72 yards to 400,000 in 116 yards. (An even more dramatic increase occurred in the years 1940 to 1943, when the number of shipyard workers increased from 102,000 to 1,336,900).

The EFC built several entirely new yards, including the world's largest, Hog Island, near Philadelphia, which eventually employed over 30,000 men and women. New workers were taught the language and traditions of shipbuilding by company sponsored newspapers, classes and experienced workers. The government sought to increase the speed of production by offering bonuses and prizes for setting construction records. The play aspect of this competition was underscored in the headlines of the April 15, 1918, issue of **Emergency Fleet News** which announced that the "New National Game of Riveting Promises Novel and Patriotic Sport." Company sponsored athletics, which included soccer, baseball, basketball and boxing, functioned in two ways to create shipyard culture. It kept the workers together in their non-work time and it reinforced the association of work skill and athletic prowess. "Good shipbuilders are expected to be good athletes," wrote the editor of the **Hog Island News** on January 18, 1918, "and there is no cause for surprise when a big yard turns out a first rate baseball team or a high-class quintet."

There was soon criticism of excessive emphasis on contests and recreation, but these methods of building company spirit were used again in World War II. Today, company sponsored athletics seem less important than in the past, although almost all the crafts in the Newport News Shipbuilding Corporation, for example, enter teams in baseball, bowling and golf competitions. Industrial recreation is only one part of management's efforts to create and maintain peaceful labor relations. However, the situation in the shipyards is made more complex by the role played by the federal government. In addition to setting wage and safety standards in private yards doing government work, the existence of federally controlled Navy yards created a situation in which Navy yards welders, electricians and boilermakers were also government employees, a status which may have added some "small pleasure" to their work.

The physical layout of shipyards is another important factor in establishing the context for work and play. Most shipyards are linear, stretching along the waterfront for a mile or more and occupying as much as 250 acres of land. The huge buildings housing the mould loft, machine shops and fabrication shops, the acres of steel storage along railroad tracks, and the towering cranes by the shipways and outfitting basins, constitute an imposing sight. Much time is spent walking to and from work in a yard and it is possible to become lost in unfamiliar areas. During World War II, when the yards operated around the clock, a novelist described one yard at night as a "city in a fairy story" (Saxton 1958:125). By both daylight and flood lights, a shipyard offers a dramatic setting for the performance of the workers. In a shipyard, workers are out of sight of supervisors or foremen for long periods of time. Delays in getting material or equipment to the appropriate crews inevitably occur. The perennial charges of loafing made against workers by managers stems in part from these delays. The loafers smoke, read papers, talk and occupy their time in various ways. Once work begins there is still opportunity to play. The most frequent type is probably fantasy play. As one welder observed, "when I pulled that welding mask down, my mind went a thousand miles away. My head, my eyes, my hands knew what they were doing, but my mind was away from the yard. Every welder knows how to do that to survive" (Mergen 1977).

Other kinds of play arose in response to work created problems. Augusta Clawson (a Special Agent of the Vocational Division of the U.S. Office of Education, who worked as a welder in a Portland, Oregon, yard in 1943, to check on the efficacy of the training programs for women) learned a sign language which allowed her to communicate with other welders despite the noise of construction (Clawson 1944:92). She also sang and screamed to relieve her tedium, safe in the knowledge that she couldn't be heard. Other observers have noted the importance of nonverbal communication in industrial settings. Like joking and occupational argot, sign language, "requires relatively exuberant acting, and willingness to go out on a limb. It's important nontechnical uses involve jokes created to break the routine of repetitive and demanding work" (Meissner 1976:264). Although my examples come for workers who recall their experiences in World War II, fantasy play and sign languages almost certainly continue as part of the behavior of contemporary shipyard workers.

This may not be the case with some other forms of ritual play. A crane operator at Newport News Shipbuilding Corporation recalled that in the 1930's a man would go down into an unlighted area of a ship with portable lights only to find that someone had unplugged his cord at the switchbox as a joke. Apprentices were sometimes sent for nonexistent tools, such as a flag pole key. Retired workers think that this kind of play on the job has declined in recent years, partly because supervision is stricter, and partly because they feel that younger workers are less deeply involved in their crafts. Pride in doing a job with skill has many of the attributes of play. Workers compete among themselves to do good work. The crane operator cited above boasted that he "could put the hook chains into a five gallon bucket from a distance of 135 feet up in the air, and with about a 60-70 foot boom" (Mergen 1977). Clawson writes of the satisfaction she felt in learning to do good welds and in the conditioning of her body to work under difficult physical environments.

The difficulties and danger of shipyard work serve to create close group feeling and to raise the stakes in the games played on the job. All the workers I have interviewed have spontaneously mentioned the constant hazards of their work, the frequency of injuries and even death in the yard. Although saftey measures have increased enormously since 1917, the accident rate for shipyards is still high. The men are fatalistic about dying of some work related cause, but refuse to quit because they are convinced they can beat the odds. In a less serious situation, Clawson found that "the discomforts were a source of fun. I'd climb up and do a tack [weld]. I'd come down dripping [from the heat], and one of the men would pick up the blower and turn it full upon me. Sometimes it would blow off my hat, and invariably it took my breath away. But it cooled me off, and I'd climb up, and repeat the performance" (1944:162-163).

Clothing worn by shipyard workers, like the uniforms of other occupations, has a symbolic as well as a utilitarian function. The novelist Chester Himes described the feelings of a black sheet metal worker in a Los Angeles shipyard as he put on his coveralls, safety boots and "tin hat": "Something about my working clothes made me feel rugged, bigger than the average citizen, stronger than a white collar worker—stronger even than an executive. Important too. It put me on my muscle. I felt a swagger in my stance when I stepped over to the dresser to get my keys and wallet, identifications, badge, handkerchief, cigarettes" (1945:12). The play element of costuming was also noted by Clawson: ". . . when I had finished my shopping tour, I came to my room and had a private showing of 'What the Well-dressed (?) Welder

Will Wear.' I was so tired at that point that I didn't expect anything to draw a laugh out of me; but honestly, when I tried on the blue work shirt, blue denim overalls, blue denim jacket, leather overalls, leather jacket, leather gauntlet gloves, and helmet, I howled" (1944:16).

Play in work is evidenced in other ways. During the wars, when each ship completed was considered a step toward victory, the launching ceremonies were occasions for brief periods of celebration. (In leaner times the emphasis is on keel layings which celebrate the beginning, rather than the end, of work.) Lunch time has always provided an opportunity to continue or to begin playful activities. Photographs of meal times, shift changes and pay days suggest that these movements were used to make and renew friendships, collect contributions for injured workers or sick relatives and conduct union business. Katherine Archibald, who worked at Moore Dry Dock Company in Oakland, California, in the summer of 1942, supports this conclusion, while Clawson adds another dimension by using a sports metaphor to describe lunch time as "a time out in a critical basketball game" (Archibald 1947:216; Clawson 1944:97). While friendship continues as a positive factor in shipyards workers' attitudes toward their work, romance was added in World War II, when thousands of women came to work in the yards. Sex play of various kinds is mentioned by Clawson and Archibald, but today's workers seem unperturbed by the presence of women on their crews. In Newport News, for example, race still seems to be a more disruptive factor than sex. While some workers gamble with dice and cards during unsupervised moments, others take the opportunity to proselytize for their religious sect, or argue fine points of Biblical interpretation. Profanity and obscenity are used in extremely subtle ways to initiate novices and solidify group feeling. Word games, involving threats and promised violence, take place among workers without serious consequences, but tensions become real when a foreman tries to play (Ryan 1977).

The competitive spirit, company sponsored athletics, day dreaming, joking, tricks, gossip, costuming—all have important functions in making shipyard work more like play. Despite the fact that labor organizations arise because of serious grievances between employers and employees, organization, and especially strikes, often take on many characteristics of play. Leaflets and picket signs exhibit considerable imagination and creativity. A typical example of the recreational element in an organizing drive is the advertising copy which appeared during the attempt by the Industrial Union of Marine and Shipbuilding Workers of American to win a representation election at Fore River Shipyard in 1941. Beside a drawing of a young woman was a headline which proclaimed: "I Want A Husband! With Job Security. I'm looking ahead—my man must be a Union man." In the two hundred fifty words which followed, the writer developed the play image by saying, "Don't get me wrong. I'm not a gold digger—just a smart girl who wants to finish the game without an error. . . a man who doesn't belong to a Union is starting out with two strikes on him." The playful tone of this appeal is, of course, enhanced by the baseball metaphor, a literary device which may reveal a good deal about the writer's attitudes toward his work.

Except for launchings, there is little in the behavior described above that is unique to shipyards. The abundance and diversity of such behavior, however, is noteworthy. Like their British counterparts, American shipyard workers have developed leisure in their work. Despite their great variety, government reports, union correspondence, newspapers, novels, autobiographies, interviews and photographs provide evidence which is in general agreement on the main features of the shipyard workers' work culture. Beginning in 1917 and continuing through 1945, and beyond, the federal government has exerted enormous influence on the style of shipyard work. By encouraging in-inovative ideas in management in 1917, the government created an atmosphere in which workers felt free to observe the traditional rituals of their crafts and to take advantage of new play-like activities, such as riveting contests and patriotic parades. In World War II, new kinds of workers—women, blacks, high school and college graduates—stimulated the development of new forms of play on the job. But shipyards are not completely isolated from their surrounding communities. Workers' attitudes toward work and play are shaped by the mass media, schools and other large institutions. There are subtle, but important differences in attitudes toward work and leisure between southern shipyard workers in Newport News, urban shipyard workers in Baltimore, Maryland, and New England shipyard workers in Fore River, Massachusetts. The content of work and play, and of play in work, is ultimately the result of the "interplay" of local and work place influence (Pilcher 1972; Mergen 1974).

Like other workers, shipyard workers seek job satisfaction or, at least, job tolerance by free, playful, ritualistic activities (Roy 1959-60; Green 1965, 1968, 1971). They also seek to control production by informal work rules (Montgomery 1976). The folklorist Archie Green has described "a custom jealously guarded in San Francisco shipyards [of] pick-up time or the 'right' to get tools together and remove overalls five minutes before quitting time." Yet these same men worked around the clock in the 24 hours before a ship's launching, to be rewarded with a drink and newly minted silver dollar (1965:64).

The management, the manipulation of time, is the ultimate playful activity of the shipyard worker. He or she learns to recognize the moments in and out of the yard which are free from immediate necessity and sieze them for play. Csikszentmihalyi (1975) has proposed that play is a flow between boredom and anxiety. Play, I think, also forms the "flow" between the rhythms of work and the rhythms of family and individual life. Ship construction takes many months. The pace of work and the shipyard setting are both conducive to the kinds of play which create unity between self and environment. On both sides of the Atlantic this play takes the form of day dreaming, loafing, joking and gossiping. Changes in work rules, personnel and technology can alter the content of these activities, but they cannot destroy them. Anthropologists and historians should describe the specific content of these playful activities and explain the ways in which work and play affect one another. From this research, we may be able to contribute to the fuller development of every worker.

REFERENCES

Archibald, Katherine, 1947, Wartime Shipyard: A Study in Social Disunity. Berkeley: University of California Press.

Brown, Richard and Peter Brannen, 1970, Social Relations and Social Perspectives Amongst Shipbuilding Workers—A Preliminary Statement. Sociology 4:71-84, 197-211.

Brown, Richard, Peter Brannen, Jim Cousins, and Michael Samphier, 1973, Leisure in Work: The "Occupational Culture" of Shipbuilding. In Leisure and Society in Britain. M. A. Smith, S. Parker, C. A. Smith, Eds. London: Allen Lane. pp. 97-110.

Clawson, Augusta, 1944, Shipyard Diary of a Woman Welder. London: Penguin.

Clegg, H. A., A. Fox, and A. F. Thompson, 1964, History of British Trade Unions from 1889. New York: Oxford.

Csikszentmihalyi, Mihaly, 1975, Beyond Boredom and Anxiety: The Experience of Play in Work and Games. San Francisco: Jossey-Bass.

Goodenough, Ward, 1963, Cooperation and Change. New York: Russell Sage.

Green, Archie, 1965, American Labor Lore: Its Meaning and Uses. Industrial Relations 4:51-68.

1968, The Workers in the Dawn: Labor Lore. In American Folklore. T. Coffin, Ed. n.p.: Voice of America. pp. 281-292.

1971, Only a Miner: Studies in Recorded Coal-Mining Songs. Urbana: University of Illinois Press.

Himes, Chester, 1945, If He Hollers Let Him Go. New York: Signet edition, 1971.

Meissner, Martin, 1976, The Language of Work. In Handbook of Work, Organization, and Society. Robert Dubin, Ed. Chicago: Rand McNally. pp. 205-279.

Mergen, Bernard, 1968, A History of the Industrial Union of Marine and Shipbuilding Workers of American, 1933-1951. Unpublished Ph.D. dissertation, University of Pennsylvania, Philadelphia, Pennsylvania.

1972, Blacksmiths and Welders: Identity and Phenomenal Change. Industrial and Labor Relations Review 25:354-362.

1974, The Pullman Porter: From "George" to Brotherhood. South Atlantic Quarterly 73:224-235.

1977, Unpublished interviews with retired shipyard workers in Newport News, Virginia.

Miller, Raymond Charles, 1969, The Dockworker Subculture and Some Problems in Cross-Cultural and Cross-Time Generalizations. Comparative Studies in Society and History 11:302-314.

Montgomery, David, 1976, Worker's Control of Machine Production in the Nineteenth Century. Labor History 17:485-509.

Pilcher, William W., 1972, The Portland Longshoremen: A Dispersed Community. New York: Holt, Rinehart and Winston.

Roy, Donald F., 1959-60, "Banana Time:" Job Satisfaction and Informal Interaction. Human Organization 18:158-168.

Ryan, T., 1977, Letter to author.

Saxton, Alexander, 1958, Bright Web in the Darkness. New York: St. Martin's Press.

Schwartzman, Helen, 1976, The Anthropology of Work and Play. Paper presented at the Northeastern Anthropological Association Meetings, Middleton, Connecticut.

Stearns, Peter, 1975, Lives of Labor: Work in a Maturing Industrial Society. New York: Holmes and Meier.

Thompson, E. P., 1963, The Making of the English Working Class. New York: Vintage Books.

Turner, Barry, 1972, Exploring the Industrial Subculture. New York: Macmillan.

United States Shipping Board, 1917-1919, Record Group 32, National Archives and Record Service.

## ORGANIZATIONAL DANCING: HOW PLAY WORKS IN A COMMUNITY MENTAL HEALTH CENTER[1]

Helen B. Schwartzman, Institute for Juvenile Research, Chicago

> But should the play
> Prove piercing earnest,
> Should the glee glaze
> In Death's stiff stare,
>
> Would not the fun
> Look too expensive!
> Would not the jest
> Have crawled too far!
>
> Emily Dickenson

Work:Play, Labor:Leisure, Reality:Fantasy—a series of recognizable and powerful Western dichotomies used by layman and scientist alike to organize, structure and also to study the social world. Of course, anthropologists have frequently pointed out that many cultures do not constitute their worlds by the use of these particular contrasts (see Bohannan 1963:219; Norbeck 1971:48). Nevertheless, we persist in imposing these distinctions on other societies when we have not yet critically evaluated their validity in Western societies. And, finally, we have even begun to incorporate these oppositions into the formation of our own anthropological societies.[2]

In order to develop a viable ethnographic approach for the study of these activities, anthropologists must begin by critically questioning the traditional play/work dichotomy of Western societies. This paper is an attempt to outline such an approach. As anthropologists, we cannot assume and, in fact, have evidence to the contrary, that the phenomena of work and play are mutually exclusive activities which can best be studied independently. Nor can we assume, given the history of our discipline's lack of concern with these topics, that relationships between work and play in culture are clearly understood. For example, in responding to our own culture's devaluation of play, ethnographers have been reluctant, until recently, to consider seriously the investigation of this phenomenon.[3] And, curiously, in adhering to our own field-**work** ethic, we have produced both "theoretically vague and ethnographically superficial" studies of work and the work context in complex societies, according to a recent paper by Johnson (1975). Since we are starting from a history of neglect, it seems important to emphasize that an anthropology of play necessarily entails an anthropology of work; and, of course, the opposite is also true.

PLAY IN WORK

Studies by sociologists and psychologists (e.g., Csikszentmihalyi 1975; Parker 1973) indicate that certain Western workers actually do experience their jobs or occupations as providing them with the pleasures and satisfactions thought to be part of the play experience. It is also true (although the topic cannot be pursued in this context) that play-forms may be experienced as painful or "work-like," Bohannan states:

> In the past, Westerners have assumed that work is painful and that play gives pleasure, when they actually should know (if they would examine the situation critically) that work is sometimes painful and sometimes gives pleasure, and play is sometimes pleasant and sometimes unpleasant (1963:219).

Csikszentmihalyi (1975) has recently conducted a psychological investigation of the experience of "flow" as a play form in certain traditional games and sports (e.g., rock climbing, chess) as well as work (e.g., surgery) activities. According to Csikszentmihalyi, flow is the experience of acting outside the parameters of worry and boredom (1975:38).

> In the flow state, actions follows upon action according to an internal logic that seems to need no conscious intervention by the actor. He experiences it as a unified flowing from one moment to the next, in which he is in control of his actions, and in which there is little distinction between self and environment, between stimulus and response, or between past, present, and future. . . one of the main traits of flow experiences is that they usually are, to a less or greater extent, autotolic—that is, people seek flow primarily for itself, not for the incidental extrinsic rewards that may accrue from it. Yet one may experience flow in any activity, even in some activities that seem least designed to give enjoyment—on the battlefront, on a factory assembly line, or in a concentration camp (1975:36).

Anthropologists, however, are less likely to focus on the study of individual motivations and feelings about work or play, than they are to investigate the general social system or culture of an occupational group or a work context, such as a factory or bureaucracy (e.g., Clinton 1975; Conkling 1975; Johnson 1975; Tway 1975). It is important to recognize here that play forms may, in fact, become a part of this work-based culture. And, they may even transform this culture into something which **should** be work, but **looks** like play. An analysis of "dancing" in a community mental center located in the Midwest reveals how play and work may become fused and also confused in particular social contexts.

## ORGANIZATIONAL DANCING: MIDWEST COMMUNITY MENTAL HEALTH CENTER

Between January, 1975 and July, 1976, I was involved, along with three other researchers (Don Merten, Gary Schwartz and Anita Kneifel) in the study of a community mental health center located in a low income, multi-ethnic community of a large Midwestern city. This study was designed to investigate the historical development of what I will call the Midwest Community Mental Health Center (MCMHC), parti - cularly in reference to the influence of the following three contexts of a center's activities: 1) the community or neighborhood context; 2) the organizational context created by center staff interactions with each other, with community residents, and so on; and 3) the bureaucratic context, established by the relationship existing between a center and its major funding sources.[4]

Midwest CMHC was funded by an NIMH staffing grant in 1971 as a free-standing comprehensive CMHC. According to the grant proposal, a community board was ultimately responsible for center operations and for the hiring of a director. The grant stressed community participation of individuals as board members, the use of para-professional staff and a consortium model of service delivery to a specifically designated catchment area. This particular catchment area contained a large number of "at-risk" populations, the most obvious of which were numerous ex-State mental patients who had been "dumped" or "deinstitutionalized" (depending on who you talk to) into the community during the 1960's. In fact, many community residents referred to this neighborhood as a "psychiatric ghetto."

Midwest CMHC began enthusiastically with much talk of its being a new solution to the mental illness/social problems of the area, and a feeling that this was **the** community's mental health center. However, the Center quickly encountered and seemed to engender, criticism both from within and without (from affiliated and non-affiliated agencies, board members, staff, etc.). At the end of the first two years, Center programs were established and a variety of services were being offered. However, hostile and suspicious cliques and factions had by now been formed and there was a tendency to constantly personalize issues and scapegoat individuals as the cause of all the problems.

This seems a most unlikely context for the development of something which anyone would be willing to refer to as play. And yet something did develop which Center personnel designated, and seemed to recognize and respond to, as a type of play form. I also believe that this activity, when measured against definitions of play in the literature, meets at least some of the major criteria of play. Whether **we** will feel comfortable calling this activity play remains to be seen. At the very least the existence of this activity in this context (and I believe it has analogues in many other work contexts) needs to be examined, and perhaps it will help to underline the importance of reconceptualizing our understanding of both play and work in specific sociocultural contexts.

One of the most significant and frequent social events at the Center was "the meeting"; and there were many different kinds—staff meetings, cabinet meetings, supervisors' meetings, committee meetings, board meetings, and so on. Certain meetings were considered to be boring or "a drag" and one only went because "you had to," while others were attended voluntarily and often enthusiastically. When the Center first opened we have been told that staff spent close to 70% of their time in "meetings".

Meetings were ostensibly held in order to solve a problem, make a decision, or deal with a particular issue. However, the significant feature of **certain** meetings was that "nothing was accomplished"—issues did not get resolved, problems were not solved and decisions were not made. Instead, the participants engaged in a type of meta-social commentary or critique of themselves and their relationships to one another in the context of the Center. Frequently this commentary appeared in the guise of a discussion of a specific problem or issue, or it would turn into a general discussion of all problems and issues. It was always concerned with a struggle for whose definition of Center "realities" was to be accepted.

At the Center certain individuals called this activity "dancing." This term denoted the particular type of complex social negotiations and commentary as described above, and the process is similar in some ways to Geertz's description of the Balinese cockfight as "a Balinese reading of Balinese experience; a story they tell themselves about themselves" (1972:26). In a meeting where dancing took place, specific problems, crises, or solutions would quickly become part of the collective dance and in this way the "reality" of the problem would be transformed into the "unreality" of the dance, which was itself a comment, at another level, on the "realities" of life at the Center.[5]

In fact, there was nothing more exciting than a "crisis" meeting at MCMHC because it was frequently the occasion for a very dramatic "dance," complete with heroes and villains, as well as much crying and shouting.[6] During the 1½ years of our fieldwork there were various actual plays and entertainments (e.g., singing and dancing) held at the Center, but no play or dance drew as many staff, council and community individuals as a budgetary crisis meeting, or the Annual Meeting of the Council.[7]

Actually, any meeting could turn into a dance. I attended a series of meetings of Center "management" held in the fall of 1975 to decide on strategies for dealing with an upcoming election to establish if a majority of the workers wished to be represented for collective bargaining purposes by an AFL-CIO union local. At the first of these meetings, held with the Center's lawyer, the discussion shifted almost immediately from consideration of specific legalities and strategies to follow in trying to convince people to vote against unionization, to a general discussion of all the problems at the Center. Each person enumerated his/her beliefs as to the cause of the Center's problems and a lengthy list of problems developed. This list, however, had been created and enumerated many times before. It was always enthusiastically, and dramatically, discussed, and then promptly forgotten, only to be "re-invented" at the next meeting.

As many people in this meeting believed that certain other people, also attending this meeting, were **the cause** of all the problems, a variety of disguised references and phrases were used as ways to refer to (and yet not really seem to be blaming) these particular people. For example, whenever the clinical director used the phrase "lack of accountability"—i.e., "the cabinet is not accountable"—she was specifically referring to the Center director and what she felt was his inability to hold people responsible for their actions. When one of the specialized program directors suggested that the problems stemmed from "the reorganization process," this was an indirect criticism of the clinical director, who was in charge of the "reorganization" process. And so the discussion would continue in oblique and convoluted ways. At the conclusion of the meeting, it was suggested that everyone should come to the following week's cabinet meeting with ideas for procedures, how to deal with problems, and so forth. As everyone stood up to leave, one of the outpost directors commented that "maybe we do need a union after all." An interesting conclusion to a meeting that was ostensibly held to figure out ways to avoid having staff vote for the union. As might be expected, the Center's lawyer looked quite confused and bewildered all during this meeting. After giving up on attempts to suggest specific strategies for management to use, he finally said, at the conclusion of this meeting, that this certainly was "a most unique discussion," because "in most businesses, management meets, decides what to do, and then does it, and that is that."

Of course, this was "a most unique discussion" in his experience, but it was actually quite commonplace at MCMHC. Many other meetings were also characterized by this circuitous and confusing dancing process. For example, our research group followed the activities of one particular "Drug Abuse Task Force" for a year. This group met every week and included Center staff as participants as well as individuals from other agencies in the community. The group decided to write a proposal to secure funds to coordinate drug abuse services for the area. At the end of a year, the proposal was completed after a long and very complex negotiation process. Shortly thereafter, **the proposal was lost.**

A second group was established at the Center to develop "a coherent and consistent intake procedure." This group met for several months in the late summer and early fall of 1975. A variety of procedures were discussed, systems were outlined and charts were drawn. One example is provided here (Figure A) which reflects what can only be described as a diagram of a non-intake system. At each meeting, the procedures that people thought had been agreed upon at the previous meeting had to be re-negotiated again and again, particularly if a new participant (with a

## MCMHC Proposed Intake System
### August 8, 1975
### Figure A

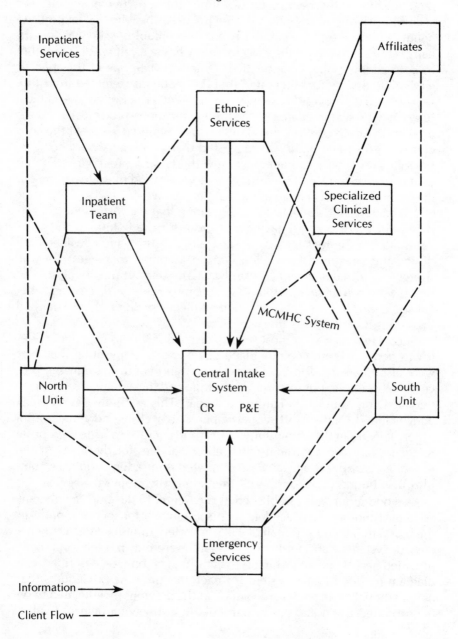

Information ———→

Client Flow ————

new viewpoint) had joined the group. To my knowledge, these meetings never produced a "coherent and consistent" intake system. Instead, the one in operation, which is the one that **works** (or, at least, seems to), gradually evolved in a hit-or-miss fashion over time.

Dancing occurred in various contexts and involved various routines and patterns. The most elaborate forms involved a complicated system of pretending to say or know something in order to define "reality" in one way, or to find out something about the way someone else was defining their "reality," and then using that information to redefine the situation. Of course, in this instance, some individuals were better "dancers" than others. As one informant put it, for some people this ability was developed as a "real art":

> . . . and it takes you hours to figure out that *in reality* they haven't told you anything, but they may have, in fact, *acted* in such a way that you *assumed* they knew more than they *really* did, and you told them a whole bunch. So if you put two or more people like that together. . . then you get a dance.[8]

What was it like to work (?) in this Center? A place where meetings went on forever and became more and more convoluted creating yet again another committee or subcommittee to establish a policy to deal with a particular problem which would soon become lost in the mass of memos, minutes, and confusing charts and diagrams.[9] What was it like when the development of an intake system, or a strategy for a union election, became the format for a dance instead of the place for a decision? For some it was terribly frustrating and they either resigned or were fired. Others, however, described it as "fun" and "totally involving," at least for a time (even though they recognized that "it was certainly no way to run a business"). As some staff put it, "It was undignified, unprofessional, just plain craziness and it was fun in a way. . . It had nothing to do with service. It wasn't based on evaluations; it wasn't based on productivity and it wasn't based on budget." Or, "When the place started we were so into the whole process. . . it became your life. . . and it used to be fun, that was the great part." Another person on the volunteer community board expressed her involvement in the meetings. "Well, you felt you couldn't, you couldn't miss a meeting because so much was happening. . . I remember one time my mother was in the hospital and I kept saying to the doctor. . . couldn't you keep her a couple more days, because I've got this important meeting." A number of ex-staff members described their present job as "just a job," or as "much less intense," " a place where you can keep your sanity intact, but not as much fun, really not as much fun, nobody is as interested in people."

## DEFINITIONS OF PLAY

Huizinga's (1934:13) classic definition of play characterizes it as: 1) a free activity which is situated outside "ordinary" life and recognized as being "nonserious"; 2) an activity which is intensely absorbing for the player; 3) an activity connected with no material interest or profit; 4) behavior which proceeds within its own boundaries of time and space according to fixed rules; and 5) something which promotes the formation of groups which surround themselves with secrecy and which emphasize their difference from the "common" world by disguise or in other ways. Play occurs as a contest **for** something or as a representation **of** something. Caillois (1961) critiques Huizinga's definition of play for being at once too broad and too narrow (see Ehrmann 1968). However, Caillois also established a similar listing of play's characteristics: 1) it is a free or voluntary activity; 2) it occurs in a separate time and space; 3) it is uncertain and unpredictable for its course cannot be determined in advance; 4) it is unproductive; 5) it is controlled by conventions which suspend "ordinary laws"; and 6) it is fictive, accompanied by an aware-ness of "unreality" or a "second reality" in comparison to "everyday" life.

More recently Stephen Miller (1973) has attempted to define a series of "leitmotifs" of play. Most specifically, he argues (after Bateson 1955, 1956) that play is a **context** or a **frame**, i.e., a mode of organization of behavior, or "one way of fitting the pieces of activity together." This can best be understood, according to Miller, by discussing the way ends and means, or goals and processes, are orchestrated.

> We have said that play is activity, motor or imaginative, in which the center of interest is process rather than goal. There are goals in play, but these are of less importance in themselves than as embodiments of the processes in-volved in attaining them. Process in play is not streamlined toward dealing with goals in the shortest possible way, but is voluntarily elaborated, compli-cated in various patterned ways. The patterns can take the shape of rules, symbols, or just "galumphing" (1973:97).

Another way of putting this is that play is the crooked, not the straight, line to the end of the road.

> Play is not means without the end; it is a crooked line to the end; it circum-navigates obstacles put there by the player, or voluntarily acceded to by him (1973:93).

## FUSION AND CONFUSION

In looking at the dance at MCMHC, can it be said that it is anything which Huizinga, Caillois, or Miller would call play? First of all, meetings, as has been said, were often attended voluntarily and fre-